KNACK
MAKE IT EASY

UNIVERSAL
DESIGN

KNACK

UNIVERSAL DESIGN

A Step-by-Step Guide to Modifying Your Home for Comfortable, Accessible Living

Barbara Krueger and Nika Stewart

Medical Review by Gail M. Sullivan, MD, MPH

Principal Photography by Mark Davidson

KNACK
MAKE IT EASY

Guilford, Connecticut
An imprint of Globe Pequot Press

KNACK®
MAKE IT EASY

Copyright © 2010 by Morris Book Publishing, LLC

ALL RIGHTS RESERVED. No part of this book may be reproduced or transmitted in any form by any means, electronic or mechanical, including photocopying and recording, or by any information storage and retrieval system, except as may be expressly permitted in writing from the publisher. Requests for permission should be addressed to Globe Pequot Press, Attn: Rights and Permissions Department, P.O. Box 480, Guilford, CT 06437.

Knack is a registered trademark of Morris Book Publishing, LLC, and is used with express permission.

Editor-in-Chief: Maureen Graney
Editor: Katie Benoit
Project Editor: Tracee Williams
Cover Design: Paul Beatrice, Bret Kerr
Text Design: Paul Beatrice
Layout: Melissa Evarts
Photo Research by Marilyn Zelinsky-Syarto
Front Cover Photos by Mark Davidson photographed at Sun City Shadow Hills by Del Webb; © Dorel Juvenile Group 2008. All Rights Reserved.; Courtesy of Diamond Cabinets; and Courtesy of Levolor. Back Cover Photo © Shawn_tsk | Dreamstime.com.
Interior Photos by Mark Davidson with the exception of those listed on pages 237–41.

The following manufacturers/names appearing in *Knack Universal Design* are trademarks:
DustBuster®
Formica®
Oxo Good Grips®
Roomba®
Sulatube®
Swiffer® Sweeper

The information in this book is true and complete to the best of our knowledge. All recommendations are made without guarantee on the part of the authors or Globe Pequot Press. The authors and Globe Pequot Press disclaim any liability in connection with the use of this information.

Library of Congress Cataloging-in-Publication Data

Krueger, Barbara.
   Knack universal design : a step-by-step guide to modifying your home for comfortable, accessible living / Barbara Krueger and Nika Stewart ; medical review by Gail M. Sullivan ; principal photography by Mark Davidson.
       p. cm.
   Includes index.
   ISBN 978-1-59921-613-3
   1. Universal design—United States.   2. Dwellings—Barrier-free design—United States.   I. Stewart, Nika.   II. Sullivan, Gail M.   III. Davidson, Mark.   IV. Title.   V. Title: Step-by-step guide to modifying your home for comfortable, accessible living.
   NA2547.K78 2010
   728.087—dc22
                                                              2009044926

Printed in China

10 9 8 7 6 5 4 3 2 1

Dedicated to Ma

Barbara (Moldofsky) Krueger

With loving gratitude to the wind beneath my wings, Rob. Thank you for giving me your shoulders—so I could lean on them and stand on them.

I dedicate this book to the talented designers with whom I have the honor of working every day. I am inspired by your continuous passion and desire to make the world a more comfortable and beautiful place.

Nika Stewart

Acknowledgments

Just as Knack had many people involved in production of this book, many people also paved the way for my arrival here. Colleagues, both professional and volunteer, provided opportunities for me to develop knowledge and skills. Those openings built upon childhood messages that encouraged creativity, original thought, and affirmation there was a way to be whatever I wanted. This publication is a tribute to all of them.

Barbara (Moldofsky) Krueger

Photographer Acknowledgments

Many thanks to Pulte Homes & the Communities of Del Webb (www.delweb.com and www.pultecom) for permission to photograph its Sun City Shadow Hills property in Indio, California.

Mark Davidson

CONTENTS

Introduction viii

Chapter 1: Life Cycles
Life Cycles xii
Fine Motor Challenges. 2
Visual Challenges 4
Just Not as Agile 6
Mobility Challenges 8
Memory Loss 10

Chapter 2: Entries & Doorways
Entry Doors. 12
Thresholds 14
Around the Car 16
Exterior Door Hardware. 18
Interior Doors: Quick Fixes 20
Remodeling Interior Doorways 22

Chapter 3: Flooring Treatments
Hard Surface Flooring. 24
Carpeting 26
Flooring Edge Treatments. 28
Area Rugs 30
Throw Rugs. 32
Patterns 34

Chapter 4: Kitchen Work Surfaces
Kitchen Counters 36
Revealing Edges 38
Sinks 40
Counter Workspaces. 42
Wheelchair Modifications. 44
Faucets & Sink Helpers 46

Chapter 5: Kitchen Storage
Pull-out Shelves 48
Shallow Pantry Shelves 50
Interior Cabinet Modifications 52
Drawers 54
Wheelchair Accessible Storage. 56
Dementia Safety Adaptations 58

Chapter 6: Kitchen Appliances
Stoves 60
Wall Ovens 62
Built-in Cooktops 64
Microwaves 66
Selecting Appliances 68
Placement of Appliances 70

Chapter 7: Arthritis Hand Aids
Door Handles. 72
Levered Faucets 74
Soap & Water Helpers 76
Kitchen Tools 78
I Can Manage But 80
Vacuums & Brooms 82

Chapter 8: Bathroom Fixtures
Bathroom Sink Adaptation. 84
Bathroom Faucets 86
Medicine Cabinets. 88
Toilets 90
Grab Bars 92
Emergency Call Buttons 94

Chapter 9: Tubs & Showers
Bathtubs 96
Tub Fixtures 98
Transfer and Bath Seats 100
Shower Stalls 102
Shower Fixtures 104
Shower Enclosures 106

Chapter 10: Living & Dining Rooms
Sofas 108
Also Keep in Mind 110
Easy Chairs 112
Tables & Storage Furniture 114
Living Room Lighting. 116
Dining Chairs 118
Dining Tables 120

Chapter 11: Home Office & Den
Bookcases 122
Televisions 124
Desks 126
Computers 128
Laptop Tables 130
Organizing Paperwork 132

Chapter 12: Bedrooms
Bed Height 134
Sharing a Bed or Using Twins 136
Mattresses 138
Bed Transfer Slings .140
Emergency Pull Cords 142
Light Controls 144

Chapter 13: Storage & Organizing
Closets 146
Drawers & Shelves .148
Linens 150
Collectibles 152
Photographs 154
Memorabilia 156

Chapter 14: Halls & Stairs
Hallways 158
Chair Rails & Banisters 160
Illuminated Light Switches 162
Elevators 164
Stairway Helpers 166

Chapter 15: Color Considerations
The Aging Eye 168
The Effects of Yellowing 170
Contrasting Walls & Floors 172
Making Edges Distinct 174
Combining Patterns 176
Minimizing Linear Elements 178

Chapter 16: Windows & Treatments
Patio Doors 180
Custom Windows 182
Sliding Windows 184
Window Coverings .186
Light & Glare 188
Remote Controls 190

Chapter 17: Lighting
Skylights 192
Ambient Lighting 194
Recessed Lights 196
Task Lighting 198
Sensors on Lights 200
Switches & Switch Plates 202

Chapter 18: Other Elements
Thermostats 204
Smoke & Gas Detectors 206
Home Security 208
Garage Door Openers 210
Organizing for Travel 212
Adapted Telephones 214

Chapter 19: Landscaping & Gardening
Garden Lighting 216
Softscape vs. Hardscape 218
Levels & Topography 220
Gardening with Arthritis 222
Practical Mobility Solutions 224
Gardening Alternatives 226

Chapter 20: Resources 228

Glossary 234
Photo Credits 237
Index 242

INTRODUCTION

Knack Universal Design focuses on a design and building approach that believes interior spaces, especially people's homes, can be made more accessible to all, regardless of their mobility and ability. This book is written for seniors, empty-nesters, adult children of seniors, as well as the younger population facing physical challenges. It suggests hundreds of ways for you to make your own surroundings barrier free, and to help others do the same.

Full-color photos, sidebars, and concise descriptions make it easy to recognize what topics are covered and how the information can be a benefit. This book covers easier-to-live-with appliances, fixtures, flooring, lighting, electrical considerations, color choices, traffic flow within the house and between inside and outside, and structural adaptations. *Knack Universal Design* helps you to be better informed and able to adapt an environment to live within it to the fullest capability.

Which chapters apply to you?

Unless you are already aware of failing eyesight, a diagnosis of a progressive physical, muscular, or neurological disease or ailment, or have a strong tendency toward one of these built into your genes, you probably don't know which design approaches in this book might apply to you as you age. But if you are honest about the general progression of human aging, you will recognize that many of these ideas could apply to you sometime in the future. If you have the opportunity to replace or refresh things in your home, why not err on the side of planning ahead instead of being caught short later on? If you are replacing faucets, why not pick ones that will serve you well in the years to come? If you are re-carpeting all or part of your home, why not pick a texture and color that will serve you safely into the future? If the children have moved out and you are preparing for the next passage of your own life by redoing the old house, or relocating to a smaller one, or to a resort area, keeping in mind the aging accommodations covered in *Knack Universal Design* will put you in a better position to cope with what life deals you.

What about helping your parents?

Adult children of seniors are all too aware of the failings of their parents. Their health is not so good; their vision is getting worse; arrangements in their old home do not accommodate their needs as they could; they are forgetful; they lose track of investments; but they are fiercely independent.

These signs of progressing age, if dealt with proactively, don't have to take away a parent's independence.

Of course, it is one thing to know what can make everyday life easier and quite another to actually get one's parents to institute changes. Unless parents have been declared to be incompetent by a court, we must take the role of advisors and educators. Practice techniques to get a point across to reluctant listeners. Recognize the barrier to following up on your pointers from your parents' point of view. Is it your interference they object to rather than the advice? Is it recognition of their own failings?

Every change starts with an idea. Approach your parents with the assumption that they have not considered modifying their environment. Make them aware of what is possible or what can make everyday chores easier to perform. Give them alternatives to think about. With this book under your arm you can suggest, present, and clarify for them what changes would better accommodate your mom's arthritis, or make navigation at home easier for Dad with his advancing glaucoma. Maybe arming yourself with this information will enable you to paint a picture of life once again being easier for your parents or other older relatives with just some minor updates in their house.

Realistically, will Mom be able to take care of Dad? Vice versa? What changes in their environment might make it easier? Facing what your parents need to make their life

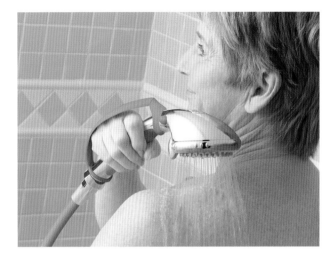

easier is also the first step for you to realize what might be in your own future. It could be the first realization that your own home and lifestyle could benefit from barrier-free changes.

What your genes can tell you

With awareness of what ailments affected your grandparents, parents, aunts, and uncles, you get an inkling of what could possibly be in your own aging future. Does diabetes run rampant through the family? Did it take their sight? Leave them without a leg? Does arthritis show up in many family members? Does it affect their hands, knees, shoulders? Sometimes the way it shows up in families is just that specific. Does Parkinson's crop up in several relatives?

This is definitely not a scientific way to predict the path your genes will take, or that the tendency toward some impairment will actually manifest itself in you. But it could be the path of your aging process. If there is some way to consider the chance for that, when you replace minor or major items in your home, you will be ahead of the curve should that failing befall you.

Your early life may also be a probable predictor. If you had polio as a kid, your senior years may find you dealing with post-polio syndrome. After you worked so hard at ten years of age to rehab your right leg muscles so you could run again, they may now be failing. The course of post-polio syndrome means that by the time you are seventy your right leg muscles might be failing. You could be in a wheelchair or using a motorized scooter.

You may have been a champion runner in your youth and now your knees or hips are paying you back for the pounding abuse you gave them. What course will that take? What modifications can you make in your home and garden to keep from compromising your hobbies in retirement?

Remember, your genes are from your parents. So heed the advice you would give them. How should you modify your own environment in the years to come to face aging more wisely than those before you?

A range of suggestions to meet your needs and budget

It is on purpose that some of the ideas covered within this book are not major home renovations. Just as everyone's aging process is unique, homes and financial statuses are unique. People's long-range plans differ, as well. Sometimes it only takes a new application of paint on one wall to clarify a space. Maybe it's just a matter of replacing some twenty-year-old knob faucets with new lever-handled ones. How costly is it to replace doorknobs with levered door handles? It may only take awareness of how life will be easier or that there will be one less challenge to face every day if a small modification is made.

Maybe the old tub would be easier for Mom to use if she bought a portable transfer seat. Add a telephone shower attachment and make the whole daily washing routine easier. Don't re-carpet or re-paint the walls, just re-paint

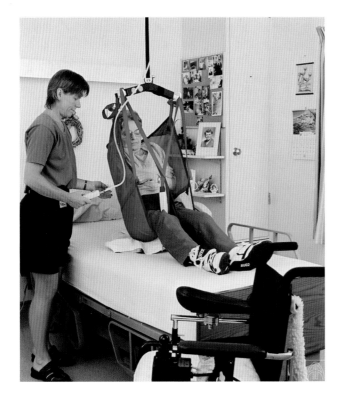

or spreads that seem relevant to your life or your parents' life. Or you can read it cover to cover and get a comprehensive picture of the freedom the full scope of barrier-free living can provide.

The more you understand how color and design modifications can facilitate everyday life, the better prepared you can be to modify your surroundings to make them work for you. The more familiar you are with the products developed to accommodate universal housing, the more aware you will be of the possibilities whenever you shop for home appliances and gadgets. Certainly this book does not show every product on the market in any class of products. But it does include typical accommodating products in their class. Use this book with a bit of imagination, and growing old could be just another phase in your full life.

Where to begin

Evaluate what is difficult now and likely to get more difficult with time. Then think through what type of budget you could realistically designate to tackling a challenge. Then, review the options suggested herein for modifying the environment. You may find that you can do more than you thought within your budget. Or you may find that what you fell in love with is beyond your means, but you'll settle for a lesser solution. To get to barrier-free living, you have to start somewhere.

—Barbara Krueger

the baseboards. Where there are less costly modifications that can accommodate barrier-free living, we have included them. We also show some Cadillac options so you will see that a home doesn't have to look institutional to be accessible or universal.

Does this entire book apply?

Only parts of this book will ring true for you. But the idea of the book applies to all of us lucky enough to grow old. You can flip through the chapters stopping only at the sections

LIFE CYCLES
What your aging process might look like

Wisdom, experience, and a stronger sense of self . . . these all come with growing older. Yet aging also can bring new challenges, such as diminished vision, declining agility, and memory loss. Slower recall of trivial information and names, feeling aches when bending to get something from a lower shelf, and stumbling over obstacles become more common.

The aging process occurs little by little over time, and at different rates for different people. It depends on a combination of genetic and environmental factors, and lifestyle choices. Though genes have a very powerful impact on how a person ages, the speed and severity of symptoms can be influenced by behavior. A healthy lifestyle including exercise, a healthy diet, social involvement, and spirituality can significantly improve functional ability and enrich the overall feeling of well-being.

While there is a range of individual responses to aging,

Vision

- Aging eyes are less able to absorb light, making it more difficult to see in dim lighting.

- At about the age of forty, near vision acuity starts to decrease.

- A person with decreased vision will have trouble seeing the shapes in a room with a muted color scheme.

- If there is a family history or early diagnosis of serious vision decline, design a home that is easy to navigate.

Agility

- Arthritis, back pain, injuries, certain health conditions, and medications can all affect a person's ability to move easily.

- First, become aware of the many modifications and products available to facilitate comfortable, accessible living.

- Then incorporate the appropriate solutions into your home.

- In many cases, it is possible to "age in place" in a comfortable, barrier-free home by making simple modifications.

there are inevitable alterations in our body. These changes are not necessarily debilitating. Disease is not automatically part of aging. But the physical transformations—as slight as they may be—can affect a person's lifestyle.

As these changes occur, it is easy to become unhappy or feel out of control. The great news is that we do have control over our attitudes and how we choose to deal with infirmities or limitations. We don't have to let our aging disrupt us negatively. There are simple steps that can be taken to ensure comfortable, even luxurious, living.

Memory

- Aging is associated with slower recall of trivial information, like where the keys are— especially if they weren't placed in their usual spot. Put things in the same place every time for easier recollection.

- Wise planning and organization can help everyone function better. Create memory triggers by posting photos of objects where they belong.

- For most dementia illnesses, the best strategy is structure. Keep things in their correct places and keep activities at the same time each day.

Anticipating the Aging Process

- Aging takes its toll on our senses: Vision, taste, touch, and hearing decline over time for most people.

- The rate of decline differs from person to person based on genetics and life experiences.

- Loud music causes loss of hearing and very spicy foods dull our taste buds to subtle seasonings.

- Planning a home with a "just in case" attitude can make aging in place as barrier free as possible.

1

FINE MOTOR CHALLENGES
Simple design features can keep joint and muscle pain from slowing you down

When the usual aging process affects activities of daily living, universal design offers practical solutions. People of advanced age can compensate for their diminished physical capabilities through planning, creativity, and technology. There are many simple strategies and devices that are available to help people overcome weakened hand-eye coordination and joint stiffness affecting fine motor skills.

By surveying the home, it is possible to identify potential problems that need to be addressed. The kitchen is a perfect place to make adjustments to accommodate people with motor skill challenges. For greater comfort and ease of operation, install easy to grip handles on all kitchen cabinets and

Better Grip Handles

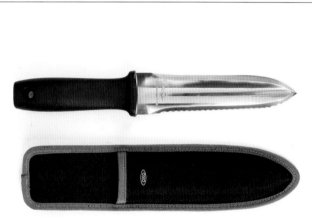

- Small, narrow, metal handles are not ergonomically designed and are very difficult and painful for arthritic fingers to grasp.

- Padded handles are softer and thicker so gripping them securely is easier and more comfortable.

- Replace the tools and utensils used most often or add padded adapters that fit onto existing tools to make the biggest difference in everyday life.

Fat Pens

- Simple solutions are available for common-use items, like fatter pens that require less of a grip to hold.

- Think about which everyday items have become challenging to use, and look for products that alleviate the struggle.

- If fine finger manipulations are painful or difficult, choose newer utensils and tools that are designed especially for hands with joint mobility challenges.

replace smaller appliance knobs with larger ones. And think creatively: Install cabinet doors and kitchen drawers that can be opened with the aid of other body parts such as wrists, arms, elbows, and forearms. It is a good idea to relieve the hands and fingers of tasks that can be accomplished by other means. Jar opening devices are essential for people with muscle weakness, joint pain, or decreased fine motor skills.

Throughout the home, replace standard door handles with lever-type handles. Select ones that are easier to grip and can be moved without the use of fingers, wherever possible. This will ease the burden of opening and closing doors for people with arthritis.

If the home has windows or doors that are stuck or difficult to operate, replace them with newer and better fitting ones. As with cabinets and drawers, opt for doors that can be opened and closed with the aid of other body parts such as legs and shoulders.

And, of course, remote control makes the operation of appliances, electronics, lights, and window treatments easier and less taxing on the muscles and joints.

Front Door Grip

- The simple act of unlocking and opening a door can be extremely difficult if the latch is not easy to release.

- Turning a doorknob requires a firm grasp and the ability to rotate the wrist. One or both of these actions can be a problem for someone with arthritis.

- A thumb latch is easy to push down, and a U-shaped handle is easy to grip.

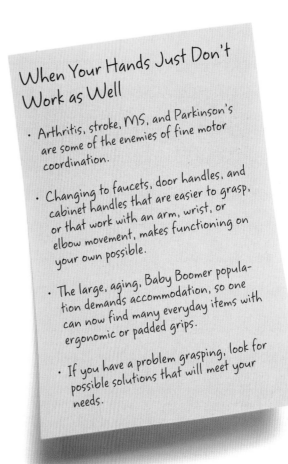

When Your Hands Just Don't Work as Well

- Arthritis, stroke, MS, and Parkinson's are some of the enemies of fine motor coordination.

- Changing to faucets, door handles, and cabinet handles that are easier to grasp, or that work with an arm, wrist, or elbow movement, makes functioning on your own possible.

- The large, aging, Baby Boomer population demands accommodation, so one can now find many everyday items with ergonomic or padded grips.

- If you have a problem grasping, look for possible solutions that will meet your needs.

VISUAL CHALLENGES

Good lighting, appropriate color choices, and familiar furniture layout assist declining vision

As part of the normal aging process, the eye's lens loses flexibility and begins to yellow, and the retina receives less light. This leads to visual challenges that can affect safety in the home if not addressed.

As the eye becomes less flexible, it is harder for it to adjust its focus. Close-up items often need to be held farther away to be clear. Reading glasses can help and are needed by many people after age forty.

The yellowing of the eye not only reduces illumination, but it also changes the perception of colors. White objects may appear yellow, and it is more difficult to distinguish between blues and greens.

Blurry Words

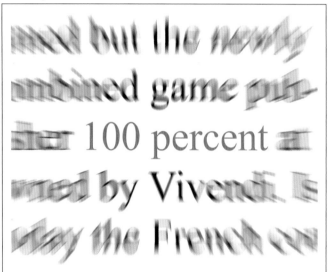

- Inexpensive drugstore magnifying glasses can help farsighted people read small print.

- Large print books, available in libraries, bookstores, and on the Internet, can reawaken the love of reading for those with poor vision.

- Look also for books on tape, often read in the author's voice.

- Purchase portable magnifying screens or rulers to read oven dials or dishwasher buttons.

Controls on the Stove

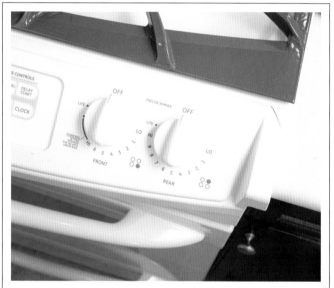

- Stove knobs and digital stove controls can be hard to read for those with poor vision.

- Upward-facing control knobs are usually illuminated better than front-facing ones. Consider an additional overhead light to make reading even easier.

- Before purchasing a new stove, look to see that the dials and controls are clearly marked and easy to understand.

It becomes more challenging to see clearly in dim light. Night vision declines. It is harder to discriminate between similar colors, so stronger color contrasts need to be used. Better lighting should be installed throughout the home, with additional task lighting in needed areas. People in their sixties need three times more light for comfortable reading than those in their twenties. Muscles in the pupil respond less to changes in lighting, and it is more difficult to manage glare. Light dimmers and glare-controlling window treatments can help.

Down a Hallway

- Hallways can be uncomfortable or tenuous to navigate for those with poor vision. They may be dark, with light coming only from doorways to side rooms.

- When possible keep doors to rooms along the hall opened during the day to maximize light.

- To illuminate a dark hallway and make it safer for travel, add recessed ceiling or track lights that are controlled by illuminated switches at both ends of the hallway.

Depth Perception

- Depth perception may be a challenge for those with poor or uncorrected vision problems. When focusing on something close-up, surfaces in the background can become a fuzzy blur.

- By using contrasting colors or shades, the various levels in a room and surface edges become easier to distinguish.

- Counters are viewed from above as we perform tasks. Beyond the counter edge is the floor, which can be out of focus. Using contrasting colors between counter and floor is helpful.

JUST NOT AS AGILE

Home adaptations and technology can compensate for physical limitations

As the body ages, tasks and activities that were at one time routine may become more challenging to perform. Reduced physical exercise can cause muscle mass deterioration as well as diminished range of motion. Consistent exercise helps the body maintain strength and flexibility, but even active adults may notice that certain activities involving reaching,

bending, stretching, or turning are sometimes accompanied by aches and pains.

Some reduced physical abilities occur from injuries and may ease over time, especially with physical therapy and exercise. Older bodies, however, require more time to heal than younger ones. Despite the physical limitations that

KNACK UNIVERSAL DESIGN

Reaching

- It is necessary to tilt the neck back and raise arms above the shoulder in order to reach items placed above the head.

- A fully extended arm cannot hold as much weight as a bent arm.

- If reaching overhead items has become difficult, store only rarely used items on the top shelf. Heavy items should be placed down low.

- For people using wheelchairs for mobility, objects stored on high shelves are out of reach.

Stairs

- Hip or knee problems can make climbing or descending a staircase tricky.

- When we can't see clearly to the bottom of the staircase, tenuous descent is made harder because the bottom of the stairs appears fuzzy. Good light can give confi-

dence by clearly illuminating the entire staircase.

- A good handrail can offer confidence in descending the stairs and be a strong aid in climbing them.

increase with injury or disease, there are ways to ease the burden on the body. The increased sensitivity toward those who are physically challenged, and the growing market of the eighty-plus population, has spawned a focus on technological advances that address physical abilities versus limitations. Inventors are continually conceiving gadgets and aids that simplify everyday tasks, making activities of daily living more manageable and convenient.

Devices and aids such as jar openers, easy-to-grip door handles and faucets, remote controls, and chair lifts enable people to perform much of the same activities as in their fitter days, while relieving the strain on muscles and joints. Simple changes can alleviate muscular stress on the body. Longer-term problems may require more extensive and expensive solutions. In some cases, doctor-prescribed modifications and devices are covered by government programs or medical insurance providers. Ask a professional for advice.

Vacuum

- Many household chores require bending, flexing, pushing, pulling, and gripping. When these physical movements become challenging due to poor muscle tone or a debilitating disorder, alternatives should be sought.

- When certain household tasks cannot be delegated, lightweight tools are attractive alternatives.

- If a heavy upright vacuum is hard to push, it may need repair. Or consider replacing it with a new lighter-weight model that is easier to use.

When Bending, Stretching, or Walking Is Challenging

- Recognize when what used to be doable becomes challenging, and remember that safety is the first concern for long-term quality of life.

- If reaching and bending are difficult, rearrange storage so items used daily are between mid-thigh and shoulder height.

- If stairs are difficult to climb, use the banister, and perhaps a properly fitted cane used as directed to keep yourself using the stairs safely for as long as possible.

- If household appliances are too heavy or difficult to use, look for new models that do the same job, but are lighter and easier to use.

7

MOBILITY CHALLENGES
When exercise and medication don't solve the problem, adaptation is the key to improving mobility

People experience varying degrees of decreased mobility if they have not continued to stay physically active over the years. Walks that used to be easy and pain free can feel burdensome and strenuous. It may take a much shorter distance to become winded and fatigued. Routine tasks such as climbing stairs, carrying groceries, and gardening may seem more

difficult or altogether impossible. Strength, stamina, and balance are all susceptible to erosion, but can be maintained or regained if worked on.

Meeting with a professional will help to determine if there is a long-term prognosis of decline. People who understand their physical limitations are better able to make needed

KNACK UNIVERSAL DESIGN

Tripod Cane

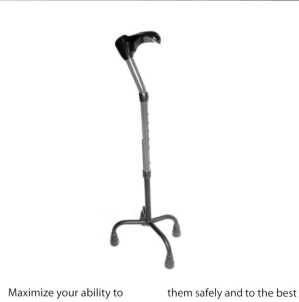

Walker

- Maximize your ability to get around and stay active with a walking aid that meets your specific abilities. Safety should be a priority.

- A variety of cane aids are available, but a professional should fit them specifically and individually. Users need to be trained on how to use

them safely and to the best advantage.

- When a simple cane is not enough to offer stability tri- and quad-canes may be options.

- Walkers can help people stay mobile longer.

- Satchels can be added to walkers to carry small items, and some walkers come with seats, so the user can turn and sit down.

- Standard-width walkers are wider than interior door-

ways, and doorways may need to be widened.

- Crutches might be an option for stairs, which are unmanageable with a walker. But crutches require more fitness and are not a realistic alternative for the elderly.

adjustments to their home. The use of appropriately pre-scribed mobility aids can also increase functioning in the home environment.

If mobility decreases, be sure to get advice on the best types of exercise or therapy for bringing back full function and strength. While you are working to improve the body's function, some modifications can make everyday tasks easier to perform.

Technology provides solutions that can help people remain mobile, capable, and independent. For many mobility challenges, there is a device or aid that can help compensate for diminished physical ability.

Wheelchairs and Doorways

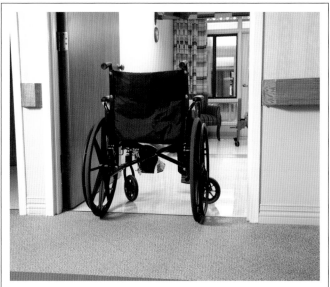

- People in wheelchairs come upon many obstacles in a standard home, not the least of which can be narrow doorways.

- Wheelchairs are not only needed by people who are paralyzed, but also by those who are unstable when walking with a cane or walker alone.

- Manual wheelchairs can be replaced by motorized scooters.

- Medical insurance, Medicare, or Medicaid will often cover the cost of either.

Wheelchair Stair Ramp

- Short stairways of one or two steps can be handled with ramps, provided they are wide enough for the wheelchair.

- A temporary solution to accommodate a visitor in a wheelchair is to place two 12-inch-wide heavy planks at wheel width apart over one or two steps. The planks can be stored in a vehicle and brought out as needed.

- Some wheelchairs can navigate high thresholds and short steps.

MEMORY LOSS
Organizational solutions can help people cope with remembering

Memory loss is often associated with aging, but the normal brain does not experience a severe memory deficit. If there is acute absentmindedness and an inability to understand, a doctor should be consulted to see if there is a diagnosis of Alzheimer's or dementia.

Common signs of usual memory loss are poor recall and forgetfulness. By making some minor adjustments in life's daily routines and taking advantage of organization and memory aids, it is possible to minimize the impact of poor recall and forgetfulness.

The best way to cope with forgetfulness is to reduce or eliminate clutter in the household and try to keep a specific place for everything. The fewer unnecessary distractions and obstacles that are in the home, the better. This is especially true if two or more people share the same residence.

Creating and maintaining organized systems within the

Front Door with Photo(s)

- Dementia can cause progressive memory loss over time. In some patients, distant memories seem to be retained over more recent ones.

- Dementia patients may recognize photos of childhood homes or family from years ago long after their memory of daily activities disappears.

- Use photos at doorways and on walls inside rooms to help someone with dementia recognize the area.

Tray with Reminder Keys

- Pictorial memory cues act as reminders and decrease frustration.

- Because someone with dementia can lose the ability to read, pictorial cues are a helpful solution.

- For those who don't have dementia, but are simply forgetful, use picture, word, or letter cues to lessen the occurrence of misplaced keys, glasses, purses, etc.

- A large calendar placed in a visible area can act as both a verbal and pictorial reminder.

home for routine tasks promotes familiarity and can aid memory. When commonly used items—such as keys and shoes—are stored in the same place each time, people are more likely to locate them without any trouble.

Planned routines are also helpful to keep people with memory loss oriented. When the same sequence of events happens each day, people are more likely to be able to rely on repetition to orient.

Automate as many tasks as possible so there is less to concentrate upon and less chance for error: set up auto-pay for bills, set timers for watering the lawn, and put the thermostat and the home alarm system on a predetermined schedule.

Work with a reliable person to set up a week or month of pills in special pill boxes to keep track of medication regimes. The boxes come with separate compartments for morning, noon, and night, and with compartments for seven or thirty-one days.

Writing down important information, to-do lists, schedules, appointments, and notes helps jog the memory and can be a valuable aid to keep life on track.

Keys on a Hook

- Simple organization makes it easier to store items and find them when needed—without aggravation.

- Place things where they are used. For example, store the dog's leash, sunglasses, and keys by the door.

- Keep a few extra keys near the door to remind you to place the keys there when you come back home.

Pill Organizers

- To cut down on the likelihood of serious mistakes, put systems into place that support important daily activities.

- There are many helpful gadgets that can compensate for forgetfulness.

- Pill organizers are helpful, reminding you not only to take the correct pills on time on the right days, but also to refill the prescription before it runs out.

ENTRY DOORS

Designate at least one entrance as your easy-access doorway and keep it safe and accessible

There is nothing more essential to any home than an easily accessible entryway. Most homes have several entrances, and some will be simpler to modify for easy access than others.

If there are any mobility concerns, plan to have at least one entrance without steps. If possible, eliminate all steps at the main entry door. But if it's too expensive to make such a change, or it interferes with the curb appeal of your home, consider reworking a side entrance.

All entranceways should have sufficient light-ing. This is not just practical, but aesthetic as well: Lighting around the front of your home adds drama and sophistication. You may want to put the front door light on a sensor so it always turns on

Entry Door Handles

- The type of entry-door hardware should be dependent upon the abilities and needs of the occupants.

- Curved, modified "U-shaped" hardware with a thumb latch is the simplest to open for those with finger and hand dexterity and grasping issues. Round knobs can be difficult to turn.

- If there is a security screen door, make sure it is also simple and painless to open.

Patio Slider or French Doors

- There are many options for exterior doors. Patio and yard access doors may slide or swing in pairs (French doors).

- Lock modifications are possible on patio and French doors that allow for effortless opening and closing.

- Large glass doors present a danger because they are hard to see when closed. Mark them clearly so that no one mistakenly tries to walk through a closed glass door. Mullions are a safe option.

when someone approaches. Focus the light on the door lock, ensuring clear visibility for putting in the key and unlocking the door.

Shelter from the elements is another concern. Select as the easy-access entrance one that is protected by a porch or overhang. Or designate one where you can easily add an overhang above the door. It is a lot easier to unlock a door once you are out of the rain, wind, or midday sun. The covering will also keep water, ice, and snow from building up around the door.

GREEN ● LIGHT

An automatic garage door opener offers safe access into a garage for someone in a wheelchair. The remote button in the car opens and closes the door without the driver having to get out of the car. After exiting the vehicle and getting into the wheelchair to enter the house, a button next to the entry door will close the garage door when pushed.

Screens

- A screen can add safety when installed behind a large glass panel door because its mesh pattern acts as a reminder that there is a closed door.

- But many screen locks are small and difficult to turn or move. Choose screens with larger locks that are much easier to manipulate.

- To prevent getting locked outside accidentally, set the screen to be permanently unlocked.

Garage Door Sensor

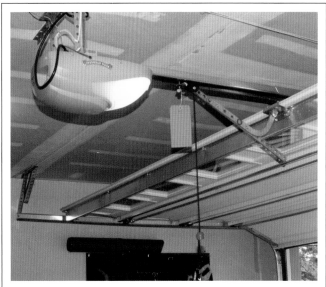

- A garage door sensor, which signals when the garage door is left open, can be installed inside the house by the company that installed the garage door opener.

- For those who are a bit forgetful or absentminded, especially when it comes to closing the garage, sensors provide a safe reminder.

- Get in the habit of checking the door or sensor before going to bed at night or when home alone.

THRESHOLDS

Create easy access throughout the home and make getting around safer

Going from room to room is something people take for granted when they are young and agile, but those simple transitions can be hazardous for those with even slight mobility issues. Varying levels, high thresholds, and flooring changes increase the risk of falling. To make moving about the home—and getting in and out—trouble free, make adjustments in the doorway thresholds.

The first threshold to consider is the entry door. A level entrance area with smooth access from the outside is ideal. But before you take a sledgehammer to your front door steps, consider adding a ramp. Access ramps can be wood, steel, aluminum, or concrete. For a more natural look, you can

Entry Thresholds

- Doorways represent transitions from one space to another and thresholds are designed to be part of the transition.

- A change in level in a doorway may present an obstacle for someone with agility challenges or poor vision.

- To prevent tripping over a threshold, add a small bevel or ramp. Sometimes this can be installed under the carpeting, and outside it can be gradual enough to fit under the entry doormat.

Patio Door Thresholds

- Patio door thresholds include not just the flooring change from inside to outside, but also the door runners and frame.

- An elevation change is necessary to protect the interior from significant rainfall, but the step should

- be modified to make the entrance more accessible.

- A small ramp can be added to a single step to create a smooth access.

modify your landscaping to create an easy entry. Relandscaping to create a smooth access to the front door is the ideal choice for appearance and resale value.

Inside the home, wherever possible, eliminate threshold obstacles. Thresholds should be kept flush with the surrounding floors. A change in color or pattern should highlight a raised threshold. Wherever a flat floor meets carpet, a smooth transition is needed so that people who shuffle or use walkers can maneuver easily from space to space.

Garage: House Entry

- Entry from the garage must be convenient since passing through it is often done with packages in hand.

- A doorstop is a convenient way to keep the door opened while entering or exiting.

- Banisters are not required for one or two steps, but if your garage steps lack one, add it for safety.

- If a banister is not enough support, install an entrance ramp for safety if space permits.

Flooring Transitions

- Falls may be caused by decreased vision, balance, or lower extremity strength. Diminished judgment due to dementia or sedation medication can also lead to accidents.

- A common place for tripping is at the transition from hard flooring to carpet.

- Reduce your risk of falling by installing a transition strip that visually emphasizes the edge and makes the transition smoother.

- When wearing slippers around the house, avoid a backless style to decrease the likelihood of shuffling.

AROUND THE CAR
Establish an accessible, convenient space for getting in and out of the car

Getting in and out of the car should be as quick and easy as possible. For those with mobility challenges, extra space is required.

Wheelchair users need a spacious garage. A van with a side lift requires a two-car garage. If the garage does not have enough space for a wheelchair to be maneuvered next to the car door, street or driveway parking may be necessary. An alternative is to have the chair lift into the back of the van. The cost of a lift may be defrayed by insurance. Many car manufacturers have the ability to install these specialized lifts for free.

Whatever spot is chosen for parking the car, make sure it is

Extra Space to Get In

- It is sometimes necessary to park only one car in a two-car garage to leave room for wheelchair access.

- When planning the garage space, consider how and where the wheelchair will go into the car or van. Will it go behind the driver's seat,

- into the trunk, or in the back of the van?

- For less hip strain, turn sideways and swing the feet outside the car to exit. Reverse the sequence to get in.

Look for Level Ground

- Park on level ground for easiest transfer to wheelchair or motorized scooter.

- If the chair or scooter is stored in the back of the van or car, having level ground in back is most important.

- If the wheelchair user must walk from the back of the car to the driver's door, level ground is needed all around the car.

level. If the driveway has a slope, it is a poor choice for wheelchair access parking.

If the car is parked in the garage, the space should be clutter free. Obstacles will not only make getting in and out of the car more difficult, but they can also cause dangerous accidents. Make sure all items stored in the garage are placed out of the way and off the floor. Garage shelving can be installed for clean organization. If you are parking your car on the driveway or the street, consider adding an overhang. During bad weather you will appreciate the protection.

Electric Garage Door Opener

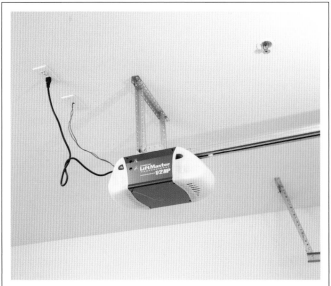

- An automatic garage door opener is an important safety device, especially for anyone living alone.

- Automatic openers come with an electronic eye that prevents them from closing when something is in the way. Older models may close until they hit something, and then reverse themselves.

- Electric garage door openers have a release lever that enables them to operate manually if the electricity goes out.

Garage Door Keypad

- An electric garage door opener is controlled from a button installed next to the door jamb at the entry to the house from the garage.

- Open and close the garage door as needed when you go between the house and the garage.

- As long as the electricity is working, you do not have to go outside the garage door to lift it open.

EXTERIOR DOOR HARDWARE
Modify door hardware to make entering and exiting easier

Mobility and fine motor skill challenges can affect the ability to open a door easily. To make getting in and out of the house easier, door hardware can be changed. These improvements are simple, quick, and inexpensive.

The first thing to do is to replace the standard doorknob with a lever handle, or fit it with a rubber or plastic adapter that converts the existing doorknob into a lever. Standard knobs need to be grabbed and twisted, which can be difficult

or cause pain. Lever handles can simply be pressed down by a fist, forearm, or elbow.

The knob on the interior of the door should be exchanged for a lever handle, as well, for safe and unproblematic exits. Assure that it is easy and quick to operate.

Exterior visibility from the *inside* of the entry door is crucial for safety and security. If the door is lacking a peephole, install at least one. It is best to have two peepholes so that

Getting Inside

- Hardware choices can add beauty to a door, but make certain the door handle and lock are easy to use.

- Easy-grip levered door handles are especially important for arthritic hands.

- If multiple keys are needed to unlock the door, highlight them with colorful plastic rings to tell them apart easily and quickly.

- Levered or modified "U-shaped" entry door handles are the easiest to grasp and turn.

Getting Inside: Part II

- Arthritis or paralysis from a stroke can impair the ability to grasp and turn a doorknob.

- Levered entry door handles are easier to grasp and turn and can even be controlled with a closed hand, an arm,

- or elbow. Hand, wrist, or finger agility is not needed.

- Exterior door handles can also be installed on a door along with a separate deadbolt lock.

any family member can use one without bending or stretching. If there is a resident in a wheelchair, the lower secondary peephole should be installed 42 to 48 inches from the floor.

MAKE IT EASY

Add beauty while creating easier door access. Comfortable, easy-to-operate exterior door hardware comes in a large variety of finishes and styles. Choose a handle that makes a dramatic statement on your front door. Decorative side plates can add the look and feel while the handle is still updated for simple, modern use.

Getting Outside: Easy Egress

- Levered door handles are available in countless designs and finishes.

- If someone is in a wheelchair, the original door handle might not be at a comfortable height. It may require that a new door be installed so that the handles can be mounted at the appropriate level. Another option is to add a second handle with a lock to the existing door.

- If a door needs to be opened from a wheelchair, and it opens in, there needs to be enough room for the door to swing clear of the chair.

Getting Outside: Limiting Egress

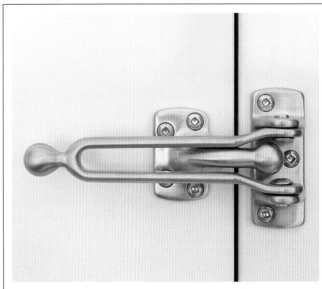

- Patients with dementia can wander outside and get disoriented and lost, so it is a good idea to safeguard the exit doors.

- Don't make the exterior doors too difficult to unlock in case of a fire emergency.

- Devices used to limit egress should be obvious to, and in reach of, non-affected persons but not in direct view of those not meant to use them. A simple latch installed above eye level is an inexpensive solution.

INTERIOR DOORS: QUICK FIXES
Make passageways easier to maneuver with a few modifications

With universal design, many of the modifications involve *removing* things from the home. For example, simply taking down an interior door will give you several extra inches of space to get in and out of a room. All unnecessary doors can be removed for easier transitions throughout the home. In all doorways, at least 32 inches of clear width is needed for smooth wheelchair or walker access. That means that the door needs to be at least 36 inches wide, because when a 36-inch door is open, there is only about 32 inches of clear space. If any of your doors are narrower than that, you'll want to remove them.

Removing interior doors will also create a more open feeling. Think about how great it is to have comfortable, wide openings between rooms. And an open floor plan is much more accessible.

After doors are removed, pay attention to flooring changes

Narrow Doorways

- It is not necessary to have a door in every archway or opening.

- When only a few extra inches are necessary to create easy wheelchair passage, and privacy or quiet is not needed, simply remove the door. That will usually provide 4 extra inches in the opening.

- Leave the hinge flanges in place so that the door can be reinstalled at a later date if desired. Remove them if a bit of extra room is needed.

Folding Screens or Bi-fold Doors

- If privacy is needed and the original door restricts wheelchair or walker access a bi-fold door attached at one side of the doorjamb is a simple and inexpensive solution.

- Folding screens come in different vinyl colors while bi-fold doors, generally made of wood, can be painted to match décor or contrast.

- Either bi-fold doors or folding screens can be an option for creating privacy when a conventional door needs to be removed but privacy is still wanted.

in the thresholds. If a room has a different floor from the hallway and it isn't flush, install a bridge or small ramp to make the transition smooth.

Of course there are some doors that you will want to keep, like the bathroom (unless your guests don't mind!). For those doors you must keep, consider changing your knobs. Levered door handles can be easily operated by anyone and are especially convenient for those with hand mobility issues. Even if someone has difficulty gripping or twisting a doorknob, he or she can use an elbow, forearm, closed fist, or wrist to open a door with a lever.

Another thing to consider with door handles is the ability to lock and unlock quickly and easily. With decreased fine motor skills, it is difficult to twist a tiny button. Choose handles with large locks that unlock automatically when the handle is pushed down from the inside.

Levered Door Handles

- Hard to grasp or turn doorknobs can be replaced with levered handles fairly easily and inexpensively. They can be changed out by any handyman with a screwdriver.

- Levered door handles are available with or without locks.

- When choosing a levered door handle with a lock, make sure that it is easy to engage the locking mechanism.

- Adapters can also be purchased that fit over an existing knob and convert it to a lever.

Easy Locking and Unlocking

- Select a locking levered door handle that unlocks with just a push of the lever.

- If someone is likely to accidentally lock himself or herself in a room, purchase door handles that have a safety release on the non-locking side and keep the unlocking device handy— perhaps on the top of the doorjamb frame above the door.

- A less expensive option is to tape over the locking mechanism. This may be sufficient to prevent a person with dementia from locking the door.

REMODELING INTERIOR DOORWAYS
Create practical solutions that are also beautiful

If the quick fixes aren't sufficient, you can remodel your interior doorways to create functional solutions that are gorgeous as well.

When a narrow doorway needs to be widened to accommodate wheelchairs, a contractor will take off the door jamb, remove the casing, and create a wider opening. If there is a threshold—blocks of wood or tile—have it removed completely to create a flush transition in the doorway. Once the

expanded doorjamb is installed, you can add a wider door, but if it is feasible, leave the door off completely for more ample access.

Switching from a traditional hinged door to a pocket door can provide approximately three to four feet of additional usable wall space. Instead of opening into a room, the door slides into the wall, hiding from view when opened. This is a perfect option if you need to use more of your space without

Pocket Door: Bathroom

- Bathrooms can be too small for a wheelchair or walker, especially when they have an inward swinging door.

- Although costly to add, pocket doors can provide the room needed to make a bathroom accessible.

- A pocket door with a glass inset allows light to be shared by an adjacent room space while the door is closed.

- Pocket doors are often used to provide privacy in bathrooms between the toilet and the washing area.

Pocket Door: Room 2

- When a doorway is too narrow, redoing the jamb to accommodate a pocket door can be done to add the extra width.

- Extra wall space can also be gained without an opened door in the way.

- In a wide doorway, two pocket doors—one on each side—can replace a set of double doors, recovering a lot of needed wall space otherwise taken up by two doors opened onto adjacent walls.

sacrificing needed privacy. Pocket door designs are limitless. Semi-transparent decorative glass doors add chic style, providing some privacy while allowing light to filter through. Choose the highest quality hardware for the pocket doors so they slide easily, and be sure to choose a U-shaped door pull.

A less expensive remodel is to replace the standard door hinges with offset hinges. Offset door hinges are designed to swing the door clear of the opening, providing access to the full width of the doorway frame. This adds about 2 inches of additional clearance.

After the doors and jambs are complete, get out your paint can. If vision is a concern paint all doors, moldings, and jambs in high contrast to the walls around them. Also consider adding contrast at all thresholds to give them emphasis.

Before investing in replacing a door or doorway for accessibility be sure that the space inside the bathroom or narrow kitchen will accommodate a turning wheelchair (60").

Widening the Doorway: Room 1

- A wider doorway may be needed to provide more light and to allow wheelchair access.

- Measure and decide on the additional width needed in the doorway before you begin a widening project.

- Offset hinges can provide two extra doorway inches. If more width is needed, approximately 4 inches can be gained by removing the door.

- Consider the loss of wall space when beginning a door-widening project, and make a plan for rearranging the furniture, if necessary.

Widening the Doorway: Room 2

- A creative way to widen a doorway is to open as much of the wall space as possible. This will tie two rooms together and create an open floor plan.

- This kitchen opening allows more space for entering the kitchen from the dining area by eliminating the inches needed for a standard doorjamb.

- The larger opening also allows light from the kitchen windows to illuminate the dining area.

HARD SURFACE FLOORING
Hard flooring surfaces have advantages when mobility is a challenge

Whatever hard surface flooring you choose—vinyl, tile, marble, terrazzo, clay pavers, or stone—make sure it is non-slip. Balance difficulties and the potential for falling can increase with age, so flooring choices are important.

Tile and stone flooring with unglazed, non-slip finishes are better choices for entranceways and bathrooms because of their ability to withstand water. Smaller tiles mean more grout and better traction.

Avoid heavily textured tiles. Very uneven surfaces are difficult for wheelchairs and walkers.

Vinyl flooring is low cost and easy maintenance. It is also great for wheelchairs and softer in case of a fall. Some comes with padded backing for extra cushion.

Remember that continuous, smooth floor surfaces are the easiest to use, as well as the safest.

Vinyl and Linoleum

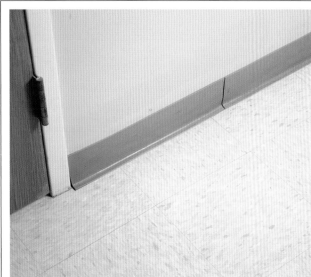

- Vinyl and linoleum are inexpensive hard surface flooring choices.

- They can be designed to imitate the look of other floor surfaces, like wood, tile, or stone.

- The wide choice of color and patterns makes it easy to select a pattern that creates needed contrast with other design elements in the home, accommodating those with poor vision. Contrast the flooring with the walls, counters, and any window treatments that hang to the floor.

Tile

- Tiles are available in gloss or matte, with smooth or rough textured finishes. They are made of porcelain or clay.

- Place the tile sample on the floor and view it while standing. Make sure it will contrast with the surrounding wall, baseboard, and counter.

- To reduce the chance of slipping, choose a textured finish tile for the bathroom or kitchen. In a small space, select matte tiles because they reflect less light and create fewer glares.

MAKE IT EASY

Varying floor texture and color is a way to help someone distinguish different rooms. They can recognize the kitchen with linoleum flooring, the carpeted living room, bathrooms with tiles, etc.

YELLOW LIGHT

Although hard surface to hard surface transitions work well for wheelchairs and walkers, low pile or indoor-outdoor carpets or low, dense pile carpet can be a good alternative when osteoporotic bones and instability are a concern. Any fall can be dangerous, but carpeting offers a bit more padding than does hard surface tile or stone.

Stone

- The natural quality of stone provides interesting variations in color and texture, but some products are cut with an irregular surface that can be a tripping hazard.

- If the irregular cut surface is desired, be sure the edges of the stones are installed evenly to minimize the opportunity for tripping.

- Glass that is dropped onto stone floors will break easily, as will frail bones.

Wood

- Select a wood color or stain that will create a strong contrast with the wall or floor-length draperies. Because wood is a natural product, variations in the grain are not controllable, but stains can darken the overall floor to provide the necessary contrast.

- Also consider the contrast between the flooring and the furniture that sits on it.

- In areas that may get wet, consider protecting the wood with a rubber-backed rug or vinyl mat.

CARPETING

Select carpeting that suits your lifestyle but won't trip you up

The right carpet not only provides greater comfort, but also increases safety in the event of a fall and saves energy by adding warmth. When choosing carpeting, consider both the functional and aesthetic requirements of the household.

There are many beautiful carpeting options that work in a universal design home. Look for a smooth texture with a low pile (no higher than a half inch). Tight weaves and dense knotting provide longer durability and more safety, which is especially important for canes, walkers, and wheelchairs—and, of course, pointy high heels.

Avoid plush carpeting, as it is too thick and soft for comfortable mobility. People with wheelchairs or walkers and those with balance problems will have a hard time moving around on carpet that is too plush. If you need a carpet pad, choose a dense pad that isn't too soft. A deep pad will create a spongy surface that is unsafe for anyone with decreased balance.

Low Pile

- The shorter the pile or nap of the carpet, the easier it is to move a wheelchair or scooter across the surface.

- Low-pile carpeting is available in wool, cotton, silk, bamboo, and synthetic fibers.

- Synthetic fibers require the least maintenance, because they do not grow mold and can more easily release stains. They also tend to cause less allergy problems.

Sculpted Pile

- Sculpted pile, or carpet with alternating high and low surfaces, is considered a patterned carpet.

- The varying depths make moving a wheelchair more difficult than on an even or short-pile carpet.

- The uneven height and low texture can lead to tripping, especially for those who shuffle.

- It is also not friendly to those who wear high heels.

On the other hand, if you or a family member is prone to allergies, use carpeting sparingly, and vacuum it often. Some people are allergic to wool and should choose carpets made from synthetic, bamboo, or silk fibers. Other people are allergic to substances in the dust that collects in the carpet, rather than to the carpet itself, so cleaning regularly will alleviate symptoms.

You'll need to create a seamless transition where your carpeting meets another floor. Flooring installers can help ensure that your travel from room to room is smooth.

Wall-to-Wall Carpets

- Solid-colored wall-to-wall carpet creates a uniform background for the furniture in the room, which simplifies coordination of the room's elements.

- Wall-to-wall carpet is safer than rugs because there are no edges for tripping.

- Good contrast between the color of carpeting and the color of furniture and walls makes navigating within the room easier.

- Some carpet stains may be harder to clean than spills on glazed tile, but carpet is easier to maintain than real wood floors.

Carpet Pad

- A thick, soft carpet pad creates a spongy, unsteady surface for a wheelchair.

- Those who are unsteady on their feet will also find it hard to balance on a thick pad.

- Carpets can be glued directly to the floor to avoid any pad difficulties.

- A thin, dense carpet pad is the best choice. It will not be spongy to navigate, but will still give the added padding needed to cushion falls and help the carpet wear longer.

FLOORING TREATMENTS

FLOORING EDGE TREATMENTS
Simple home modifications can aid perception, reducing possible bumps

Because of the eyes' decreasing ability to distinguish spatial differences, the edges of steps and walls should be specially treated to minimize the chances of potentially dangerous stumbling and falling. If walls are the same color as the floor, it is difficult to see where one ends and the other begins. This perceptual difficulty can lead to accidents.

Wherever there is a change in level, a strong contrast must be created: a distinct pattern alteration, a vivid color contrast, or a bright strip of paint to mark the edge.

Edges occur all over the house, and they should all be treated for maximum safety. The most dangerous ones are the edges of stairs. Add a strip of bold color on the front of

Wall and Floor Edges

- Solid, darker-colored carpets provide the best contrast for light walls.

- With multicolored tweed or sculpted pile carpets, consider the *overall* hue and make sure it contrasts with the shade of the wall.

- Maintaining a similar color hue on all floor surfaces, carpeted or not, helps people with poor vision stay floor-wall oriented throughout the house.

Contrasting Baseboard

- When the floor and walls are a similar color, paint the baseboard in a contrasting hue or color.

- Choose flat-finish paints rather than gloss to minimize glare.

- A satin finish has a bit of sheen, but is more washable than flat-finish paints.

- Even if the walls and floor are different textures, a contrast in color is still needed to provide safety to those with poor vision.

the top edge of each step so that each tread is seen clearly and separately when walking down. A contrasting color on the risers will make them easier to see while walking up.

If stairs are not carpeted, apply strips of reflective tape to the edges. They aren't noticed in daylight, but can be very helpful during evening hours. If contrast is needed during the day, add a contrast color strip to the stair edges.

Don't forget other small steps in the home, like single step-down rooms. If the flooring in the room and on the step is too similar in appearance, treat the front edge of the step with a color or pattern that stands out.

Reduce visual confusion and the chances for accidents by treating the edges where walls meet the floor. Light walls in a room with dark flooring help to define the difference.

If the walls and floor are similar in shade, you can simply paint the baseboard molding in a contrasting color to create an effective edge treatment.

Top of Stairs

- A change in flooring material just before stairs can warn even a blind person that there is a level change ahead.

- Those with poor vision may have to count steps as they descend a staircase unless each step is distinctly marked as separate and the bottom of the stairs is also clearly marked.

- Good lighting is imperative on stairs.

Bottom of Stairs

- For staircases that have multiple landings, and those that change direction at landings, treat each landing as if it is a separate flight of stairs.

- Clearly mark the top and the bottom of each series of steps. Pay particular attention to the edge of the landing before the next group of stairs.

- Falling up the stairs results in bangs on one's legs or arms. Falling down the stairs can be fatal.

AREA RUGS

Well-planned area rugs can add beauty and still be safe

Area rugs add warmth and beauty and are often a needed accessory to complete a room's décor. But they must be used strategically to create the biggest impact while supporting safety in the home.

Area rugs help define a space by establishing parameters of a seating group or a particular area. They also serve to create harmony and pull all of the elements in that space together. In an open floor plan, they work to create visual distinctions between different areas without the need for large obstacles, like furniture, walls, or doors.

On glossy or light-reflecting floors, area rugs act to block distracting glare. Their texture absorbs the shine, making the light in the room more balanced and even.

Create a visual guide down a hallway using a long-running area rug. The added color or pattern contrast on the floor will help eyes navigate an otherwise tricky space.

Create an Edge Effect

- For safety, choose area rugs that contrast in color to the floor so that they can be seen easily.

- Area rugs can be created from traditional carpet materials or even made of rubber or vinyl solids. New materials for rugs now include bamboo and recycled plastic. With the many materials available, finding a contrasting color to the floor should be easy.

- A rug that contrasts with the surrounding floor will be even safer if it is anchored to the floor with tape or has a non-slip pad underneath.

Use an Area Rug as a Runner

- A carpet runner can stretch the entire length of a hall-way, or a series of small area rugs can be used.

- Use a non-slip pad under a runner or non-slip tape for safety.

- Pay special attention to the rug edges because anyone who shuffles can trip on them. Avoid fringed rugs.

- Be aware that someone with dementia could see the edges of the rug as a barrier and refuse to cross onto it.

Area rugs make a sitting area cozier, often adding needed color and accent. They can even act as interesting artwork. But they may cause hazards in doorways and other highly traveled areas.

Where an area rug could cause accidents, create an "area rug" with contrast flooring that is flush with surrounding floors. This will identify a specific area visually, without adding unwanted obstacles.

Designate Spaces

- In a large, open room used for multiple functions, area rugs can define specific areas.

- Place coordinating rugs in a large space. One can designate the game area; another can specify the TV seating.

- For a dining area, choose a rug that is large enough so that all chair legs are still on the rug even when the chair is pushed away from the table.

Designate Areas by Rug Placement

- Area rugs for adjacent spaces should have walking space between them.

- Choose area rugs for the amount of contrast they present with the flooring beneath.

- Contrast can be from a distinctive pattern or from a color change.

- Avoid fringes at the edge of rugs. Even if short, they can be a tripping hazard.

- Secure large rug edges with special tape so they do not curl up after many people have walked on them.

THROW RUGS

Take extra precautions with smaller, scattered rugs

The compact size of throw rugs can lead you to believe they are innocuous. But loose throw rugs hold the potential for great danger. These rugs often cause stumbling, tripping, and falling, sometimes leading to serious injuries. The safest thing to do is to remove them from the home. That being said, there are a few things that can be done to make throw rugs a bit safer.

Select only thin rugs—¼-inch high at the most. Avoid all fringe and trimmings at the edge. Look for non-fabric materials like linoleum or vinyl. Vinyl floor mats are popular because their edges are thin. But if they start rolling up—which they often do—get rid of them immediately.

Although non-skid floor mats protect larger area rugs from sliding, a smaller throw rug needs to have double-sided tape applied around all edges to ensure better stability.

A common use of the throw rug is as a welcome mat inside

Throw Rug with Rubber Backing

- Use throw rugs sparingly around people who are unsteady on their feet. If they are needed to catch water drips, use rubber-backed rugs.

- There is little danger of slipping from a bit of water on the floor if you are in a wheelchair, but in a home shared with a mobile person, a rubber-backed rug beveled at the edge is the best choice.

Non-fabric Area Rugs

- Area rugs that can be sponged or mopped like the rest of the floor are low maintenance and usually durable. Use them wisely though; they are slippery when wet.

- Purchase a remnant of vinyl or linoleum at a flooring store and trim it to fit the space.

- Custom-painted vinyl throw rugs can add a cheerful, decorative touch to a room.

the front door. This can be used for brushing off dirt and drying wet shoes. Clean, dry shoes do lead to fewer accidents when walking through the house, but that benefit needs to be weighed against the risk of the potential for tripping by the door.

Non-skid Underpads

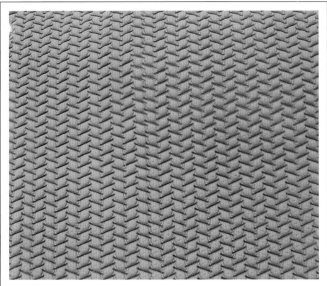

- Carpet pads made of natural rubber provide a comfortable, safe, non-skid surface. Place them under all area and throw rugs.

- Pads made from 100 percent rubber will not stain floors.

- Underpads can be easily cut, making it a snap to fit any size floor covering. Pre-cut sizes are also available.

- Avoid spongy underpads that can be dangerous for those who are marginally mobile.

Tape to Anchor Corners

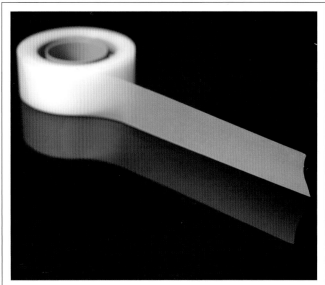

- Carpet tape is an option for anchoring rugs to the floor. Pay special attention to the rug corners.

- When purchasing tape, look for a brand that will not damage the flooring surface underneath. For wood finishes, test a small piece of tape in a corner of the floor before using permanently.

- It is not necessary to anchor the corner of a rug in the corner of a room.

PATTERNS

Use this design element cleverly to establish comfortable spaces

Patterns are an important part of a universal design home. They contribute to the overall design, add drama and interest to an otherwise plain décor, and provide needed contrast and visual direction. Using the same pattern throughout a space can help set the area apart in an open floor plan. But because patterns can affect how proportion and depth is perceived, they must be selected wisely.

When many colors or line directions are used in a pattern, it becomes busy to the eye. This can be confusing or even disturbing. Stick with subdued patterns to create a calm atmosphere.

Remember the size and scale of the space. Small patterns are too active for large spaces. Not only will relaxing be difficult, but vision can be impaired.

Deliberately changing patterns on the floor or wall between two spaces is a good way to provide contrast. Specific

Patterned Carpets

- Flooring patterns that appear bright and colorful in a small sample may look softer or much lighter when installed on a whole floor. They may not contrast enough with the surrounding walls.

- Consider other patterns in the room when selecting a carpet pattern, and make sure it doesn't clash or make the room too busy.

- A sculpted carpet creates its own pattern with light and shadow.

Tile-created Patterns

- There is a large selection of flooring that can be laid as individual vinyl, rubber, or carpet tiles. They are economical because they can be purchased in small quantities and are do-it-yourself projects.

- Soft rubberized ones are even available to lay outdoors over brick or concrete.

- If choosing contrasting tiles to create a pattern, be sure they are not going to create a line or barrier for a person with dementia.

functional areas can be visually delineated, and doorways or stairs can be more easily sensed. A floor or wall pattern can also be directional, easing the way down a challenging hallway.

Note that pattern is not simply what is seen in fabric and flooring. Light creates patterns; furniture layouts establish patterns; the placement of accessories reveals their own patterns.

Color Changes on the Floor

- When planning for aging in place, choosing colors becomes more than just a matter of making decorating decisions.

- For those with poor vision, color changes on a floor or between a floor and a wall can trigger identification of where they are in the home.

- Since flooring can be a big remodeling expense, it is best to anticipate what might be needed in the future, with decreasing vision or memory.

Pattern Delineating Doorways

- Embedding a contrast carpet square in front of a doorway breaks up the hallway.

- The contrasting color acts as a memory trigger and delineates the doorway.

- Since carpets are often cut and pieced together in long hallways, the labor expense can be minimal.

- In an apartment hallway, a contrasting entry mat in front of the door will create the same effect.

KITCHEN COUNTERS

Providing work surfaces at varying heights improves a kitchen's usability

A traditional kitchen, with its standard countertop, presents an obstacle for many older people. A 36-inch work surface height is standard. But for wheelchair users or those bent over from osteoporosis, this height can be tiring, uncomfortable, or impossible to work with.

In a universal design kitchen, there is a mix of counter heights to suit a range of functions and a variety of users and conditions. A 42- to 45-inch counter—the standard height of a bar—is okay for some standing tasks, but is too high for serious counter work. A counter of 36 to 38 inches is more comfortable for standing while cooking and washing dishes. And a 30- to 32-inch counter height is comfortable for both

Formica Counter with Straight Edge

- Formica counters are available with a right angle edge. Unlike a bullnose edge, right angles tell you exactly where the counter edge is.

- Formica has been around a long time and is one of the least expensive counter material choices.

- It is easy to see the end of the counter when Formica counters are made with a right angle edge. Other materials offer a right angle edge as an option.

- There is a wide selection of shades and aggregate colorations available from different manufacturers.

Upscale Counter

- Fancy, multi-curved counter edges can add architectural interest to a kitchen.

- Almost all counter surfaces reflect light and create a glare, a hazard for those with poor or compromised vision.

- Fancy edge treatments, however, make it harder to distinguish the true edge. Overhead lighting can create glare on counters and make the true edge hard to see.

- Straight edges clearly show the edge.

seated cooks and people working in wheelchairs.

A compact kitchen may not have room for such a collection of workspaces. An alternative is to install an adjustable counter. These can be purchased ready-made or custom-made to your specifications. They can be raised or lowered as needed for any kitchen task, and can even double as a sit-down table.

If a complete kitchen remodel isn't in the budget, there are low-cost solutions. A small table can be used as a lower-height surface. Kitchen carts and islands are available in any height. They can be added to a kitchen for additional counter space. Many come with casters and can be rolled out of the room when extra floor space is needed.

Tiles and Grout

- Tile size determines how many grout seams there will be on the counter.

- Grout needs to be sealed from time to time to keep it impervious to water and to prevent mold from growing.

- If you seek low maintenance counters, tile may not be a good choice.

- Although cutting on the tile surface is not recommended, it does stand up to occasional cutting better than Formica.

The Case for Different Counter Heights

- Standard kitchen counter height is 36 inches. This may be a few inches low for a tall person but high for someone short or bent over due to osteoporosis or osteopenia.

- Working from a wheelchair requires a counter height of 30 to 32 inches. Add a counter at this height if space allows, in any kitchen; sitting for some chores works for anyone.

- Redo a kitchen with a variable height counter. It is installed with brackets that can be adjusted to meet the immediate need.

REVEALING EDGES
Countertop edge treatments will keep you from going over the edge

Consider visual cues with kitchen counters. Because the eye can't always be counted on to judge edges and differences in levels, you'll want to use contrast to identify the countertop perimeter.

Accent colors, patterned borders, and complementary edge-fascia materials help make edges stand out. Combine light and dark colored materials for strong visual contrast since it's not easy to distinguish similar hues.

A raised-edge detail on countertops is another great way to provide a visual and tactile indicator of the countertop edge. It's also an easy way to prevent spills from dripping onto the floor. You can create your own raised edge in a contrasting color by adding a curved bullnose to a counter.

Another option is to create the contrast on *top* of the counter. Add a touch of color all the way around the top edge so the perimeter is clearly seen.

Tile with Edge Slightly Raised

- Installing a bullnose tile on the edge of a counter will create a raised lip that prevents things from rolling off.

- Remember that where the sink and counter meet is also an edge.

- With an under-mount sink and tile counter there is a bevel that rolls to the sink.

- A top-mounted sink creates a barrier that prevents pushing liquid easily off the counter.

Rounded Corners at Counter Ends

- Islands and counters that extend into the kitchen should be installed with rounded corners or oval shapes.

- Because bumping into edges is common to everyone, rounded corners will reduce the chances of bruising.

- Finish all counters and islands in the kitchen with the same shape edges to create a harmonious design.

- Retain the top clean edge to avoid things inadvertently falling.

To reduce the chances of inadvertent bruising, eliminate all sharp corners at the ends of countertops. There is a wide variety of countertop material choices that can be made with rounded edges, from granite to Formica to ceramic tile. If replacing your countertop is impossible, install edge protectors around the sharpest edges.

Edge with Contrast

- Use an edge tile on a counter to emphasize that the end of the counter is "here."

- The most emphasis comes from an edge of contrasting color bull-nose tiles.

- A Corian, Formica or Silestone counter can also emphasize the edge with a 1-inch, inlaid contrast color stripe.

- Consider labor cost as well as material cost when deciding on a counter modification or remodel.

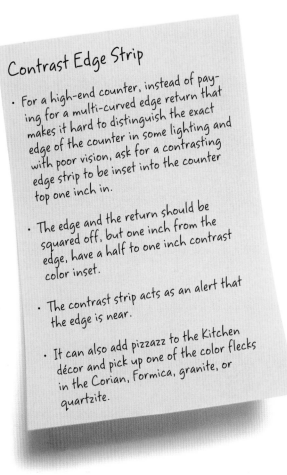

Contrast Edge Strip

- For a high-end counter, instead of paying for a multi-curved edge return that makes it hard to distinguish the exact edge of the counter in some lighting and with poor vision, ask for a contrasting edge strip to be inset into the counter top one inch in.

- The edge and the return should be squared off, but one inch from the edge, have a half to one inch contrast color inset.

- The contrast strip acts as an alert that the edge is near.

- It can also add pizzazz to the kitchen décor and pick up one of the color flecks in the Corian, Formica, granite, or quartzite.

SINKS

Everything 'bout the kitchen sink

The sink is probably the most used appliance in the kitchen, so it needs to be convenient and trouble free. By choosing the right one, kitchen work becomes more comfortable. There are specific features that need to be considered when purchasing a new sink: depth, material, style, and hardware.

A double-basin sink allows more room for food preparation. Install a trash disposal on one side so that cleanup is quicker. When preparation and cleanup can be done in one place,

less strain and movement is required, making kitchen work more efficient.

Select a sink that has its drain offset to the rear so that pipes come down at the back. What if your sink has an inconveniently placed drain? By using a tub-bend pipe, the drain can be moved closer to the rear of the under-counter area, providing knee room, if needed, and more ample storage space.

Sink Ideas

- Pick a sink that adds to the beauty of the kitchen, but don't sacrifice function and durability.

- Kitchen sinks come in stainless steel and enameled cast iron. Stainless steel, cast iron, and enameled finishes come in different weights and thicknesses.

- The heavier the weight and thickness, the more durable and costly.

- Stainless steel sinks may scratch, but do not chip when heavy pots are dropped in them.

Stainless Steel Sink

- Choose a stainless steel sink for its durable, low-maintenance finish.

- Because the stainless steel surface does not scratch easily, germs are less likely to get caught in grooves where they can thrive.

- Stainless steel sinks can be under-mounted or top-mounted, so you can select the model that works best for you aesthetically and functionally.

Install the sink close to the front of the counter, and if possible, mount a single-lever faucet on the side of the sink on the counter surface for easiest access.

Some universal design kitchens modify the area under the sink to allow for wheelchair access. For this purpose, choose a sink with a narrow basin—5 to 6 inches—to allow comfortable knee space when the wheelchair rolls under. It will also allow anyone to sit in a chair while working at the sink. Another benefit of a shallower sink is that less bending and leaning into the basin is required to reach items.

Since legs under the sink can get close to its underside, the sink should be heavy-gauge stainless steel so that it is heat resistant. A shield can also be built around the sink for more protection.

Double Sink of Uneven Sizes

- Double sinks are practical when dishes are washed by hand; dishes can be soaped in one sink and rinsed in the other.

- With a dishwasher, it is mostly pots and pans that are hand washed. Use the second sink for a small dish drainer and keep counters clear for food prep.

- Washing and drying dishes in a double sink will reduce the chances of wet counters and floors.

Double Sink with Center Disposal

- If you have the room, a large sink with a center garbage disposal will add convenience and safety.

- The raised center section guards against unwanted items falling into the garbage disposal in the sink.

- A cutting board that fits over the small center section comes in handy.

- Choose a cutting board with an opening so pushing vegetables into the disposal is easy.

COUNTER WORKSPACES

Put counters where you need them

In a universal design kitchen, placement of counters is key. They should be located where you really need them to make your kitchen work much simpler.

It's most important to have space around stoves, ovens, and microwaves. When you take out a heavy, hot dish, you want to be able to set it down quickly. Be sure to have a trivet or other heat-resistant counter protector nearby if your surface is not heat proof.

It's also very practical to have sufficient space near the sink, since this is the primary food preparation area for most cooks. With easy access to water and the disposal, you can prepare foods and get rid of your waste all in one area.

Counter space around the refrigerator is a convenience. It provides a place to rest items as they are pulled out or put away.

To make any kitchen task easier to accomplish, make sure

Counter Work Areas near Stoves

- Remove clutter from counters near the stove so they are available for hot pots and dishes.

- Cooking utensils should be stored close to the stove, either in a nearby drawer or in an upright container on the counter.

- If counters are not heat resistant, keep at least one hot plate or trivet handy.

Counter next to Wall Oven

- It is important to have adequate counter space next to a wall oven or wall-mounted microwave.

- The relationship between the height of the oven door or microwave and the countertop determines the amount of bending or reaching involved when

- transferring heavy pots from the hot oven, or carrying dishes from the microwave to the counter.

- Plan relationships thinking through the tasks and motions, and keep in mind your abilities.

there is enough light. Under-cabinet lighting is a terrific way to flood your countertops with light, eliminating shadows caused by ceiling lights. They will also add a dramatic accent to the kitchen. Under-cabinet lights come in many styles and shapes and are available in home centers, hardware stores, and even some office supply stores. They are fairly easy to install. Make sure they are installed under the front of your upper cabinets to cast light onto more of the work surface. If your countertop is dark or glossy, choose a fixture with a frosted covering to minimize potential glare.

What if you don't have sufficient counter space? For quick fixes in the kitchen, consider products that add the equivalent of more counter space: a rolling cart, an over-sink cutting board, a drop-leaf shelf placed in front of the counter or at the end of an island, or rising storage shelves in cabinets for heavy mixers or food processors.

Work Areas next to Sink

- For stress-free food preparation, make sure the counter areas near the sink are clean and clutter free.

- Place appliances used every day, like coffee pots and can openers, in easy-to-reach corners so they don't interfere with food preparation and cleanup.

- Other heavy portable appliances should also be kept out on counters because they can be awkward and difficult to retrieve if stored in low or high cabinets.

Under-Cabinet Lighting for Counter Tasks

- Ceiling lights are appropriate for general kitchen illumination, but they don't provide sufficient light for specific counter tasks.

- Poor lighting needs to be resolved to make tasks easier for those with poor vision.

- Task lighting can be installed under the upper cabinets to illuminate the countertops. Fixtures can be hard wired, or portable and plugged into an outlet.

WHEELCHAIR MODIFICATIONS
Make your kitchen more accessible for family members in wheelchairs

There are many modifications that can make a kitchen accessible for people in wheelchairs. Some of these alterations may be easy enough for a local handyman. Others require reconstruction.

When altering your kitchen, the key factors to consider are creating sufficient room for the wheelchair to easily maneuver, ensuring counters and appliances are at a convenient height, providing sufficient knee space, and keeping all essential items within reach. Clearing knee space under a sink requires modification of the cabinets underneath. Kitchen designers should specify a shallower sink so the wheelchair can fit comfortably underneath, and place it at a height of 32 inches. The faucet can be mounted on the side of the sink for easier reach. A pull-out spray hose is helpful as well. Install a scald guard over the plumbing to prevent leg burns.

You can modify the cabinets under counters and cooktops

Counter with No Cabinet Below

- For someone in a wheelchair, the ideal work or eating area is a counter that is 32 inches high with no cabinets below.

- Straight, right-angle counter edges without curves and bevels work best for wheelchair access.

- Specially made cabinets that look like standard ones are available with removable parts that can be removed for wheelchair accessibility.

Sink with No Cabinet Below

- Making a sink accessible to wheelchairs requires eliminating the cabinet below. It may also require relocating the plumbing so it is out of the way.

- Hot water pipes may need to be insulated to protect knees from their heat.

- Consider the depth of the basin when making a sink purchase; shallower basins allow for more leg room.

to create easy access for wheelchairs. These countertops should also be at the lower height of 30 to 32 inches. A pull-out cutting board or drop-leaf shelf can be added to create additional working space.

To reduce the need for bending and stretching, install pull-out shelves on all remaining lower cabinets. In the upper cabinets, lower the bottom shelf for comfortable reach and add open racks for dishes below the upper cabinets. Replace the hardware on all cabinets with U-shaped handles.

Lower Placement of Counter

- Planning a wheelchair accessible kitchen from scratch is the ideal situation.

- Counter height, pull-out lower cabinet shelves, and all appliances can be selected to accommodate the individual user.

- Use a professional when adapting an existing kitchen that requires changing counters, cabinets, or appliance locations.

A Wheelchair in a Galley Kitchen

- Galley kitchens are efficient with little walking from side to side and between appliances, but they can be difficult for a wheelchair.

- With at least 56–60 inches from side to side, there is ample wheelchair turning room. Opened lower cabinet doors, an opened dishwasher or oven door can become obstacles.

- If you can live without cabinet doors, eliminate them.

- Replace a standard dishwasher with a drawer washer.

- Install an oven with a side-opening door.

KITCHEN WORK SURFACES

FAUCETS & SINK HELPERS
Get help from a few simple sink buddies

Who would have believed that by simply upgrading sink accessories, life could be more convenient? Most sink accessories are installed in holes provided in the sink by the manufacturer (two or three hole are most common, but four or five holes can come on large sinks). To add accessories for sink use without replacing a sink, a hole can be drilled in the counter top to accept the "gadget." Its base plate will cover the edge of the drilled hole.

The main accessory is a faucet. An easy-to-operate faucet is so important. It is easiest to use if it is operated by a single lever, instead of knobs. A tall spout works best to accommodate large pots and tall pitchers. An integrated pull-out spray head with a gooseneck attachment provides a longer reach, allowing users to direct water where needed. Most come with a button that turns the spigot into a spray faucet.

Add a built-in soap dispenser and fill it with liquid dish

Single Lever Faucet

- A single-lever kitchen faucet is compact and easy to use.

- Unlike a rear or side lever, it doesn't interfere with the backsplash or adjacent gadgets.

- A single lever above the spout can be operated with either the right or left hand.

- The faucet lever can be raised or lowered with the side of a hand or a closed fist—eliminating the need for gripping.

Pull-out Spray Attachment

- A pull-out sprayer is a convenient sink option.

- It can reach all corners of the sink for easy cleaning and is even handy to use when washing hair in the sink.

- A faucet can be selected with a pull-out sprayer

attachment installed right in it so it does not take up extra space on the back of the sink.

- Optionally, a pull-out sprayer can be installed separate from the faucet if the sink has an extra hole for it.

detergent. This eliminates the need for bending or stretching to retrieve the dish-soap every time the dishes need to be washed.

A separate filtered water faucet can deliver only cold water, or both cold and instant hot-water. Instant hot water delivery right at the sink accelerates many kitchen tasks, like preparing hot drinks or soups or accelerating the time to boil pasta. Avoid units that have twist grips, choosing ones with a lever release. Hot- and cold-water dispensers are available in finishes and styles to coordinate with your existing kitchen hardware.

Soap Dispenser Pump

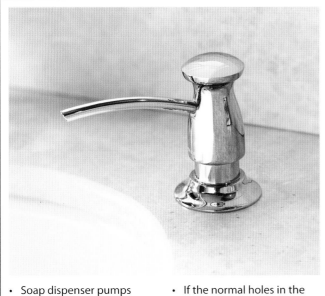

- Soap dispenser pumps are helpful additions to a kitchen sink. They conveniently store soap for quick, easy access, and they never tip over.

- Choose a dispenser that is easy to operate with a closed hand.

- If the normal holes in the back of the sink are hard to reach, locate the dispenser near the front of the sink with an extra hole drilled in the countertop.

Drawer Dishwasher

- A drawer dishwasher is a convenient alternative to a standard model.

- One dishwasher drawer holds about half the capacity of a standard dishwasher.

- You can install one drawer or two, one above the other. They can be run separately, or both at the same time.

- A drawer installed directly under the counter requires little bending to load or unload.

PULL-OUT SHELVES

Shelves, trays, baskets, and bins on gliders use space efficiently and keep things within reach

Adding pull-out shelves (also known as roll-out shelves, roll-out trays, gliding or sliding shelves) to your kitchen cabinets will not only make it easier to gain access to your things, but it will add more storage room and keep things more organized. Instead of having to bend down to reach into a standard cabinet and pull out something stuck in the back, you

can simply roll out a shelf and grab whatever you need.

There are many styles of pull-out shelves. Standard gliding wooden shelves can hold pots, canned goods, or cleaning supplies. Sliding wire or mesh baskets are deeper and will hold miscellaneous kitchen items like plastic bags or cleaning supplies. Pull-out tray bins with custom dividers help

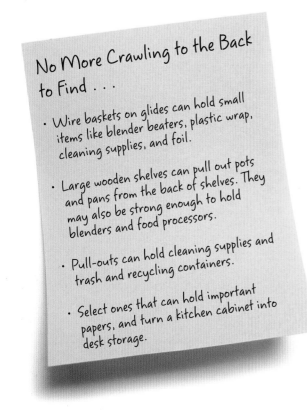

No More Crawling to the Back to Find . . .

- Wire baskets on glides can hold small items like blender beaters, plastic wrap, cleaning supplies, and foil.

- Large wooden shelves can pull out pots and pans from the back of shelves. They may also be strong enough to hold blenders and food processors.

- Pull-outs can hold cleaning supplies and trash and recycling containers.

- Select ones that can hold important papers, and turn a kitchen cabinet into desk storage.

Wire Pull-out Baskets

- Items that tend to topple over or roll around are contained nicely in pull-out baskets.

- Pieces that should be organized together but are mismatched in size and shape can be stored in a wire basket.

- Finding anything buried in the bottom shelf is difficult, but pull-out baskets make locating and retrieving items much easier.

- Most large hardware stores offer easy-to-install pull-out baskets that can be mounted in existing cabinets by a homeowner.

organize small appliances, cutting boards, and other odd-shaped items.

A pull-out bin for the trash container is another good use of gliders. With careful planning you can install the pull-out trash bin where you do most of your food preparation, making it easier to dispose of garbage.

To organize paper or store files, a pull-out shelf or bin can also be installed in the part of the kitchen where you make phone calls, pay bills, and schedule appointments.

Wooden Slide-out Shelves

- When ordering new cabinets, specify slide-out shelves in matching wood.

- Slide-out shelves can be shallow—ideal for storing pots and pans, or deep—better for holding stacks of breakable dishes.

- Consider replacing both top and bottom shelves in the lower cabinet with pull-out shelves to double the accessible space.

- Gliding shelves make storing, organizing, and retrieving kitchen items simple and convenient.

Trash Container Pull-out

- Set the trash container in a pull-out glider for efficient and tidy garbage disposal.

- Line the pull-out container with a trash bag so that tossing garbage is quick and clean.

- Specialty trash container pull-out shelves hold the bins steady so they never fall over or spill.

- Many pull-out devices can be retrofitted in existing cabinets, so a complete remodel is not necessary.

KITCHEN STORAGE

SHALLOW PANTRY SHELVES

Proper pantry shelving can make the difference between chaos and convenience

KNACK UNIVERSAL DESIGN

Pantries located within easy access to the food preparation area provide effective solutions for storage issues. But the shelves are what make the pantry convenient and accessible.

Shallow pantry shelving—12 inches deep or less—offers effortless retrieval of any item. No more guessing or trying to remember where things are stored. Because the shelves are shallow, boxes and cans are all on display, making it much easier to find everything.

In pantries that have deep shelves, install dividers to keep items from being pushed to the back.

If more storage is desired, it is better to add more shallow

U-shaped Shelves for Easy Access

- A walk-in pantry should have shallow shelves on three sides for easiest access.

- With shallow shelves, there is less chance of older items getting shoved to the back when new groceries are added.

- Group items by type so they can be found quickly.

- Store rarely used items on the upper or bottom shelves.

Pull-out Swing Shelves

- Customized swing shelves expand storage space.

- Narrow pull-out swing shelves can be installed in any closet to add space and ease of accessibility.

- Multiple sections make everything easy to organize and find.

- Swing shelves are usually narrow, making them convenient for storing canned goods and other small kitchen items. Things stored in the back are easily located by pulling out the front sections.

shelves than to deepen the existing ones. Although deeper shelves store more items, the smaller items will get hidden, making it more difficult to use the older items first. Adding shelves does not have to mean going higher. Installing pull-out shelves or swing shelves will provide added storage—sometimes doubling or tripling the space—without causing extra bending or stretching. Modifying your existing pantry to include these additional shelves is a great investment.

When choosing materials, opt for solid shelves because items tend to tip over on wire.

Pull-out Pantry Storage between Studs

- Narrow pull-out shelves take advantage of unused wall space in a kitchen and are ideal for storing heavy items like canisters and bottles.

- The small size of the shelves limits the number of stored items, so shelves never get too heavy.

- Store most frequently used heavy items at a height between your thighs and shoulders for easy access without bending or reaching.

Inside Door Spice Rack

- Interior cabinet door shelves are ideal for storing spices.

- Because small spice jars are difficult to find when stored on deep shelves, interior door spice racks offer organization and ease of accessibility.

- Mount the spice rack in a convenient location so spices are easy to grab when preparing food.

- Spices are sensitive to heat, so don't locate them too close to the oven, stove, or dishwasher.

KITCHEN STORAGE

51

INTERIOR CABINET MODIFICATIONS
Adapt the cabinets to make items easy to find and retrieve

Items stored at the back of cavernous cabinet shelves are not only hard to find, but difficult to retrieve. Simple modifications can make cabinets more accessible.

Add sliding shelves on the lower cabinets. Pots and small appliances stored on the bottom shelves are hidden completely in the dark unless they can be pulled out into view. Sliding shelves make tracking down items easier and reduce the need for bending.

Add shelves on cabinet doors to create easier storage space. Slim shelves reveal everything right on the door and make reaching into the cabinet unnecessary. For increased accessibility, modify the cabinet hinges to allow the doors to swing open 180 degrees. Interior shelving in these cabinets needs to be made shallower to accommodate the door shelves.

Upper and corner cabinets can use lazy Susans. Hard-to-reach items in deep cabinets become more available when

Door Shelves for Small Items

- Interior door shelves are handy for storing many small kitchen items.

- Frequently used items can be stored on door shelves so that they are not in view but always close at hand.

- Spices and paper goods are lightweight and ideal for wire shelf add-ons.

- Consider door shelves or door-mounted racks for any cabinet, including in an entertainment area.

Accommodating Door Shelves

- To accommodate added door shelves, existing interior shelves must be modified; deep shelves must be made narrower.

- Consider replacing the shallower shelves with pull-out baskets or sliding trays so that accessing hidden items is not a struggle.

- Add small baskets and shelf dividers on the pull-out trays to keep small kitchen items organized and easy to find.

they can be spun around to the front of the shelf. A single, inexpensive lazy Susan can be purchased in a home supply store and simply placed on a shelf. A professional can install multi-tiered turntables, typically used in corner cabinets. These revolving shelves, which are available in many styles and variations, allow the greatest access in areas that are difficult to reach.

To keep cabinet items from toppling into disarray, add shelf dividers. Wooden brackets can be installed permanently for the greatest stability. This is best for cabinets containing heavier appliances and utensils. Temporary portable dividers can also be purchased ready to use and are great for storing and organizing pot lids, dish towels, hot plates, and small containers. They are available in many materials, including wire, acrylic, and plastic. Think about the desired function before buying shelf dividers, as you will want to match their strength and durability to your needs.

Portable Stands

- Portable wood and wire racks help to tidy up a cabinet and add more storage space.

- Inexpensive stands can be placed on permanent cabinet shelves or pull-out trays.

- These racks are ideal for storing hot plate trivets, pot lids, and dishes.

- In smaller cabinets, consider installing a narrow pull-out organizer. These are available in sturdy plastic or wire.

Platters and Tray Dividers

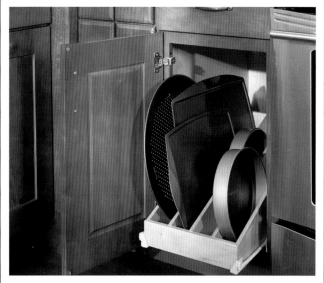

- Large platters and trays can be hard to store and difficult to retrieve if stacked on top of each other on a shelf.

- Vertical dividers in a relatively tall cabinet allow for safe storage with one or two platters in a section. Retrieval is convenient and the chance for breakage is greatly reduced.

- Removal of a shelf can provide the height needed for vertical storage.

DRAWERS

The right type of drawer hardware can make the difference between struggling and comfort

You want drawers that glide in and out easily, are easy to open and close, and are suited by location and depth to the contents stored in them.

Typically, the drawers just below counters are shallow and ideal for storing silverware, mixing and cooking utensils, and plastic and foil wrap. Deeper kitchen drawers lend themselves

to storing linens, potholders, plastic containers and lids.

When considering what goes in which drawer, keep in mind where items will be used and locate them for greatest convenience. Items in lower drawers will be accessed by bending, so do not place large or awkward-to-lift items there.

Container and kitchen stores offer drawer adapters and

Safety Glides with Lock Stop

- Check that all kitchen drawers open and close smoothly.

- To make the kitchen storage more user-friendly, drawer glides can be added or replaced to make older drawers slide more easily.

- Make sure all drawers have a safety stop so that the drawer never pulls out all the way and drops to the floor.

In-drawer Knife Racks

- Horizontal knife blocks or knife racks organize cutting utensils and fit nicely into a drawer.

- A jumbled pile of knives is dangerous to sift through; an in-drawer knife rack keeps the knives safely separated.

- Utensil dividers in drawers can organize all of the kitchen silverware.

- If there are no separate drawers available for storing knives, a countertop knife block is an option.

dividers that customize standard drawers into organized spaces. The most common one is a silverware divider which keeps spoons, forks, and knives separated and neat. But flexible dividers are available that allow you to create your own shapes and spaces within drawers.

Good organizing makes kitchen chores easier.

Spice Jars on Angle in Drawers

- Customized drawers allow for better organization and accessibility.

- An angled drawer spice rack is a great way to store and organize herbs and spices. The drawer rack holds bottles and tins at an angle, making labels easy to read at a glance.

- Look for racks that can install in existing drawers.

- Locate these shallow drawers accessible to the food prep area and away from heat generating appliances.

- Deep drawers can hold dish towels and aprons or baking pans and pie tins.

Door and Drawer Pulls

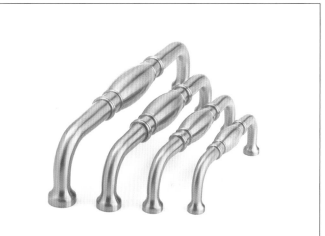

- Large, easy-to-grasp cabinet door pulls are essential in a universal design kitchen.

- U-shaped pulls that allow space for a thumb or four fingers are easy to grasp and are recommended if anyone in the household has arthritis.

- With good drawer glides, a firm grip is not necessary. Just a slight tug or nudge will open or close the drawer smoothly.

KITCHEN STORAGE

WHEELCHAIR ACCESSIBLE STORAGE

Creating more efficient storage makes kitchen work more accessible to people in wheelchairs

For people with limited mobility, the most effective kitchen storage solution is exposed shelving. Wheelchairs and walkers—even tired unstable legs—can get in the way of opening doors, so the more things are kept out in the open, the better.

Because of limited overhead and lower reach capabilities,

gain added storage under upper cabinets or lower on a wall—not more than 50 inches high. Mug holders, pothooks, and open slots make for convenient storage solutions and can add beautiful style to the kitchen.

Kitchen storage should be provided in locations that are convenient to the work areas. Pots should be stored near the

KNACK UNIVERSAL DESIGN

Wheelchair Accessible Storage

- Pull-out gliding shelves make things in the back of cabinets accessible.

- Open vertical storage under upper cabinets makes dishes easy to store and take down.

- Narrow pull-out pantry racks put all items right there in front of you.

- Wall-mounted pots and pans are easy to reach.

Pull-out Glides for Shelves

- Pull-out shelves provide access to the full depth of cabinet shelving.

- Consider how far a person in a wheelchair can reach and grasp, and make sure the shelf is no wider.

- Seat-height shelves can hold heavier items, but lower shelf items should be lighter in weight to make lifting them from a seated position easier.

stove, food prep bowls and utensils close to the open counter workspace, and dishes in the vicinity of the eating area.

Install pull-out shelves in existing lower cabinets so that stored items can be brought into view and retrieved easily. Turntables, or Lazy Susans, can be installed to help find things in deep cabinets. Upper cabinets can be lowered to provide accessibility or under-cabinet racks can be added. Leave 12 to 15 inches above the countertop to keep the surface usable.

Upper Cabinet Plate Storage

- Plate racks installed under the upper cabinets make an attractive and accessible place to store everyday dishes.

- Racks can be added to an existing kitchen if there is sufficient height above the counter.

- Dish hutches add additional open storage space and can be placed at a height accessible from a wheelchair.

Hanging Pots

- Pots hanging near the stove are convenient for wheelchair accessibility.

- Pot lids can also be hung from hooks so they are easily retrieved. If lids have a "U" handle on top, they can be hung on the pan handles and save space.

- Decorative hooks will complement the style of the kitchen and add architectural interest.

- Look for solutions that are convenient, creative, and stylish.

KITCHEN STORAGE

DEMENTIA SAFETY ADAPTATIONS

Extra precautions are necessary when living with a dementia patient

Kitchen storage requires extra safety considerations when living with someone with dementia. Because dementia can be a progressive problem, what is safe today may not be safe tomorrow. A kitchen should be designed for the future, and storage safety must be planned to always stay ahead of the condition's progression.

When considering how to protect someone from harm, think about "childproofing" the kitchen. Whatever would normally be done to safeguard children is a good idea when a person with dementia lives in the house. Lock up dangerous items, like chemicals, cleaners, and knives. Put safety locks on cabinets and drawers containing anything that could

Living with a Housemate with Dementia

- Education about dementia progression can keep you one step ahead in adapting your home for safety. Anticipating hazards in advance is the job of the caregiver.

- A knife block may be convenient, but a hazard for someone with dementia.

- Latches on drawers and cabinets containing sharp or dangerous objects are a must.

- Chemicals and cleaning supplies need to be behind locked or safety-latched doors as well.

Locks on Drawers and Doors

- A person with dementia needs to be protected from certain items in the kitchen: cleaning supplies, vitamins and medicines, chemicals, and sharp objects.

- Safety locks installed to prevent small children from accessing cabinets can prevent dementia patients from gaining entry as well.

- Plastic drawer and door latches allow minimal opening to let the appropriate person release the lock.

be potentially harmful. Install safety plugs in electric outlets. Add stove knob covers to keep patients from accessing and turning on the gas or a hot electric stove.

Even if a person once knew to avoid something, he or she may forget or not understand anymore. Memory loss can appear to come and go, so don't be fooled into becoming careless with safety during periods when your housemate seems to be his or her old self.

Don't wait until an accident occurs to plan for what may come. When caring for a person with dementia at home, safety precautions must be considered at all times. If another person comes in to relieve you, make him or her aware of the precautions and that he or she understands the reasons for them.

Caring for someone at home is a big commitment and drain on the caregiver. The guardian's health and emotional well-being should be taken into consideration when adapting a home.

In-drawer Knife Storage

- Keep all sharp knives and cutting utensils in locked drawers for safety. Install dividers to keep knife access safe for those who should access them.

- If a simple drawer-locking device is not sufficient, resort to more elaborate locks.

- When someone who lives in the home does not understand or remember the safe use of products and utensils, convenience must be sacrificed for safety.

Chemical Storage

- Those with dementia or severe visual impairment may ingest harmful chemicals or apply them to their skin.

- Keep cleaning supplies and medications behind locked doors.

- Vitamins and supplements in large quantities can be harmful and should be stored safely out of their access.

- Consider the automobile and garden chemicals stored in the garage, and keep them in locked cabinets as well.

STOVES

Today's safer and simpler kitchen appliances benefit everyone

When selecting a stove, you will notice that there are quite a few options. Some choices make it easier to see and use the stove. Here are features to look for and consider.

Smooth cooktops, available with some electric stoves, make sliding heavy pots on and off burners easy. If you have a gas stove, look for grates that are level so that moving heavy pots from one burner to another is safer.

Consider stoves with controls on the top. Top controls, as opposed to controls on the front face of the stove, are usually easier to see. The exception is when cooking from a wheelchair, where front controls are best for reaching and seeing. If controls are on the back face above the burners, they can be readable, but they require reaching and that can be a problem for some people. Choose a stove that offers controls in contrasting colors for added visual assistance. If there is some visual impairment, you can add a texture to the controls.

Top Control Knobs on Stoves

- Top control knobs may be toward the front, side, or back part of the stove. Ones toward the front are easier to read and reach.

- Consider the needs of the household, and choose a stove with knob location that works best.

- For wheelchair accessibility, dials located close to the front edge are good. Ones on the front face are best but may be harder to read with overhead lighting.

Easy-to-Read Controls

- Make sure the numbers or words on the controls contrast and are easy to read.

- Replace all worn stove dials with newer, easy-to-read controls. Look for dials with numbers and words that are large and well marked so they stand out.

- Digital controls may be easier on the hands, but they require more complex thinking, so make sure this will work for the household.

If you buy an electric stove with a smooth cooktop, be sure it has lights to indicate when the burner surface is hot. And look for a downdraft feature to draw the heat away from you as you cook, or install an overhead exhaust fan. You can also install special cover plates over the stovetop burners that limit how hot they can get and automatically shut off the stove if it reaches a certain temperature.

For wheelchair access, stoves need to be low. There are also several cooktops that are adjustable. These are incredibly convenient because they can accommodate all the cooks in your household. Add plenty of open shelves nearby to make grabbing needed ingredients and cooking utensils a breeze. And also make sure to keep a fire extinguisher in an accessible spot near the stove.

Electric Glass Cooktop

- Black electric glass cooktops will reflect overhead lighting and may create distracting glare, so opt for a light color.

- The flat surface on electric cooktops makes sliding pots around effortless and decreases the likelihood of tipping and spilling.

- A light will warn if the surface is still hot, alerting you to the danger.

- Be aware that someone with dementia may not connect the light to heat and danger. If necessary, disable the stove or remove the knobs when not in use.

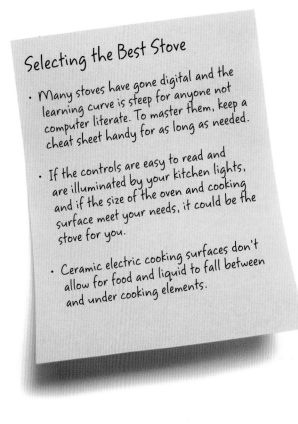

Selecting the Best Stove

- Many stoves have gone digital and the learning curve is steep for anyone not computer literate. To master them, keep a cheat sheet handy for as long as needed.

- If the controls are easy to read and are illuminated by your kitchen lights, and if the size of the oven and cooking surface meet your needs, it could be the stove for you.

- Ceramic electric cooking surfaces don't allow for food and liquid to fall between and under cooking elements.

WALL OVENS

Optional features can make your wall oven easier to use

A wall-mounted oven provides advantages that traditional ovens cannot. Instead of stooping to take out heavy, hot dishes, a wall oven can be set at a height where it is most comfortable. When purchasing a wall oven, there are several options to consider.

Think about an oven with a side-swing door, rather than one that has a door opening down. A side-swinging door requires less body movement, is safer because it requires less reach, and is much easier to open and close.

A single wall oven may be preferable to a double wall oven or an oven/stove combination. Single ovens can be mounted at a convenient height, eliminating the need for bending or stretching. The oven should be mounted so that the bottom of it is about 6 inches below the counter top. If needed, separate ovens can be installed according to individual family members' needs. Ideally, all ovens should be placed in close

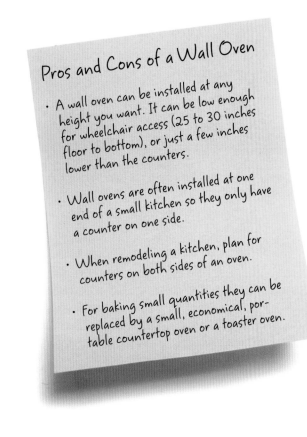

Pros and Cons of a Wall Oven

- A wall oven can be installed at any height you want. It can be low enough for wheelchair access (25 to 30 inches floor to bottom), or just a few inches lower than the counters.

- Wall ovens are often installed at one end of a small kitchen so they only have a counter on one side.

- When remodeling a kitchen, plan for counters on both sides of an oven.

- For baking small quantities they can be replaced by a small, economical, portable countertop oven or a toaster oven.

Distance from the Floor

- The distance from the floor is less important than the oven's relationship to adjacent counters.

- An oven mounted no more than 6 inches below the counter is convenient for moving pans from the oven to the counter.

- When a double oven is needed, mount them so that the oven used most often is in the best position for easily transferring baking dishes to the adjacent counter.

proximity to easily accessible, open counter space.

Easy-to-read controls are important. Many ovens are available with LED screens showing large lit-up numbers that can be seen easily, even in dim light. A touch screen is simpler to use than knob controls for arthritic fingers, but digital controls may require a learning curve. If there are severe visual challenges, a flat touch screen will be difficult. When sight is limited, choose larger buttons in contrasting colors that are *not* flush with the control panel. These buttons are easier to recognize and can be found by touch.

With a side-opening door, consider a pull-out shelf directly under the oven, where you can rest hot pans as you pull them out.

Side-opening Oven Doors

- Side-opening oven doors allow users to get closer and more easily lift items with bent elbows.

- When the door is opened, the escape of hot air should be enough to alert cooks not to touch the oven edges.

- There should be counter space on the open side of the door to easily place hot items as they are removed from the oven.

- If counter space is sparse, install a heavy-duty pull-out shelf below the oven.

Use of Nearby Countertop

- Keep nearby countertops clutter free to provide an easy, safe place to rest hot pots and pans as they come out of the oven.

- Store potholders and needed cooking utensils in easy-access drawers or cabinets near the oven.

- If there are no convenient drawers nearby, mount suction hooks on a cabinet or wall to hold potholders and commonly used utensils.

BUILT-IN COOKTOPS
A built-in version of a stovetop offers benefits

A built-in cooktop, accompanied by a wall oven, is an alternative to the traditional standard stove. As far as cooking function, the cooktop and stovetop are similar, and both are available in electric or gas. But there are benefits and challenges to consider when deciding which is best for the kitchen.

When a cooktop is installed into the countertop, a separate oven is required. The benefit of the separate oven is that it can be mounted at any convenient height, instead of being attached below the stove.

A built-in cooktop is set into a cutout in a countertop and dropped in. There is no space between it and the adjacent counter. This means that drips and spills—even papers and other small objects—cannot disappear through a crack. Glass electric cooktops are thin and sit almost level with the countertop. No ledge means easier cleaning.

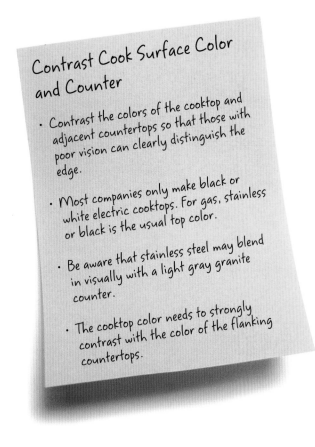

Contrast Cook Surface Color and Counter

- Contrast the colors of the cooktop and adjacent countertops so that those with poor vision can clearly distinguish the edge.

- Most companies only make black or white electric cooktops. For gas, stainless or black is the usual top color.

- Be aware that stainless steel may blend in visually with a light gray granite counter.

- The cooktop color needs to strongly contrast with the color of the flanking countertops.

Countertop Cooking Surface with Top Controls

- Top-mounted controls are illuminated by overhead lights, making them easy to read.

- Reading top-mounted controls is also easier because they can be viewed straight on without bending.

- Hard-to-read dials can be lifted off and replaced with new, easier-to-read controls. Or existing controls can be marked with nail polish.

- Top mounted controls are hard to read from a wheelchair.

Most built-in cooktops have controls on the top. This can be difficult for people in wheelchairs, who will have difficulty reading and reaching them. Some cooktops now come with a front fascia where the controls are located and are ideal for wheelchair access.

Top controls, however, are easier to see for those with diminished eyesight. Small numbers on the knobs can even be seen more easily when looked at straight on.

ZOOM

Electric vs. Gas: The verdict is in. Electric cooktops are safer than gas. The smooth-top system uses electricity to generate heat, and the burner cools quickly after a pot is removed. In comparison, the open flame of a gas stove is a fire hazard, especially to loose sleeves. And if a gas stove is left on, consequences could be deadly.

Front Controls

- Front cooktop controls are easier for wheelchair-confined chefs to read, reach, and operate.

- Manufacturers offer built-in cooktops with a front fascia, which contains the controls.

- Sinks with front-edge fascias can be purchased and installed to match the look of the wide appliance fascia.

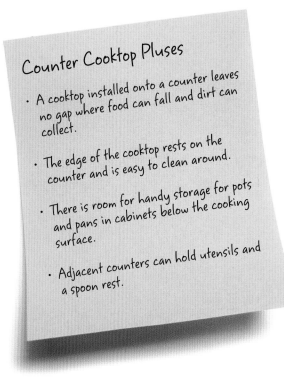

Counter Cooktop Pluses

- A cooktop installed onto a counter leaves no gap where food can fall and dirt can collect.

- The edge of the cooktop rests on the counter and is easy to clean around.

- There is room for handy storage for pots and pans in cabinets below the cooking surface.

- Adjacent counters can hold utensils and a spoon rest.

MICROWAVES

A convenient appliance meets an accessible kitchen

Microwaves are extremely useful for many reasons. They can do almost anything an oven can—in a fraction of the time. A side-swing door is simple to open for those with hand or arm weakness. The automatic shut-off makes cooking a breeze, even for family members who are forgetful.

Microwaves are safest when they are at counter height. Though most homes store them much higher, this can be dangerous. Reaching up and holding hot items above your shoulders is bad enough, but if you lose your balance, you can break a dish, burn yourself, or worse.

Place your microwave where you can reach it without bending or stretching. It should be no higher than 48 inches above the floor. If it is on the counter, be sure to leave plenty of room around it for resting hot foods as you take them out. If the microwave is mounted on the wall, install a separate shelf to act as a counter under it.

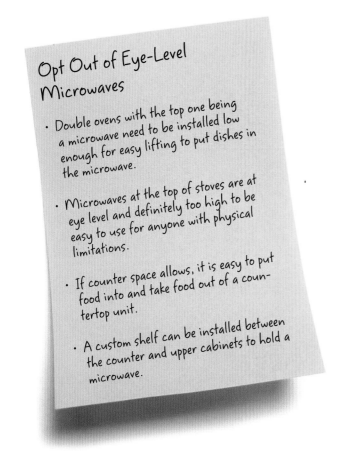

Opt Out of Eye-Level Microwaves

- Double ovens with the top one being a microwave need to be installed low enough for easy lifting to put dishes in the microwave.

- Microwaves at the top of stoves are at eye level and definitely too high to be easy to use for anyone with physical limitations.

- If counter space allows, it is easy to put food into and take food out of a countertop unit.

- A custom shelf can be installed between the counter and upper cabinets to hold a microwave.

Countertop Portable Microwaves Ovens

- Countertop microwaves are convenient, but do take up counter space.

- When purchasing a portable microwave, opt for the smallest one possible to use the least amount of counter space, unless it will also function as a regular or convection oven.

- Microwaves are more economical than traditional ovens when cooking for one person.

Although there are many options and features available with microwave ovens, choose one that is simple to understand and operate. The extra bells and whistles are rarely used, and often confuse the user. Microwaves are most often used for defrosting or warming meals, and even the simplest microwave can do that perfectly. Get a microwave with touchpad controls.

MAKE IT EASY

If using the stove or wall oven is too difficult or time consuming, cook with the microwave. Practically every meal can be prepared in a microwave. Eliminate bothersome tasks like lifting heavy pots, waiting for pre-heating, and scrubbing pans. And running the microwave for small quantities can be more economical than using a big oven!

As Top of Double Wall Oven

- Double wall "ovens" are available with a microwave as the top oven.

- Placement of the double unit requires compromise. Installation height must make using both ovens convenient. Place the center of the two units at counter height.

- Some ovens function as a microwave and traditional oven. They may be less economical but offer flexibility.

- Optional bells and whistles can make the microwave confusing. Only choose what is practical.

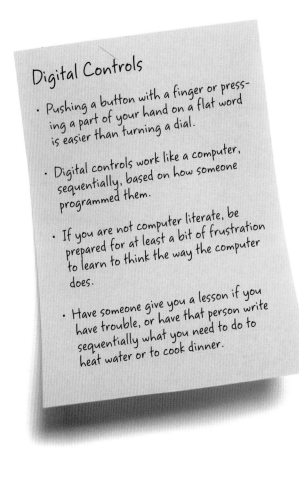

Digital Controls

- Pushing a button with a finger or pressing a part of your hand on a flat word is easier than turning a dial.

- Digital controls work like a computer, sequentially, based on how someone programmed them.

- If you are not computer literate, be prepared for at least a bit of frustration to learn to think the way the computer does.

- Have someone give you a lesson if you have trouble, or have that person write sequentially what you need to do to heat water or to cook dinner.

SELECTING APPLIANCES

Choosing the best features and upgrades will make everyday tasks feel easier

Appliances that are used many times a day need to be conveniently located and provide ease of use. With all the options available in refrigerators, washing machines, and dryers, which styles are the best? When purchasing new appliances, consider the energy-saving advantages.

Side by side refrigerator/freezers often have adjustable shelves on both sides, allowing everyone easy access to food without bending or stretching. Side-by-sides are easier to use for people in wheelchairs because the doors are smaller than on standard units.

If a side-by-side is too wide, opt for a refrigerator with a bottom freezer. Since most daily items are kept in the refrigerator

Double-door Refrigerators

- A double-door refrigerator opens so that there is always a door between the refrigerator and the counter. Consider this extra carrying distance before selecting.

- Because the doors are narrow, they make for easy wheelchair access.

- The usual water dispenser on the door may be hard for those with poor vision or unsteady hands to use.

- Double-door refrigerators require more width than a traditional single refrigerator model.

Three-door Refrigerators

- In a three-door refrigerator, most everyday items are easily found in the upper sections.

- A three-door refrigerator is less convenient than a two-door one for someone in a wheelchair because daily food is normally kept in the upper sections.

- Keep in mind that in the lower freezer section, items are piled on top of each other, so food may have to be reorganized or rotated regularly.

section, this type of unit requires less stooping.

Under-counter refrigerator drawers are another option that can blend beautifully with the kitchen cabinets. They install anywhere and provide convenient access to refrigerated storage when a large capacity refrigerator is not needed.

Front-loading washers and dryers are easier for the whole family. To take the bending and straining out of doing the laundry, mount the washer and dryer on pedestals or drawer bases so they are about a foot off the floor.

There are many optional features available in washing machines. Some offer "smart dispensers" that hold several months of detergent and softener, simplifying the washing process.

If space is an issue, check out a washer-dryer combo, which washes and dries clothing in the same unit. The downside is that wash cycles can take many hours.

Machines located near the bedroom make putting away clean clothes a snap. Make the laundry area more convenient by including an ironing board, a counter or shelf for folding and sorting, and a rod for hanging and air-drying.

Chest Freezers

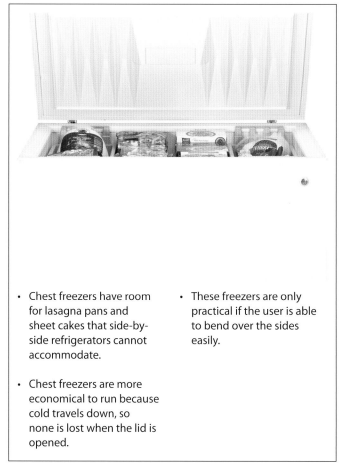

- Chest freezers have room for lasagna pans and sheet cakes that side-by-side refrigerators cannot accommodate.

- Chest freezers are more economical to run because cold travels down, so none is lost when the lid is opened.

- These freezers are only practical if the user is able to bend over the sides easily.

Elevated Dryers

- Front-loaded washers and dryers are harder to access because the openings are lower.

- Elevate the dryer at least 6 inches for more comfortable use.

- Most front-load washers and dryers have optional drawers that can be put under the units to raise them up.

- Stacked units put the dryer on the top, which may be too high for comfortable reaching.

PLACEMENT OF APPLIANCES
You've got the right equipment; now put it in the right place

Having appliances that are easy to reach and use is important, but the placement of them is just as crucial in making kitchen tasks easier.

Most kitchen designs refer to the kitchen triangle. Kitchen work is most convenient when the refrigerator, stove, and sink are aligned in a triangular shape, each one at a point. Counter surfaces should be provided next to each of the appliances. If a kitchen is set up in this way, all components are easily accessible, and tasks become more efficient.

Ideally counters should be on both sides of each of these appliances, but not all kitchens lend themselves to the ideal.

Be sure not to space the appliances next to each other or too close together. This would dramatically reduce the available counter space where it is most needed. Also, you don't want a refrigerator next to an oven. Doors can open into each other and get in the way of easy mobility.

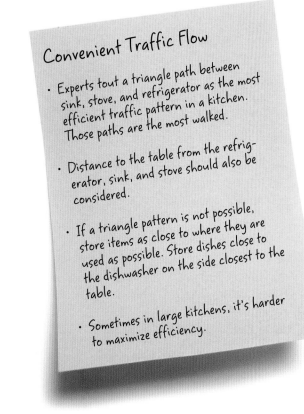

Convenient Traffic Flow

- Experts tout a triangle path between sink, stove, and refrigerator as the most efficient traffic pattern in a kitchen. Those paths are the most walked.

- Distance to the table from the refrigerator, sink, and stove should also be considered.

- If a triangle pattern is not possible, store items as close to where they are used as possible. Store dishes close to the dishwasher on the side closest to the table.

- Sometimes in large kitchens, it's harder to maximize efficiency.

Triangle from Refrigerator to Sink to Stove

- The most traveled kitchen paths are between the refrigerator, sink, and stove.

- Kitchen layout should be designed to minimize the distance between these appliances, saving steps and reducing how far things need to be carried.

- For convenience and efficiency, adjacent counters should be a part of the kitchen appliance triangle.

Since food preparation requires going back and forth to different areas in the kitchen, appliances should not be placed too far apart. A good rule of thumb to follow is to add up the sides of the "triangle" and make sure it is less than 20 feet.

For a wheelchair to maneuver in the kitchen there needs to be 60 inches between points of the triangle (or cabinets on either side) for rotation.

RED ● LIGHT

Dishwashers are available with a sani-cycle to increase water temperature for sanitary reasons. Be aware that they may also vent heat into the room during the dry cycle. Hot steam vents directly out of the front of the dishwasher and can create a hazard to someone too close to the counter.

Work Surfaces

Dishwasher to Dish and Silverware Storage

- If the sink, stove, and refrigerator are located far apart, consider adding a mobile workspace, such as a rolling butcher block in the kitchen. It can reduce how far things have to be carried in one trip.

- Because counters are so important and frequently used, never sacrifice counter space for a bigger stove, cooktop, or sink.

- With adequate counter room, it is easy to perform all necessary tasks.

- Surveys show the least favorite kitchen task is unloading the dishwasher. Convenience can make it easier.

- For convenient unloading, make sure the silverware drawer is close to the dishwasher.

- Arrange everyday dishes and glasses in a cabinet that is near the dishwasher so minimal walking is needed when unloading. But also keep in mind the distance from the cabinet to the table.

DOOR HANDLES
Adapt or modify traditional doorknobs for pain-free accessibility

Opening a door is a simple task for most people, but it can be painful—and sometimes impossible—for those with arthritis or other joint problems. By modifying the door handles or attaching a hand aid to the existing handles, door opening becomes much easier.

Levered door handles are the easiest for arthritic hands to manage. While standard doorknobs need to be gripped and twisted, levers can be pushed with a fist, wrist, forearm,

or elbow. If a doorknob cannot be replaced, purchase an adapter that fits right over the knob. These ergonomically designed extenders turn a standard round doorknob into a push lever. Some models have a slot in the handle where a cord can be looped through. A wrist can be slipped through the cord, pulling down to open the door.

Cabinet drawer and door handles should also be replaced. U- and D-shaped handles are the easiest to grasp, even with

Levered Interior Door Handles

- Levered door handles are easier to grasp and manipulate than traditional knobs.

- If a lock is needed, choose a levered handle that unlocks when the lever is simply pushed down from the inside, so no small parts need to be turned for unlocking.

- Levers are available in many finishes so they can be matched to other door hardware.

Cabinet Drawer Pulls

- U-shaped handles are easy to grasp and open, and with a push, the drawer is closed.

- Drawer pulls are easy to replace, and can usually be a do-it-yourself project.

- If the new drawer pull is a different size, the old screw hole can be filled with wood filler and touched up with paint or stain.

- U-shaped drawer pulls are available in all sizes and styles, so pick ones that fit hand size, as well as the room's décor.

weak hands or painful fingers.

Don't forget the locks on the doors. The interior of the bathroom door needs to have one that is easy to lock and open. Choose a door handle with a push button lock that unlocks automatically when the interior lever is pushed open.

While you're modifying the door handles and locks, don't forget the keys! Standard locks on exterior doors require tiny keys, which are extremely difficult to operate for those with joint problems. Key adapters fit right over keys to increase leverage with minimal stress on the fingers. One type of key adapter simply enlarges the end of the key for easier gripping. Another attaches a double opening to slip two fingers in, improving the grip.

Cabinet Door Pulls

- Cabinets throughout the home can be updated with U-shaped handles so they are easier for arthritic hands to pull open.

- Rounded U-shaped cabinet pulls are the easiest to grasp and pull.

- Avoid pulls with right angles because the edges put extra pressure on sore or sensitive fingers.

- Choose cabinet pulls to match your décor.

Bathroom Door Locks

- Bathroom doors need locks, but since a person can get locked in, select a handle that has a safety release on the outside.

- Keep the lock-releasing device handy; try the ledge above the doorjamb.

- If someone with dementia lives in the home, consider replacing the door handles with non-locking ones.

- For an easy quick fix, tape the latch inside the door so it cannot engage.

LEVERED FAUCETS

The magic lever strikes again, making sinks easier to operate

There is no doubt that a levered faucet is easier to operate than a standard round-knob faucet. But there are actually several types of levered faucets, each with its own style and function.

Widespread-levered faucet sets have a center spout with separate hot and cold water levers. All pieces appear to be separate. Widespread faucets are mounted in sinks with three pre-drilled holes. This type of faucet set works well if reaching to either side of the spout does not cause pain or discomfort.

Center-set levered faucets combine the spout and two levers on a single base unit. The operation is similar to the widespread faucet, but the levers are closer together near the waterspout. This faucet is also installed in a sink with three pre-drilled holes.

Single-lever faucets, which are mounted in sinks with only

Three-hole Sinks

- Three-hole sinks are usually fitted with separate hot and cold water controls and a center spout.

- A spout with a single-lever control can also be used in a three-hole sink if a cover plate is installed over the two unused holes. The connection between the lever

- and the pipes are made under the counter.

- When choosing a finish for the faucet, determine functional and maintenance needs, along with desired style.

Single-lever Control

- Single-lever faucets can be used just as easily with the left or right hand.

- A single-lever control can be operated with the side of a hand or arm; no gripping is required.

- With a single lever, it is easy to mix the hot and cold water to a desired temperature using just one hand.

one hole, have a spout and one lever for single-handed control. The lever is either on the side of the spout or on top. Both are simple for arthritic hands. Choose the style that seems most comfortable.

Wall-mounted faucets are also available with single- or double-lever controls. The modern, sleek look of this faucet enhances many bathroom designs. But avoid this faucet style if reaching forward toward the wall is a problem.

MAKE IT EASY

If you have standard round sink knobs, consider an easy adaptation. Arthritic faucet wraps slip right on standard kitchen and bathroom faucets. The ergonomic non-slip rubber provides better leverage so water can be turned on and off easily. They come in bright colors, making the hot and cold controls easier to see.

Utility Room Faucets

- Utility room sinks are usually characterized by deep basins. Their faucets often have a rotating long spout, and the controls are usually set wide apart.

- To make them easier to use, traditional sink knobs should be replaced with levered faucets or easy to grasp controls.

- If you are lucky enough to have a large basin sink in the utility room, think out of the box. Laundry, gardening, and many other household chores can be facilitated by using a deep sink.

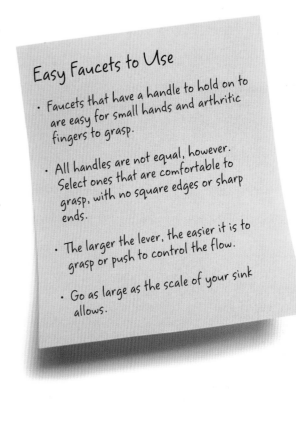

Easy Faucets to Use

- Faucets that have a handle to hold on to are easy for small hands and arthritic fingers to grasp.

- All handles are not equal, however. Select ones that are comfortable to grasp, with no square edges or sharp ends.

- The larger the lever, the easier it is to grasp or push to control the flow.

- Go as large as the scale of your sink allows.

SOAP & WATER HELPERS
Simple bath aids can make washing up a breeze

The simple act of washing up can be painful for someone with joint stiffness. But with a few clever aids, pain can be minimized.

A long-handle body washer gives people with limited reach the power to wash their shoulders and back with ease. Choose one with soft bristles for gentle cleaning, and an angled head for greater reach. Some brands are available with a pouch for liquid soap, which releases as you clean.

Instead of stooping to wash your feet, toss a foot scrubber pad on the floor of the shower, and rub your feet clean as you stand in a comfortable position. These pads, which suction to the floor, have a bumpy surface that scrubs and massages the foot. Choose one with a soap dispenser to eliminate the need to soap up the feet. The soap is released as you rub your foot over it.

Wall-mounted soap and shampoo dispensers make

Pump Soap Dispensers

- Portable, refillable, plastic pump dispensers are inexpensive and easily found in local stores.

- Keep them wherever hands will need to be washed.

- They are an economical way to add a soap or shampoo dispenser to a tub or shower area.

- Some brands of liquid soap can be purchased in plastic pump bottles to eliminate the need for refilling small bottles from a heavy, large container.

Body Brush

- With the loss of flexibility, there is an ever-increasing list of hard-to-reach body parts.

- Keeping a long-handled body brush in the tub or shower enclosure can make washing up easier.

- The longer the handle the better for most people, but if it is too long for arthritic hands to grip, a shorter handle will be better.

showering safer and easier. No more searching for each bottle and having to lift it, or stooping to retrieve soaps that have slipped out of wet hands. A convenient dispenser keeps liquid soap, shampoo, and conditioner in one location. Simply push on the large buttons to dispense a product. Mount the dispenser 40 to 50 inches from the tub or shower floor for accessibility from a standing position, or lower if it will be used while seated.

Apply body lotion easily with a long-handled lotion applicator that lets you spread cream evenly wherever it is needed.

Fill the dispenser with your favorite body balm, and massage it on.

A hair shampoo and rinse tray makes washing hair in the sink easy. A lightweight tray rests on the shoulders for upright shampooing. If being in the shower or lying back in a reclining position to wash hair is a challenge, this tray is the perfect solution.

Water Filter Attachment on Faucet

- Filtered water may be healthier to drink in your neighborhood than tap water. Filters can remove salts, chlorine, and other impurities.

- A filter that fits on the end of the kitchen sink faucet filters tap water with the movement of a lever. They are easy to find and install.

- The filter has to be replaced periodically.

Hand Lotion Pump Dispensers

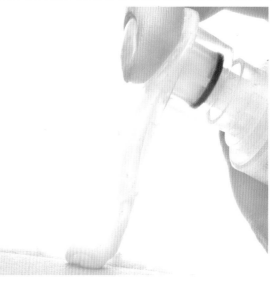

- Aging, sun, and medication can make skin dry.

- Keep hand lotion and body creams in plain sight so it is easier to remember to use them.

- To avoid having to pick up and overturn a slippery bottle and open a twist cap, buy pump dispensers of lotion.

- Keep them wherever you normally wash.

KITCHEN TOOLS

Reclaim the kitchen with joint-friendly gadgets that make tasks easier and eliminate the strain

Those with joint stiffness or inflammation can benefit from assistive kitchen tools that place less stress on joints.

Utensils with wide, non-slip handles are easier to hold, and the padding makes them feel more comfortable. Choose lightweight pans with easy-grip handles on both sides. Look for cookie sheets and baking pans with grip-style handles.

Instead of a knife, consider a rocker-style or rolling pizza cutter, which places less stress on hand and finger joints.

If you often need to open pull-top cans, purchase a ring pull tool to keep in the kitchen. This device slides under the ring on top of the can. Pulling gently opens the can.

For opening bottles, jars, and other containers, there are

Oxo/Good Grips Products

- Wide padded handles make small utensils easier to use.

- Look at the kitchen utensils in your drawers and replace utensils that have gotten harder to use.

- New gadgets make cooking and serving easier. Salad pinchers make serving

  salad easy with just one hand. Silicon-tipped pinchers help in lifting asparagus and corn.

- There are grapefruit knives, pizza cutters, potato peelers, and hand can openers with comfortable, grippable handles.

Under-counter Jar Openers

- Hand-held jar openers are a big help in opening tight caps, but they are difficult for arthritic hands.

- A jar opener mounted on the underside of the upper cabinet leaves your hands free to hold the jar, making the process less awkward and more efficient.

- The jar is slipped into the teeth device and is turned counter-clockwise with both hands.

- The biggest, widest jars can be opened with greater ease.

many styles of bottle openers. Some are small and magnetic and stay on the refrigerator. Others have chubby, easy-grip handles on one end, and a bottle-top grip on the other.

There are easy-to-use kitchen gadgets for every kitchen task. Bagel slicers, garlic choppers, cheese graters, and fruit and vegetable peelers are all available in ergonomically designed versions to eliminate strain on the joints.

········· GREEN ● LIGHT ·············

Surf the Internet for innovative hand helpers. New ideas are being invented every day, and you can find interesting items that make common kitchen tasks so much more convenient and pain free. Purchasing on the Internet is often less expensive, and you eliminate hours of driving around to search in stores.

Hand Can Opener

- If an electric can opener takes up too much important counter space, opt for a hand can opener with fat, padded handles.

- Older hand can openers can be painful and difficult to grasp and use. Invest in a new, sharp, superior product.

- Besides over time, blades dull and rust on an old can opener. A new one will be superior for ease of use and sharpness.

Plastic Sink Liners

- Plastic liners protect the sink from scratching when scrubbing pots and dishes.

- Holes in the liners allow water to pass through and can be suctioned to the sink so they are secure.

- Liners add cushion to the sink surface, which reduces the likelihood of chipping and breaking if a glass or dish slips.

I CAN MANAGE BUT...
Why not make everyday tasks easier, quicker, and less painful?

With so many innovative solutions to practically every imaginable challenge, it seems silly to live without the gadgets that make everyday tasks easier.

An electric juicer takes all the strain out of squeezing fruits or vegetables. Automatic fruit and vegetable peelers do the job while you watch. Electric pepper mills grind fresh pepper without any painful wrist twisting. And the list goes on!

Sometimes its not the slicing that's hard, but holding small items so you can slice. Slicing eggs and tomatoes is difficult for people with arthritis. But there are gadgets that hold the egg or tomato; you close the top and they do the slicing. Chopping and slicing using a standard knife can be hard on the joints. So get a food processor to electrically grate, chop, slice, and puree. Learn the difference between what a food processor can do versus a blender. Some chores are done equally well by both, but others are best done by only one.

Egg Slicer

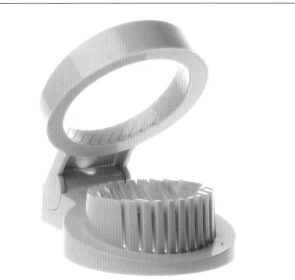

- Gripping small, slippery objects can be difficult. Doing it with a knife in your other hand can lead to trouble.

- For slicing eggs, try an egg slicer. Open the gadget, put the egg in, and bring the top down.

- The wires act as blades and evenly slice the egg.

- This device can also do a nice job on small tomatoes.

Electric Juicer

- Before purchasing a juicer, consider the following variables:

- Type of juice—a wheatgrass lover needs a different machine than someone who simply wants fresh-squeezed orange juice.

- Weight of machine—a heavy machine will need to sit permanently on the counter, taking up space.

- Ease of use—certain juice extractors require multiple steps to make one glass of juice, while others work more efficiently.

If lifting heavy objects is difficult, before buying these heavy kitchen helpers be sure you have counter space on which to keep them. If you only have enough space for one, then be sure to choose wisely.

Electric mixers have attachments that whip egg whites, knead dough, grind meat, and even make pasta. If money, space, and time allow, let technology and innovation ease your fun in life.

Countertop Cork Puller

- Countertop wine bottle openers make cork popping a breeze.

- Attach them to the counter or table edge, push on a lever, and the cork comes out.

- This simple device alleviates the strain and force needed to screw a wine bottle opener into the cork and then pull it out.

Cookie Press

- The joy of baking is another warm memory not to give up, especially if it is an opportunity for a grandma to share warm memories with grandchildren.

- Making shaped cookies from a cork-screw cookie press is hard for young hands, and impossible for arthritic hands.

- An electric cookie press is the answer.

VACUUMS & BROOMS
The dirt on painless cleaning

Lugging around a heavy canister vacuum, pushing and pulling an overweight upright, and stooping to sweep up the floor can be tedious and painful for people with arthritis. Options such as electric brooms, Swiffer Sweepers, robotic vacuums, and long-handled dustpans offer simple solutions.

Electric brooms provide a quick way to clean kitchen or bathroom floors. Many brands are ergonomically designed for fast, comfortable vacuuming. Look for electric brooms with attachments so that you can clean furniture and get into hard-to-reach corners and crevices.

The Swiffer Sweeper is an easy-to-use, lightweight product that can replace a traditional broom or a mop and bucket. It uses dry or wet cloths to double its function. Disposable cloths trap and lock dirt, dust, and hair that could be missed with a conventional broom or wet mop and make for easy clean-up.

Electric Broom

- Lightweight electric brooms are much simpler to operate than heavy traditional vacuum cleaners.

- Electric brooms can be used on both hard surface flooring and carpets.

- Choose a model that is comfortable to hold.

- Because of their compact size, electric brooms can be stored easily in the corner of a closet or near the door in the garage.

DustBuster

- DustBusters, a modern version of the old tank vacuums, were touted as perfect for cleaning car interiors.

- Because they are lightweight, some manufacturers now make them with a strap for carrying them around on your shoulder as you vacuum.

- DustBusters are handy for vacuuming high windowsills, ceiling light fixtures, and other hard-to-access spaces.

The Roomba is a futuristic appliance by iRobot that works like a spiraling pool cleaner. The disc is placed on the floor where it moves around on its own, vacuuming up dirt, dust, pet hair, and crumbs. It automatically adjusts from carpet to hard floors. A contact bumper detects walls and furniture, and sensors on the bottom prevent it from falling off ledges and down stairs. Some versions have a scheduling option. They can be programmed to turn on and begin cleaning at any set time, even when no one is home.

Long-handled dustpans replace conventional dustpans with long-handled versions so that sweeping up becomes a breeze. Dirt can be pushed into the dustpan without bending over. This is a must for anyone with back issues.

Swiffer Sweeper

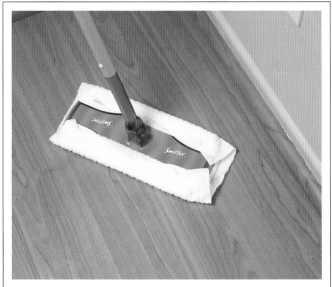

- A Swiffer is an adapted mop that uses a special, changeable cloth to attract dust and dirt to its surface.

- The handle is lightweight and easy to push.

- The swivel joint between handle and bottom makes the Swiffer easy to use for cleaning under furniture and beds, and around furniture legs.

- The wet pad option eliminates the need for a mop and bucket.

Long-handled Duster

- A long-handled duster is a valuable tool for those who should not use step stools.

- Since climbing on a stepstool is sometimes unwise, a long-handled duster makes cleaning high objects possible.

- Use the duster to clean fire alarms, recessed lights, hanging fixtures, and skylights. Also clean under furniture and reach back corners.

83

BATHROOM SINK ADAPTATION

Bathroom sinks offer unlimited opportunities to maximize comfort and create unique style

Sinks can be freestanding, mounted in the countertop, or perched on top of the vanity like a bowl. Some stand-alone sinks have an integrated countertop. These allow for plenty of floor space without sacrificing the needed work area.

When installing a sink in or on a countertop, place it as close to the front as possible. This allows easier reach to the basin and faucet. Save space and create foot or wheelchair room with a wall-mounted sink. Many of these sinks allow for concealed, behind-the-wall pipes. They project an open, airy style with their modern, sculptured look and accommodate a wheelchair or motorized scooter. They do, however, sacrifice storage space normally found under the

One-piece Counter and Sink

- When replacing a sink or bathroom counter, check out the custom-sized one-piece versions made of synthetic, durable material.

- One-piece models are durable and easy to clean, and there is no grout or glue joint between the sink and counter where mold can grow.

- Less mold is not only cleaner, but also better for allergies, which tend to get worse with age.

Counter Height

- Age-restricted housing often sets counter height at slightly higher (an inch or so) than standard counters. This requires less bending to get close to the sink for face washing.

- Loss of height often occurs with age, but bending over can also become more difficult. Counter and sink height should be a compromise between these two phenomena.

- Counter height needs to accommodate the intended users.

countertop. If pipes are exposed, create a shield to protect legs from burning.

The vanity should be at a height that is convenient for the family members using it. Taller people may have a hard time bending to lower counters, while shorter people might not appreciate not being able to bend over a sink at all.

Since vision problems can make the countertop blend with its surroundings, a distinct pattern or contrasting color should be used to distinguish the vanity from the flooring,

backsplash and walls. You can further differentiate the edge of the vanity top with a contrast strip near the front counter edge.

Use a counter edge that is square to absolutely say where the counter ends, in spite of overhead lighting glare. If counters are tiled, a raised bevel piece of tile in contrast color is a great edge.

Counter Edge Finish

- As recommended for kitchen counters, the edges of bathroom counters should be a right angle.

- Glare from the countertop caused by overhead lighting can make curved edges difficult to see, so it may be hard to see at what point the counter is no longer level.

- A curved edge may make it challenging to determine where to safely place things on the counter, but can be made safer if the edge is strongly contrasted where the curve begins.

Contrast Counter with Floor

- Since the counter is viewed mostly from above, it is important to consider the top surface color in relation to the floor color.

- Make sure that the color of the countertop strongly contrasts with the color on the floor.

- Contrasting the two horizontal surfaces helps those with poor vision naturally differentiate the two levels.

BATHROOM FAUCETS

The choices are numerous, and the final result should be safe and easy to use

Creating a universal design bathroom involves finding faucets that are easy to use by those who have trouble reaching, standing, or operating traditional bathroom fixtures.

Replace twist-handle knob or round faucets with ones that have lever handles, which are the simplest to use. Faucets are available with two levers—one for hot and one for cold—or

one single-lever control. The single lever is either on the side or on top of the spout. Single-lever faucets are usually a better choice because they allow seamless water temperature control from all cold to all hot.

Wall-mounted faucets provide a chic look for over-the-counter sinks, but should only be considered if the vanity

Single-lever Faucet and Spout

Two Faucets with Lever Controls

- A single-lever bathroom faucet is easy to use with either the right or left hand. It provides seamless switching from hot water to degrees of colder in one faucet motion.

- It prevents accidental burning that can occur by

reaching across a hot spout and touching it accidentally with your arm, to turn the left-side hot water control off or down.

- Single controls allow for mixing of hot and cold water with just one hand.

- Sometimes, for function or décor, two controls work better on a sink.

- When choosing a dual control faucet, look for lever controls that are easy to push in both directions.

- Select a finish and style that coordinate with the other elements in the bathroom.

- Be aware that faucet finish durability is dependent on climate, water type, and use.

and sink are narrow and low enough to allow easy access to the faucet handles. Installing a single-lever faucet at the side of the sink will provide the easiest reach.

Faucets are also available with spouts in a variety of shapes and sizes. For optimal comfort and style, choose a spout that is proportionate to the sink. Low gooseneck fixtures will bring the water stream closer to the front of the sink, so less bending and uncomfortable reaching is required.

Spout Sized to Sink

- The faucet spout and controls should be in scale with the size of the sink.

- Water flow from the spout should go directly into the sink drain. If water is hard, this avoids a build-up of scale in the bottom of the sink.

- Beware of spouts that arch too high; they are more likely to get in the way of face washing.

Anti-scalding Device

- Adjusting water temperature becomes tricky when finger dexterity is compromised.

- Setting the water heater to 120 degrees is a safe option, but it means that all household water temperature is lowered.

- Since hotter temperatures may be needed in other rooms, like the laundry room and kitchen, an anti-scalding device is a good option for the bathroom.

- An anti-scalding device only protects the water temperature in the faucet on which it is installed.

BATHROOM FIXTURES

MEDICINE CABINETS
Optional cabinet features can minimize possible dangers

Medicine cabinets may hold many items to which access should be controlled. They need to be practical, safe, and convenient.

Medicine cabinets open in various ways. If yours has a knob, replace it with a U-shaped handle. Some cabinets open by simply pulling on the surrounding lip. If choosing this type of cabinet, select one with a wide lip for easier access. If gripping is impossible, opt for a medicine cabinet with magnetic

spring latches, which opens by pushing on the door.

Cabinet location is important. Many cabinets are placed directly over the sink; these are often difficult to reach and cause problems with spilling and losing pills. Relocate the cabinet to an easy-to-access spot (on a return wall at the side of the sink is practical), and install it at eye level. Note that medicine cabinets *do not need to stay in the bathroom.* Place your cabinet where it is most convenient to store and take

Easy-opening Grip

- Mirrored and some metal-front cabinets have edges that are easy to grip and open.

- Even if gripping is difficult, one finger or the side of a hand can push the door open.

- Mirrored medicine cabinets can be installed on a side wall to eliminate stretching over the sink to access the inside.

Install Good Lighting

- Lighting can be from overhead fixtures behind diffusers, from lighting fixtures installed around the mirror or medicine chest, or from other ceiling or wall-mounted fixtures.

- Good lighting is crucial near the medicine cabinet.

- Choose fixtures and bulbs that give maximum light.

- Bulbs that cast yellow light should be replaced with warm, white bulbs.

- In a fluorescent fixture, choose newer fluorescent bulbs that cast more white light.

your medicine. Options on cabinets are numerous. An automatic light that goes on when the door opens is an important convenience, especially when pill bottles need to be examined. Consider a medicine cabinet with cooling capacity for medications requiring refrigeration. This eliminates the confusion of keeping pills in different places.

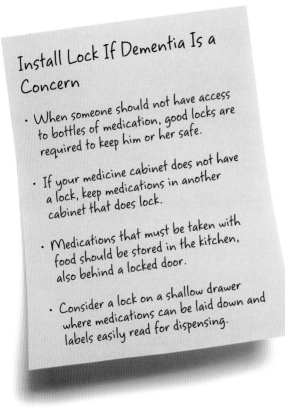

Install Lock If Dementia Is a Concern

- When someone should not have access to bottles of medication, good locks are required to keep him or her safe.

- If your medicine cabinet does not have a lock, keep medications in another cabinet that does lock.

- Medications that must be taken with food should be stored in the kitchen, also behind a locked door.

- Consider a lock on a shallow drawer where medications can be laid down and labels easily read for dispensing.

Medication Dispenser

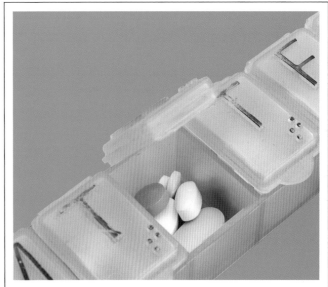

- Weekly and monthly medication holders are handy for anyone who experiences occasional memory lapses.

- Dispensers should be kept where medications are to be taken.

- Medication dispensers are available in drugstores and can often be found for free at senior and health fairs.

- Even if memory is not a concern, medication organizers are very convenient—for home or travel.

BATHROOM FIXTURES

TOILETS
Eliminate pain with an accessible toilet

The simple act of sitting on a toilet is something everyone takes for granted, until bending to a low seat becomes challenging. Accessible, comfortable toilets then become a crucial part of a home bathroom.

Standard toilets are about 14 inches high, which is a little lower than an average chair. A taller seat—17 inches high—will put less strain on legs, hips, and knees, making it easier to sit down and get back up.

Look for new toilets that hang on the wall. These can be installed at any height. Hanging the toilet not only creates a comfortable seat, but also leaves extra floor space. This is safer for walkers, gives more access for wheelchairs, and makes the floor easier to clean.

Don't forget to install grab bars on at least one side. These can be a necessary aid for sitting down and getting up. Be sure the grab bars are anchored into the wall studs so they

Toilet Grab Bar

- Difficulty sitting down on and getting up from a toilet seat may be a temporary or long-term challenge.

- Grab bars are an effective solution. Because of the weight borne by grab bars, it is crucial that they be installed into wall studs or with heavy-duty anchors.

- One bar should be placed alongside the toilet—usually on a return wall. In a narrow space, a second may be helpful installed on the wall opposite the toilet in a narrow space

- Grab bars now come in attractive styles and coordinating finishes.

Elevated Toilet Option

18"

- Many lower-body challenges require an elevated toilet for comfortable, pain-free sitting.

- Eighteen inches—the height of an average chair—is the recommended height for an elevated toilet (versus sixteen inches).

- Although a higher seat may feel strange at first, it seems normal after a short while.

- Shorter people may prefer a toilet only slightly higher than the traditional height, so a wall-mounted toilet can be hung at the chosen elevation.

can withstand the weight of a falling person.

If the bathroom is being renovated, leave at least 18 inches of free space at the front of the toilet, and 42 inches of floor space on the side. This extra space will help a person in a wheelchair move to and from the toilet and is also safer for those using walking aids.

Toilet seats are easily changeable. Some are available with padding under the outer surface for greater comfort. The toilet paper holder should not be ignored. Choose one that allows the roll to be changed easily with one hand.

MAKE IT EASY

If you're not in the market for a complete bathroom renovation, you can still make the bathroom more comfortable. Ask the plumber to put a small platform under the toilet to make it a few inches higher. You can purchase a seat that raises the height of the toilet. The seat simply rests on the existing toilet. Some elevated toilet seats come with side arms—giving you two functions in one!

Japanese Cadillac Toilet

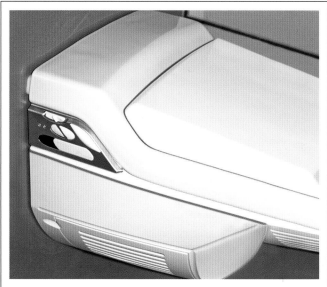

- For the ultimate in pampering and luxury, there are toilets that clean the user at the end of each use.

- A "Cadillac" toilet eliminates the need to reach and stretch in tricky, painful positions.

- A bidet can also make personal cleansing a bit easier for those with flexibility or hand agility problems.

- These rare conveniences are often very costly.

Toilet Paper Holder

- Replace old toilet paper holders that are complicated and tricky to use.

- Purchase a toilet paper holder that allows the roll to be slipped on and off effortlessly.

- Locate the holder conveniently to reach without twisting. Install it on a slight slant so that the toilet paper roll does not slip off when pulled.

- Choose a finish that matches the grab bars and towel racks for a harmonious look.

BATHROOM FIXTURES

GRAB BARS
A crucial safety tool is now available in attractive colors, shapes, and styles

Grab bars have come a long way. They now come in enough shapes, styles, and finishes to fit most decors. They are also appearing in more bathrooms. Some hotels have started adding them in all their rooms to decrease the number of falls and injuries reported.

For safety in the bathroom—for anyone who might be unstable or is susceptible to breaking bones easily—grab bars are crucial in the shower and tub and near the toilet.

Grab bars help to steady those who cannot sit down or stand up without hand supports when getting on and off the toilet.

For the same people grab bars are a steadying support for

Grab Bar in Shower—Industrial

- Grab bars are helpful for getting in and out, and moving about while washing.

- Placement of the bars should be influenced by convention as well as personal needs; think about your shower routine and how you get in and out, and install the bars where they will be most useful to you.

- If you have a shower seat, install a grab bar nearby to aid in sitting and standing up.

Attractive Option

- Although grab bars are used for medical or safety reasons, they can be attractive and tasteful, even enhancing the look of a room.

- Search hardware stores, appliance outlets, kitchen and bath specialty stores, and on the Internet for the finish and style that best fit your decor. Be sure they are intended to be used as grab bars and not towel racks.

- Grab bars need not be expensive, but remember to include the cost of professional installation in your budget.

stepping from outside to inside the tub or shower, and vice versa. They can also steady to stand up and sit down in a tub and you while you reach for the soap in the shower.

When purchasing a grab bar for the bathroom, consider the type of bar and how and where it will be needed. Position it vertically, horizontally, or on any angle in between to meet the needs of the person relying upon it.

A 1½ inch or larger diameter bar is easiest to obtain a solid grip.

Grab Bar in Bathtub

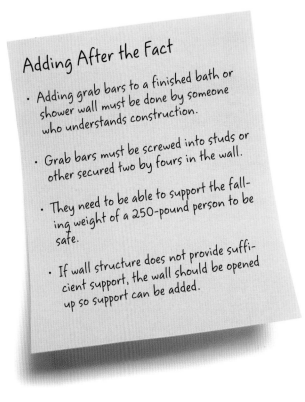

Adding After the Fact

- Adding grab bars to a finished bath or shower wall must be done by someone who understands construction.

- Grab bars must be screwed into studs or other secured two by fours in the wall.

- They need to be able to support the falling weight of a 250-pound person to be safe.

- If wall structure does not provide sufficient support, the wall should be opened up so support can be added.

- Bathtub grab bars add safety and ease the strain of getting in and out of the tub if placed on the side wall.

- On the back wall they aid sitting down and standing up in the tub. Some tubs come with a side bar

installed near the top of the tub sides.

- With more than one user, multiple grab bars should be considered.

- Grab bars on walls should always be anchored into the wall studs.

EMERGENCY CALL BUTTONS

Rest assured, knowing your loved ones have a way to call for help

Emergency call buttons are great when someone who lives alone needs to call for help

Although some senior or nursing communities may use wall-installed call systems, a portable call system is the more practical and economical way to go for a private home.

In a private setting choose a wearable emergency call button: one on a necklace or on a bracelet. No wall installations are needed and the monitor relay can sit next to the bed.

You select the device from what is offered by the service with which you contract.

In an age-restricted community or nursing home, emergency buttons call to the front desk or nursing station manned 24-7. They respond to the emergency by sending staff or calling 911.

In a privately contracted situation, the wearable call button connects to a central emergency response service. Some

Pull Cord Placement

- Age-restricted and barrier-free apartments use emergency pull cords in bathrooms, near the toilet and tub, and in the bedrooms. They connect to the front desk. The front desk then takes responsibility to send help in response.

- In a private home, it can be costly to add a wall-mounted pull cord that calls a central emergency office.

- Wearable systems are less expensive and more practical for private use.

Portable Call Button

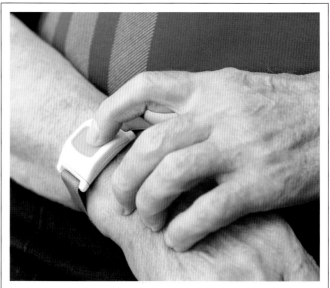

- Portable call buttons are designed to be worn on the wrist or around the neck.

- They are waterproof and can be worn in the bath or shower.

- The portable buttons connect wirelessly, through a monitor that is kept in the house, to a central emergency response service provider.

- The monitor also has a button for emergency calling, so keep it where it might be most needed, like next to the bed.

portable devices come with a walkie-talkie so the central emergency response personnel can talk to the person who pushed the emergency button. When the button is pushed, as when the cord is pulled, emergency response procedures are activated.

When you purchase an emergency button or pull cord system, you are not just buying the equipment in your possession. You are purchasing the assurance that someone will answer when you call for help. Check out the company's references and how long they have been in business.

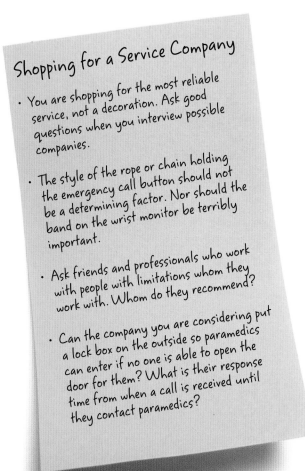

Shopping for a Service Company

- You are shopping for the most reliable service, not a decoration. Ask good questions when you interview possible companies.

- The style of the rope or chain holding the emergency call button should not be a determining factor. Nor should the band on the wrist monitor be terribly important.

- Ask friends and professionals who work with people with limitations whom they work with. Whom do they recommend?

- Can the company you are considering put a lock box on the outside so paramedics can enter if no one is able to open the door for them? What is their response time from when a call is received until they contact paramedics?

Bathroom or Special Telephones

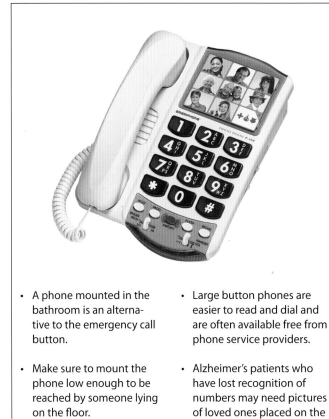

- A phone mounted in the bathroom is an alternative to the emergency call button.

- Make sure to mount the phone low enough to be reached by someone lying on the floor.

- Large button phones are easier to read and dial and are often available free from phone service providers.

- Alzheimer's patients who have lost recognition of numbers may need pictures of loved ones placed on the phone buttons.

BATHTUBS

Renovations provide safety, comfort, and convenience

Elderly and mobility-challenged people can have difficulty getting in and out of the bathtub. Replacing the tub may be expensive so consider all the options before making a decision.

For easiest and safest access, bathtub sides should be low—no more than 17 inches. But lower sides mean a shallower soak. If a deeper, more lavish bath experience is desired, consider replacing the tub with a walk-in variety. They have a watertight walk-through door. Look for optional whirlpool features available on some walk-in tubs

Modification to existing tubs can be a less costly way to make bathing easier. A wider edge on a built-in tub, created with a tile ledge and front, can aid getting in and out. A suction rubber mat may be used to ease the temperature shock of sitting directly on cold tile as you sit on it and swing your legs over.

Walk-in Tubs

- What will they think of next? A tub with a water-tight door makes getting into and out of the bathtub effortless.

- One drawback is that the bather must sit in the tub until the water drains to below the bottom level of the door.

- When medicinal soaking or a luxurious bath adds to the quality of life, a walk-in tub is a good investment.

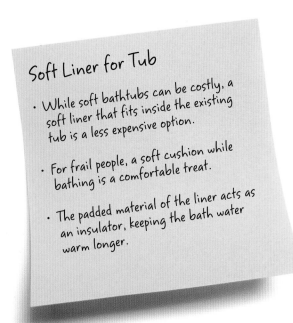

Soft Liner for Tub

- While soft bathtubs can be costly, a soft liner that fits inside the existing tub is a less expensive option.

- For frail people, a soft cushion while bathing is a comfortable treat.

- The padded material of the liner acts as an insulator, keeping the bath water warm longer.

A soft bathtub—with a polyurethane-covered foam surface—makes the bath safer by increasing slip resistance and protecting those who fall from serious impact injury.

Built-in with Edge Seat

- A wide ledge can function as a transfer seat for people who can lift their legs over the tub.

- After sitting on the ledge, move one leg into the tub at a time.

- Place a slip-proof pad on the edge and inside the tub for safety.

- The pad will also temper the shock of the cold tub surface.

Different Tub Enclosures

- Bathtub doors can be custom-made to fit any size tub and any personal needs.

- Doors can slide, swing into the tub or into the room. They can even be made to fold in sections so there is less in the way when you get in and out. Some doors cover only half of the tub leaving the part farthest from the shower head exposed.

- Choose doors that accommodate showers or baths per your lifestyle.

TUBS & SHOWERS

97

TUB FIXTURES
Make bath time enjoyable and relaxing by minimizing difficulties

The most common bath controls, located low on the center of the end wall of the tub, require bending over the tub to turn them on. If cost allows, do away with this by relocating the controls to a more easily accessible spot. Raise them higher and bring them closer to the front edge of the tub enclosure so less reaching is needed. And replace all twist and grip controls with simple-to-use lever handles.

Minimize bath time struggles by installing grab bars around the tub and shower perimeter walls. Bars can be mounted against the far wall or on a side wall, or they may come attached to the top outside of the tub.

Hot water is a real danger in a bath, especially for those who may not register heat or pain, as with stroke, paralysis, or dementia. Hot water heaters should be turned down to 120 degrees for protection. In addition to that, installing a faucet with a maximum temperature setting is the best way

Lever Control

- The ideal tub faucet has a single mixer control that allows one small movement to adjust temperature.

- In a bathtub/shower combination, faucets may be mounted on the wall above the tub, or near the tub top. One is more convenient while bathing, the other while showering.

- With a tub/shower combination, a compromise may have to be reached.

Temperature Control Faucet

- Faucets are available with an adjustable button that sets the maximum water temperature.

- The faucet automatically adjusts the hot and cold taps to reach and hold the desired temperature, preventing scalding from too hot water.

- This safety feature is crucial for a paraplegic who cannot feel the water temperature.

- It is equally important for someone who has diabetes.

to minimize chances of being scalded by hot water.

If you do not wish to install the faucets in the tub, where the manufacturer provides for them, a plate can be placed over the access and faucets can be installed into the wall above the tub. This keeps them out of the way when getting into the tub. This also provides an opportunity to add a portable, flexible showerhead, which increases bathing options.

Telephone Shower to Bathe

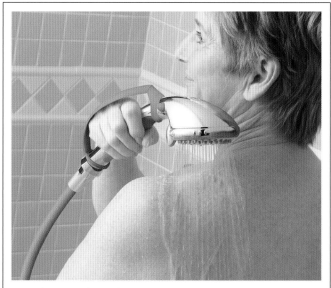

- Replacing a showerhead or a tub spout with a telephone shower extension helps anyone who needs to sit on a shower or tub seat to bathe.

- It enables moving the water spray to where it is needed—back, underarms, etc.—without the person having to move these parts into the fixed flow of the showerhead.

Shelf for Soaps and Shampoo

- When adding a new shower or tub to a bathroom, incorporate conveniently placed shelves or niches to hold soaps and shampoos.

- For an existing tub, mount a liquid soap and shampoo dispenser low on the wall, or add a shelf into a corner so soaps are accessible to someone sitting in the tub.

- Purchase soaps and shampoos with pump dispensers rather than large plastic bottles that need to be lifted.

TUBS & SHOWERS

99

TRANSFER AND BATH SEATS
Make getting in and out of the tub easier

A transfer seat is designed to allow users to move from a seated position outside the tub, to a seated position inside the tub without the danger of falling or stubbing a toe. Once on the seat inside the tub or shower they can bathe or shower comfortably and safely. Inside-the-tub seats and transfer benches are available in many sizes and styles, fitting virtually any standard bathtub and suiting any bather.

For those who are unstable on their legs, or unable to lift their leg as high as the tub side, the benefit of a transfer seat is obvious

The benefit of being safely seated in a tub or shower also eliminates the chance of slipping on the wet surface of the tub or shower bottom while washing.

A transfer board must be long enough to reach from the seat outside the tub to about half-way across the seat inside the tub. This will provide safety for someone to scoot or slide

Portable Bath Seat

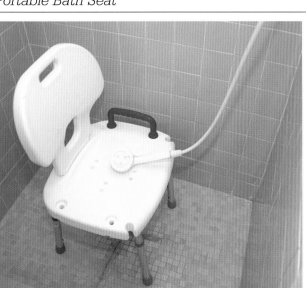

- There are many different bath seats on the market, including packable ones that fold small enough to be taken along on an airplane vacation.

- If you check ahead with your accommodations, you may find an accessible bath is available, and you can travel without your seat.

- For home use find a safe and sturdy style.

- Suction feet or rubber cups make portable bath seats safe to use wherever they are taken.

Portable Transfer Board

- A specialized transfer board makes transfer from a wheelchair or motorized scooter to a tub seat safe.

- Be sure the seat outside the tub is secured before starting a transfer. If the seat inside the tub is not built in, be sure it is not going to slip on the tub bottom.

- The transfer board can be removed while bathing so the tub enclosure door or curtain can be closed. Just slip it back spanning the two seats when you're ready to get out of the bath.

themselves from between the seats, and on and off the board.

The board must be strong enough to support the weight of the person sliding across it. Never use an improvised board as a transfer seat. It may not bear the full weight. Purchase a board made specifically for the purpose.

When using a seat inside the tub or shower, a telephone showerhead makes getting wet all over, easier. Soaps and shampoos should be kept close by.

Tub with Seat

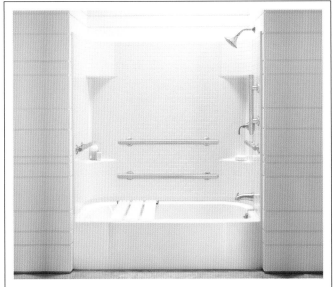

- A tub seat eliminates the difficulty of bending low into a tub for those who find it challenging.

- A seat also makes it easier to exit the tub.

- A seat can be used by anyone who feels more secure washing in a seated position.

- Lower seats allow the bather to soak in the water, while remaining in a comfortably seated position.

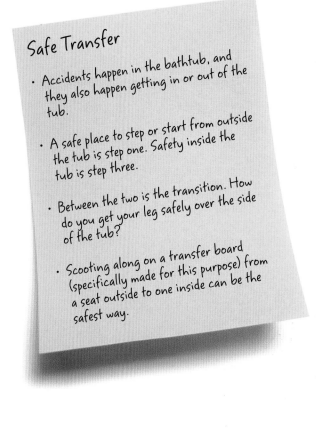

Safe Transfer

- Accidents happen in the bathtub, and they also happen getting in or out of the tub.

- A safe place to step or start from outside the tub is step one. Safety inside the tub is step three.

- Between the two is the transition. How do you get your leg safely over the side of the tub?

- Scooting along on a transfer board (specifically made for this purpose) from a seat outside to one inside can be the safest way.

SHOWER STALLS

Eliminate the risk of dangerous accidents with safety modifications

Awkward access to the shower stall is not only a nuisance; it can be the cause of accidents leading to very serious injuries. To create a safer shower environment, consider several modifications.

One of the dangerous parts of a shower stall is the threshold—the raised tile, fiberglass, or metal piece below the shower door opening, keeping water on the correct side. Not only is this difficult or impossible to get over in a wheelchair,

but it is also unsafe for those with impaired vision, people who cannot easily lift their feet, or anyone who is simply tired.

An option is to have the threshold removed entirely to provide a smooth entrée. If a threshold is needed to keep the bathroom from getting wet, switch to a mini-threshold with a flexible water dam. This soft device allows a wheelchair to roll over it but is strong enough to keep water in. A water-

Built-in Seat

- A built-in shower seat provides safety and comfort for those who prefer or are safer washing in a seated position.

- Since the seat is usually at the far end of the shower, a telephone shower attachment will add convenience.

- A portable shower chair with suction feet is an economical solution that can be moved in or out of the way as needed.

Niche for Soap/Shampoo

- A built-in shelf is an important security feature because bending to pick up soaps from the floor is not safe.

- Fiberglass shower stalls are made with niches to hold the necessities.

- Soap and shampoo dispensers can be installed in existing showers, and a rack with shelves can be hung over the showerhead.

tolerant chair can then be used for showering, eliminating the need for transfer from outside the shower to inside, and vice versa. The flexible threshold can also be walked over and is soft enough to collapse under a person's weight so it doesn't cause pain. Another danger is slipping in the shower. If the shower basin is too slick, add rubber strips or suction shapes to bottom; the ones often used in tubs.

Showering often requires bending and twisting to reach all the body parts. This can lead to loss of balance. A built-in seat in the shower stall can provide needed support and a comfortable place to rest while washing. If there is no seat built in, a portable one can be added and removed as needed.

Low Threshold Entry to Shower

- Shower doors need to have thresholds of 4 to 5 inches to keep water off the bathroom floor.

- With a grab bar for assistance, most mobile people are able to safely negotiate a low threshold.

- Be sure the surface of the shower is non-slip and that the rug outside the shower has a rubber bottom to prevent slipping.

Roman Shower

- A Roman shower is a shower that is seamlessly incorporated into a bathroom.

- The floor of the room slants slightly toward the drain, so water stays only where it is used.

- The elimination of thresholds makes a Roman shower ideal for someone in a wheelchair.

- A Roman shower is also convenient for caregivers who need to assist someone in the shower.

103

SHOWER FIXTURES

Create a soothing shower experience by increasing safety and reducing obstacles

There are many fixtures and accessories available for shower modifications that improve safety and convenience. Recessed soap and shampoo ledges provide an organized, clean way to store needed shower items without causing obstructions. A seat at the end of the shower away from the shower head makes for easier soaping and rinsing, and can double as a place to hold shampoos and soaps.

The faucet controls should be replaced with a single-lever control. That way the temperature can be regulated with the movement of one hand, from hot to cold. If cost allows, choose a faucet that marks the actually temperature of water at any of its gradient settings and with a red safety button.

Telephone Extension Shower Attachment

- A telephone extension is a flexible hose with shower-head attached.

- It can be used as a hand-held spray or slipped into a holder on the wall where it functions as a fixed showerhead.

- The spray can be directed anywhere on the body without the need for turning and bending.

- Any compatible shower-head can be used on the telephone extension.

Single-lever Control

- A single-lever control eliminates the need to struggle with two controls to create a comfortable water temperature.

- The single lever gradually changes the water temperature with the tap of a hand. A firm grasp is not necessary.

- A lever can be controlled with a wrist, elbow, or side of a hand.

- One lever contro; also means less hardware to scrub.

This allows you to set the maximum temperature mix that will be allowed.

If it is possible, when installing the new control, locate it close to the outside of the enclosure. In this position, it can be easily operated from outside the shower, so water temperature can be set and tested before entering. If it is to be used from a sitting position be sure it will be reachable.

There are many different shower spray heads. Try a handheld spray with an adjustable holder that is mounted to a vertical bar. This provides many functions in one fixture. The showerhead can be left in the mounted holder and moved up and down to spray from whatever height is personally preferred. It can be held in hand for targeted cleaning or hydro-massage, and even to rinse the shower enclosure.

Install grab bars on the back wall and sides of the shower enclosure, as needed.

Safety Button Temperature Control

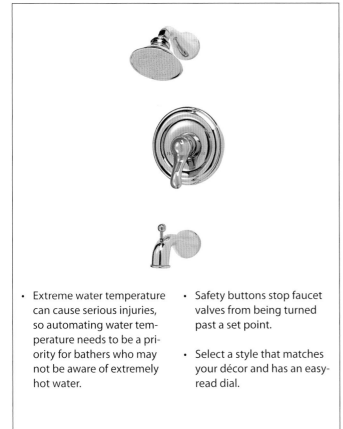

- Extreme water temperature can cause serious injuries, so automating water temperature needs to be a priority for bathers who may not be aware of extremely hot water.

- Safety buttons stop faucet valves from being turned past a set point.

- Select a style that matches your décor and has an easy-read dial.

Grab Bar

- A tiled shower may require tile replacement when installing a grab bar.

- Fiberglass showers may be less costly to retrofit.

- All grab bars must be secured into wall studs to provide enough support. If there aren't wall studs in appropriate spots, get a good installer to make the proper modifications in the wall for safety.

SHOWER ENCLOSURES
What it takes to keep the water where you want it

The ideal shower space in a universal design bathroom is a "curbless," roll-in enclosure with a built-in seat, integral shelves and niches, and grab bars for support. This accessible shower allows people of all abilities to enjoy a safe and comfortable shower experience.

With no curb or threshold, the shower floor is at the same level as the bathroom floor. People with slight mobility challenges can walk in without worry of tripping. A wheelchair user can roll directly into the shower without meeting any obstructions, or transfer right onto a shower bench or chair. There are no glass or plastic doors to worry about.

Most homes cannot be easily adapted to this kind of shower. So what can one do?

There are many upgrades and options available in shower enclosures that make them easier for most everyone to use.

Enclosure doors can swing out into the room for entry, or

Custom Tile Enclosures

- Tile enclosures can be custom-built to include many bells and whistles.

- Options include custom corner soap dishes, any size wall niche, and a built-in bench.

- Tiled showers, on the other hand, are expensive to build so they are not for all remodels. It is also harder to add attachments or additions after a tiled shower is complete (i.e., a grab bar).

Fiberglass Pre-fab Showers

- Economical fiberglass shower enclosures are prefabricated in one piece installations.

- Because they are molded into one piece, they have no grout or seams where mold can grow.

- Many prefabricated shower stalls are formed with benches, integral shelves, and offer grab bars.

- The bottom of the stall is already textured for non-slip safety.

slide side to side. Usually both of these styles provide at least 30 inches of width to enter.

Custom doors can be ordered that are fixed in place across part of the entry, or ones that bi-fold and swing completely into the shower space allowing a wider entry. They then easily fold back in place across the entry, or part of the entry.

Enclosures which do not enclose all across a shower or tub space are good for a caregiver who assists someone showering, while trying to keep themselves relatively dry.

Showers in Small Spaces

- A separate shower is a safe option for those who find it difficult to step into a bathtub.

- A small corner is all that is needed to install a one-person shower stall.

- Small showers can be fabricated from fiberglass or tile, or as a combination of the two.

- Use the same tile or fiberglass color as the bath to create a well-balanced space.

Resurfacing to Renew

- It is possible to resurface an old shower stall or tub and make it look like new.

- Resurfacing can be done over a cast iron tub and its enclosure or over a tile surface.

- Before contracting for a resurfacing job, price out a complete replacement, as well.

- Sometimes this labor-intensive job can cost more than a pre-fabricated replacement.

107

SOFAS

Create a cozy environment for relaxing and entertaining

The living room functions as a quiet relaxation space for family, as well as a conversational and entertainment area when guests arrive. Appropriate seating is the most important part of creating a comfortable and inviting atmosphere.

Choosing the right sofa can be daunting. With myriad sofa shapes, arm styles, cushion sizes, and pillow fillings, as well as unlimited fabric and trim choices, how do you know where to begin? To ensure that the seating is comfortable and safe,

follow a few guidelines. Select a sofa with a seat height of at least 17 inches for easiest sitting and standing, putting less strain on knees and back. The depth of the seat will also affect your ability to stand up without effort. Choose a sofa with a maximum depth of 18 inches. If an existing sofa has a deeper seat, add pillows or cushions to the back to shorten it.

While softer sofas may seem more luxurious, they require additional effort to get up. Opt for a firm seat and add soft

Depth of Seats/Cushions

- A sofa should certainly complement personal style and harmonize with the room's color scheme, but it also needs to fit the physical requirements and abilities of the users.

- Loss of strength and muscle tone and joint problems make it harder to stand up from a deep, soft seat and can make it less comfortable to sit in.

- If a seat is too deep, cushions in the back shorten the depth.

Height of Seat

17"

- To ensure easy transition on and off a sofa, choose one with a seat height of at least 17 inches.

- The higher height means less knee and hip bending and therefore less joint strain when standing up. It also requires less thigh

strength to reach a standing position.

- Purchase a sofa with the future in mind.

throw pillows for softness as desired.

Leave 12 to 18 inches between the sofa and the coffee table. This allows sufficient room for slipping in and out, while keeping the table close enough for comfortable use.

Height of Arms

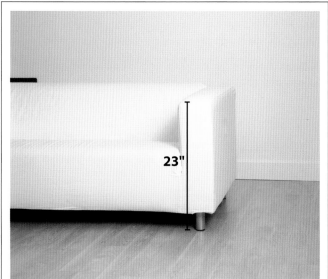

- Even if a sofa seat is low, the perfect height arm might still offer someone the leverage he or she needs to stand up more easily.

- Arms that are 23 inches off the floor are good for leveraging and lifting oneself.

- It still takes strength to lift one's body up, so be aware that not all people will be able to stand up without aid.

Placement for Natural Light

- Curling up with a good book requires a comfortable sofa and appropriate lighting.

- Placing the sofa near a window will provide good reading light during the day.

- For evening reading, make sure to have adequate, directed task lighting.

- If there is not appropriate built-in lighting, add a table or floor lamp near the reading area.

ALSO KEEP IN MIND. . .

Lighting and layout for maximum living room enjoyment

A good sofa makes for a comfortable seat, but the right placement allows for optimal comfort and security when working, reading, or relaxing with friends.

Create a conversation area in the living room by placing sofas and chairs in an L-shape. Interaction is comfortable and natural. When two sofas are at right angles, place a side table to connect the two at the corner. This makes for a convenient drink holder for those who have trouble leaning forward to the coffee table.

Keep extra throw pillows in the living room for added softness or support whenever and wherever needed. The pillows can be used on sofas and chairs to create a more comfortable sitting position, on the floor for gentle foot rests, and as extra fun seating when children come to visit. Coordinating

Keep Movable Cushions Available

- People of varying heights, shapes, and flexibility may all sit on the same sofas and chairs.

- To ensure enjoyment by all, keep extra throw pillows handy.

- Movable cushions or throw pillows help accommodate quick adaptation of the chairs and seats.

- Firmer cushions are good choices to shorten seat depth.

Place Furniture for Maximum Daylight

- To see more clearly, those with poor or failing vision need as much light as possible.

- Place furniture to take advantage of natural daylight whenever possible.

- A window that is located behind a chair will provide perfect light for reading and tasks during the daytime.

- Natural daylight not only makes tasks easier and more comfortable, but it helps conserve energy.

pillows can be left out as part of the room's décor, but keep them off the floor.

If there are large windows that provide natural light, use it to your advantage. Place seating where it can receive the best illumination. Instead of facing the sofa and chairs toward the window, which can cause disturbing or even blinding glare, position the seating backs to the light. The sun coming from behind creates the most favorable lighting, allowing for easier reading and more comfortable conversing.

Sufficient overall lighting is needed for safe navigation throughout the living room area. Sofas, chairs, tables, and other accessories all become dangerous obstacles if there is not enough light. To reduce the chance of bumping, remember to use color contrasts to distinguish all pieces from the surrounding areas. Functional task lighting should be added to the areas where reading or other chores take place. Floor lamps or table lamps placed slightly behind the task areas will illuminate them clearly.

Place Furniture near Proper Lighting for Tasks

- Task lighting is needed in the living room to make tasks—reading, crossword puzzles, knitting, etc.—easier and more enjoyable.

- Place lights above or alongside where someone will sit, rather than behind, so a shadow is not created by a head or shoulder.

- If lighting is inadequate for certain tasks, add hanging fixtures, floor or table lamps, or focused track lights.

Ambient Lighting for Mood and Socializing

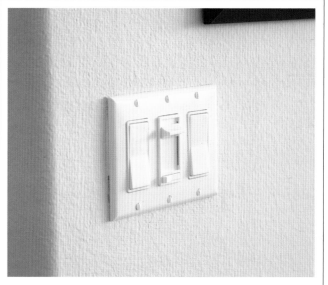

- Dimmer controls can turn overall room lights as well as task lights into mood lighting.

- Dim lights can create an ambience that relaxes and encourages casual socializing.

- Dimmer switch plates can replace most standard switch plates.

- Choose controls that allow a large range of dimming. It is then easy to adjust quickly for additional light if people need to get up and move about safely.

EASY CHAIRS

With a little planning, the easy chair can be the most comfortable seat in the home

"Easy chair" is a general term for a wide variety of chairs ranging from cozy, cushioned pieces to recliners to motorized lift chairs. When choosing an easy chair, the most important feature is that it be "easy"—easy to relax, easy to operate, and easy to get up .

First, evaluate the intended spot for the chair to identify space requirements. Understanding how the chair will fit into the environment will make ownership more enjoyable and practical. Measure recliners in their extended positions to ensure traffic in the room will not be impeded and the wall behind won't be damaged. Also consider the logistics of having the chair delivered. Will it fit through tight doorways—or

Height of Seat

17"

- The height and depth of the seat determine how comfortable a chair is.

- A seat that is at least 17 inches off the floor should be comfortable to sit in and easy for getting up.

- High chair arms can assist when getting out of the chair and also help a frail person or someone with poor balance sit down softly.

Depth of Seat

- If any member of the family has muscle tone or mobility issues, accommodate him or her by having at least one chair sized for his or her comfort.

- A chair is most comfortable when the back is supported and the knees can bend

beyond the edge of the seat.

- Shorter people can be made more comfortable with a spare cushion at their back.

will it need to be disassembled first and then reassembled once it's in the room?

The seat height of an easy chair should be at least 17 inches from the floor. This will ease the strain on the back, knees, and other joints when sitting or standing. Be sure that the chair is comfortable. Choose a fabric that feels good to the touch.

For people with mobility challenges, a power-assisted lift chair is a great option. Available in a wide range of fabrics and lift features, these chairs take much of the strain out of reclining and getting up. Lift chairs are designed to maneuver the user into varying positions smoothly and comfortably. To stand from a lift chair, press a button, and the chair gently lifts you into an almost standing position, making disembarking easy and pain free. Seat lift adaptations are also available for people who wish to convert a traditional chair into a lift chair.

Never buy a recliner, lift chair, or seat lift device before testing it. The mechanisms all operate differently, so you need to choose one that is easy to maneuver.

Height of Arms

- Chair arms come in many shapes and styles to coordinate with the mood of any room.

- For comfort and safety, arms should be evaluated by their height and sturdiness.

- For people to lift themselves out of a chair most easily, 24 to 25 inches is a useful arm height. Proper arm height also takes strain off the knees and thighs when used as support for lowering into the chair.

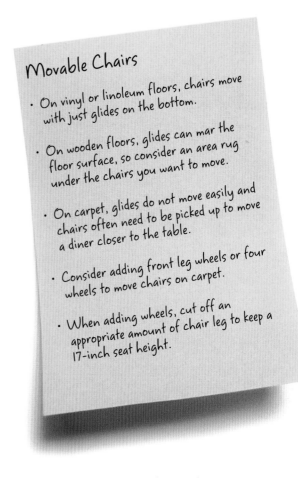

Movable Chairs

- On vinyl or linoleum floors, chairs move with just glides on the bottom.

- On wooden floors, glides can mar the floor surface, so consider an area rug under the chairs you want to move.

- On carpet, glides do not move easily and chairs often need to be picked up to move a diner closer to the table.

- Consider adding front leg wheels or four wheels to move chairs on carpet.

- When adding wheels, cut off an appropriate amount of chair leg to keep a 17-inch seat height.

TABLES & STORAGE FURNITURE
It's often the small stuff that creates the lifestyle

When designing the look and feel of your living room, here are a few things to keep in mind.

Think ahead about safety. Make sure all tables are stable and secure. Since residents or visitors may use tables to brace themselves, they need to be firm and steady. Anchor bookshelves and hutches to the wall. If any of the tables have sharp edges, attach corner protectors.

Place tables near where they will be used. Arrange them to reduce reaching and straining. Allow 12 inches of space between coffee tables and sofas for comfortable movement in and out. Add more space if walkers or wheelchairs are used. Side tables should be placed near all sofa and chair arms to provide convenient resting spots for books and drinks. Consider the function of the space, and ensure that no piece of furniture will become an obstacle. Leave open walkways to move in and out and throughout the room.

Stable Coffee Table

- Coffee tables are placed in the midst of traffic flow around seating groupings.

- They need to be durable to withstand being knocked or banged, and sturdy enough for leaning on.

- They also need to be stable enough so that glasses or vases will not topple when the table gets bumped.

- Choose the smallest coffee table that will be in scale with the other pieces in the room.

Add Corner Protectors

- All tables and furniture with square corners are potential black-and-blue producers.

- Sometimes the location of the furniture increases the chances that they will be banged into.

- Evaluate if a slight adjustment in placement or a total change in the room's traffic flow can reduce the incidence of bangs.

- Inexpensive padded corners can be purchased to soften the impact of banging into corners.

As with any piece of furniture, storage pieces and tables need to contrast with the surrounding flooring. Choose furnishings in colors that strongly contrast with the floor and other pieces that will be placed close to them.

MAKE IT EASY

How to arrange furniture: Start planning the room with the biggest pieces first. In a living room, this is usually the entertainment center or the sofa. Once that location is decided, arrange other furniture around it, keeping 3-foot-wide pathways throughout the room for easy navigation.

Tables for Lamps and Floor Lamps

- Floor or tabletop lamps can add needed lighting for specific areas.

- Since lamps can be knocked over easily, place them behind furniture or out of the flow of traffic, but where the benefit of their light can still be enjoyed.

- Know what you need before shopping for lampshades. Most will dim the light on lamps, causing them to act more as mood lighting. Some are designed to direct the light downward.

High Furniture Pieces Anchored to Wall

- High, shallow pieces of furniture are in danger of falling over when knocked or fallen into, or shaken by an earthquake.

- They should be anchored to the wall with angle hardware to prevent such accidents.

- Hardware should be mounted into wall studs and attached securely to the furniture.

- Hire a professional handyman if you are not confident you can do this yourself.

LIVING ROOM LIGHTING
The dark and light of living rooms

Before planning lighting for your living room, think about how it is to be used. Do you spend time in the living room daily, using it as a family gathering spot? Or is it a more formal room reserved for guests and special occasions? The function of your room will determine your lighting needs.

A living room that is used often needs specific lighting to illuminate tasks performed there, like reading, sewing, playing games, etc. Take advantage of natural light during the day. You may only need ambient lighting for evenings. If you don't have many windows, install overhead lighting and place floor and table lamps to easily see what you are doing.

Rooms that are used less frequently still need lighting that is appropriate for its specific use. For mood, put the general lighting on dimmers, or just use several lamps to create a soft glow. Remember that this type of lighting is only for aesthetic purposes. Make sure the lights can be turned up when

Ceiling Floods for Ambient Lighting

- Technology has made advances in the types of bulbs available.

- LED bulbs are extremely long lasting, which helps defray their expensive purchase cost.

- Choose white LED bulbs, which produce a soft white light free of harsh glare and shadows.

- Aging eyes tend to see with a yellow cast, so white light is a good solution.

Recessed Lights for Tasks

- Recessed lighting fixtures can create ambient lighting in rooms or be focused in one area for task lighting.

- Most recessed light fixtures require halogen floods, which are available in different wattages. Pick the highest wattage allowed for the particular fixture.

- An electrician can install recessed cans and connect them to a wall switch.

- Dimmer switches can always soften or brighten lighting.

company comes over so the room is safe and comfortable for everyone.

The placement of the lights is also important. The higher up the light fixture, the greater area over which it will cast its light. Ceiling lights do the best job creating ambient light. There are traditional ceiling fixtures, chandeliers, recessed can lighting, and ceiling-mounted tracks. Match your choice for ambient lighting to your décor.

Ceiling fixtures can also act as task lighting. Choose from fixtures such as chandeliers for dining, or recessed cans or track lighting with bulbs that can be directed to a special chair, a piece of art, or onto a desk. Task lighting can also often be accomplished with a table, floor, or desk lamp.

For safety, consider ceiling-installed fixtures first. Floor and table lamps may be in or near traffic pathways and can get knocked over. Never use them in a place where the wire is in the traffic flow.

Hanging Fixtures for Tasks

- If installing recessed lighting is not a realistic budget option, consider a hanging fixture for good light by a chair or desk.

- Hanging light fixtures are available with a variety of wattage choices, can be plugged into a wall outlet, and are out of the way of traffic.

- If furniture is rearranged at a future time, it is just a matter of moving one or two ceiling hooks to move hanging lights to a new location.

Portable Floor Lamps

- A floor lamp is portable, can be placed wherever needed in the room, and can be plugged into any outlet.

- The disadvantage of a floor lamp is that it can be easily knocked over by accident.

- If floor lamps complement a room's décor, place them out of the flow of traffic, preferably behind other furniture.

- If floor lamps cannot be placed in a secure location, opt for a safer lighting option.

DINING CHAIRS

If the chair fits . . . meals are more enjoyable

Dining room design can run from casual and relaxed to formal and opulent. No matter the style, you can ensure that the space is comfortable, safe, and accessible for family and guests if you follow a few guidelines.

Dining chairs are often heavier than kitchen chairs. If they are difficult to move, use lighter ones. There is no law against using kitchen chairs in a dining room. If necessary, hire a carpenter to cut the front chair legs down and add wheels so the chairs glide in and out smoothly on carpet.

Armchairs make getting up and down easier and put less strain on legs. If there is not enough room for all chairs to be armed, purchase two armchairs for the heads of the table. Those who need support can use them.

Upholstered chairs and those with padded seats should be protected from spills. A chemical fabric protector can help to prevent staining on the fabric. This type of protection can

Height of Seats

- The standard height for dining room and kitchen chairs is between 15 and 18 inches.

- The distance between the chair and the dining room table affects eating comfort.

- Leave approximately 6 inches of space from the top of the seat to the bottom of the table edge to allow sufficient room to lift out of the seat and pull the chair in.

Depth of Seats

- A 16- to 18-inch seat depth is comfortable for dining for most people.

- If someone cannot sit comfortably with their back supported, a thin cushion placed behind will help.

- Dining chairs are deeper and more padded than kitchen chairs to encourage longer sitting, but they may not be comfortable for all diners.

- To accommodate all who come to the table, consider using kitchen chairs in the dining room—or vice versa—as needed.

be embedded in the fabric or sprayed on after the seats are upholstered.

A 15- to 18-inch-high seat is comfortable for most people, but with aging, people tend to sit shorter. If a person's chin and shoulders are not high enough for them to comfortably eat at the table, place a cushion on the seat. A block or floor cushion can be set under their feet.

Dining chairs are typically deeper than kitchen chairs, so use what works best for shorter people. Cushions on the back of the seat bring a person closer to the table.

ZOOM

A dining chair with arms can make standing up and sitting down easier for someone with joint or balance problems. They also make it easier to assist someone else when scooting the chair in.

Seat Fabric

- Kitchen chairs may have removable, washable cushions. Dining room chairs are often upholstered so cushions must be cleaned in place.

- Because of the expense of reupholstering, select durable fabrics that can be protected and spot-cleaned.

- Patterns or deep colors can hide a multitude of spots.

Chair Leg Glides

- People sitting in chairs may need help moving in and out from the table.

- On carpeting, frail people can be scooted in and out from the table if wheels are installed on the bottom of chairs.

- Chair leg glides are more practical on vinyl or wood flooring.

- If chairs are pushed in and out often, consider changing a wood floor to vinyl.

DINING TABLES

Choices, choices, choices! Combine aesthetics with function for the perfect dining room table

When selecting a dining room table, it is important to consider practical features along with individual taste. With so many styles, shapes, and materials from which to choose, the purchasing decision is never easy.

The first consideration should be to ensure adequate space. Measure the room's dimensions to determine the appropriate size of the dining room table. Be sure to include enough space for people to maneuver their chairs to and from the table. If the dining room table is in a throughway, account for some extra room for people to pass behind comfortably, especially when diners are seated at the table. Strategically place the table in an optimum position in the room to facilitate proper

Height for Dining

- The top of a traditional dining table is 29 to 30 inches high.

- The width of the wood or the fascia on the edge will determine the clearance under the table.

- If an existing table is too high, shorter adults may be uncomfortable. Consider having the legs of the table shortened.

- Another solution to a high table is to add cushions to the chairs. This may lead to diners' feet dangling uncomfortably, but a floor cushion can help.

Rounded Edges

- Oval or round tables are a safe choice for a dining room, especially when a corner impact could cause excessive bleeding in elders on certain medications.

- Both round and oval tables are available with a middle leaf that extends them for larger parties.

- If a rectangular or square table is the best look for the dining room, choose one with rounded corners, or place rubber corner protectors on the table.

flow. The angle, placement, and direction of the table should complement the other furniture as well as the overall layout of the room.

Because people come in all sizes, there is no perfect height for a dining room table. What is ideal for one family member may be awkward and uncomfortable for another. Most dining room tables are approximately 30 inches high. If this is not appropriate for all family members, explore options. Purchase a shorter table or have a professional carpenter adjust the length of the legs if a smaller height is needed.

Dining room tables can be round, square, or rectangular. While it is important to choose a shape that fits best in the room, round and oval tables are safer because they do not have corners, which can cause bruising. Square and rectangular tables are also available with rounded corners. Tables of all shapes can accommodate leaves to extend the table for additional dinner guests. If the room features flexible lighting, the table can be illuminated adequately even with the extended leaf.

Placement for Room Flow

- Tables can become an obstacle to comfortable traffic flow when the room is full of diners.

- When purchasing a dining room table, consider the size with all of the chairs pulled out.

- Someone with a mobility problem should be seated where he or she can get in and out easily, but not be in the way of traffic flow. This takes special attention if the person is in a wheelchair.

Overhead Lighting and Flexibility

- Traditionally chandeliers grace the space above a dining table, but they limit where you can move a table safely.

- Consider track lighting or recessed can lights over the dining area for greater table placement flexibility.

- The table can then go anywhere in the room, without worry of a dangling obstruction.

121

BOOKCASES

Sturdy, secure bookcases provide aesthetic value and functional storage solutions

Bookcases are perfect for housing books and providing a visible place to display photographs, knick-knacks, and mementos. As with many pieces of stand-alone furniture in the home, bookcases are safer when positioned properly and mounted to a wall. Because heavy books and other objects are often placed on bookcases, do not take chances by leaving them unsecured. The books and materials that are used most often in the home should be placed on middle shelves so they are most accessible without reaching or bending. Avoid placing heavy books on high or low shelves. Reaching or bending to lift heavy or awkward-shaped objects can be difficult, so keep them within easy reach. The top and bottom shelves should

Attach to Wall

- Tall bookcases can be quite top-heavy especially when loaded with picture frames, books, and mementos.

- Built-in bookcases are the safest choice in any home.

- Anchor stand-alone bookcases to the wall with mounting hardware.

- Hire a professional who can find the wall studs and use the safest brackets.

Put Reference Books at Mid-body Height

- Frequently read books should be kept on shelves between waist and shoulder height for the greatest ease of access.

- If possible, place frequently used books in rooms where they are read, for example, cookbooks in the kitchen, craft books in the den, etc.

- Use lower shelves for books that are read infrequently or are just for show.

be reserved for decorative items or accessories that are not needed on a daily or weekly basis. Once they are positioned, they can be left in place for long periods of time.

Avoid cramming too many books on a single shelf. If books and other materials are too crowded, it becomes difficult to pull an item from its place. Leave a little space on each shelf so it is not necessary to struggle when removing or replacing a book.

Group similar books together. Create categories to avoid searching each and every shelf for one particular book. A

logical, organized system saves time and avoids frustration. Review and prioritize the items on bookcases to determine whether they should be kept on display or moved to a less accessible storage area.

If a bookcase has cabinets, be sure the doors have easy grip handles. These handles are available in many finishes and colors so they can harmonize beautifully with the bookcase style. Select bookcases that complement the décor of the room, but make sure they are safe and functional as well.

Put Mementos and Photos Up High

- Decorative items can be placed on shelves above shoulder height.

- When placed near eye level, they are at the perfect height to enjoy.

- It is easier to view higher items from across the room.

- Since decorative items are looked at and not often moved or taken down, they can be placed at less accessible heights.

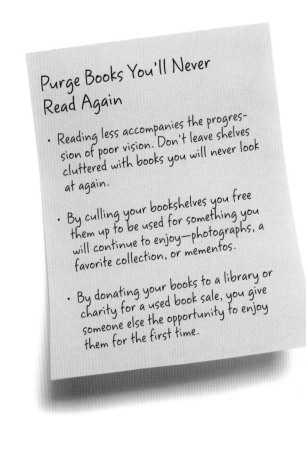

Purge Books You'll Never Read Again

- Reading less accompanies the progression of poor vision. Don't leave shelves cluttered with books you will never look at again.

- By culling your bookshelves you free them up to be used for something you will continue to enjoy—photographs, a favorite collection, or mementos.

- By donating your books to a library or charity for a used book sale, you give someone else the opportunity to enjoy them for the first time.

TELEVISIONS

Maximize the enjoyment of watching TV while minimizing the risk of problems

Watching television is a pleasure and a comfort for people of all ages. But it is important to follow simple precautions to maintain enjoyment and ensure safety.

To reduce the possibility of injury, make sure the television set is stable. Flat screen televisions securely mounted to a wall pose the least risk, as there is little chance of them toppling over. Traditional television sets are bulkier and need to be positioned soundly on sturdy tables or stands. First, verify that the table itself is stable on its own before placing the television on top. As an added measure of safety, secure the stand or furniture piece to the wall. The size of the television should be proportionate to the size of the stand.

Place on Sturdy Table or Stand or in a Cabinet

- Place a TV on or within a sturdy table or piece of furniture where it is unlikely to be knocked over or bumped into.

- When a new TV is purchased, make sure the old stand or table is adequate and strong enough.

- Wall-mounted racks are available for flat screen models, and they are a safe option.

- The cost of buying brackets and mounting a TV on the wall can be similar to purchasing a piece of furniture.

Wires Out of the Way

- Modern TVs require many wires.

- Speaker wires, electrical cords, and cables to the cable box, DVD player, Blu-ray, or digital reception box make the back of the TV and the region around it a minefield.

- Look for gadgets that wrap around the many wires and keep them together, or ones that coil up the excess cables so they don't cause tripping.

Keep all areas and walkways around the television free from electrical wires to reduce the risk of tripping. If speakers are separate from the television, mount them securely to walls to keep the surrounding area clutter free. Properly placed speakers around the room deliver better quality audio, reducing the need to turn the television up to a higher volume.

Make sure the accessories, such as the cable box, DVD player, and VCR, are secure within an entertainment unit or on an appropriate piece of furniture. To make television viewing more enjoyable, be sure to have the television and all devices hooked up to a single remote with large buttons. Consider hanging it in a pocket on a chair arm to keep it handy.

Choose a lounge chair that is easy to recline and raise for optimal viewing pleasure and position it at a comfortable distance from the television. Large-screen, high-definition televisions deliver crisper and more defined images, which is a bonus for people who have visual impairments.

Speakers off the Floor

- For safety, look to remove from the floor whatever can go elsewhere.

- With limited shelf and cabinet space, there can be a crunch to fit everything close to the TV.

- Speakers are generally light in weight and easy to mount on the wall near the ceiling or into the ceiling itself.

- The best sound is produced when they are separated. Putting them at opposite ends of a wall gives the effect of surround sound.

Comfortable Viewing

- Surveys indicate that seniors spend more time in front of the TV than do younger adults.

- Plan to have the most comfortable chair in the room be the TV chair.

- Recliners are available in a variety of fabrics and colors, and with reclining levers and optional memory dials.

- Consider durability of the fabric when ordering.

DESKS
Organize to create an efficient and trouble-free workspace

A desk often functions as the work surface for many household tasks. Keeping it organized not only saves time and makes work more efficient, but the removal of clutter provides a safer home office environment.

Make a list of all supplies used for projects done at the desk. Group those items according to each task and store them in desk drawers or portable organizers on the desktop surface. Keep the most frequently used items in the most easily accessible places, such as the top drawer or an opened cubbyhole. Reserve the desktop only for current projects.

Be sure to keep a small trash bin within close proximity of the desk for convenience.

If you are in the market for a new desk, look for practical features that will facilitate organization and provide maximum comfort. Drawers need to slide easily and be equipped with drawer stops. Matte surfaces are preferable over glossy

Organize for Chores Performed

- Only items presently being worked on should be out on the desktop.

- If a countertop does not have lower cabinets, handy cubbyholes can be added to the back so it can be used as a desk.

- Keep a calendar next to the phone to jot down appointments and for quick reference.

Portable Organizers Improve Efficiency

- More economical than buying a new desk; visit a large stationery store to see the selection of vertical and horizontal portable organizers.

- Browse for items that organize papers, hold multiple files, or group pens, paper clips, and other odd bits.

- Set dates twice a year to sort through papers, organize them, and purge what is not needed. Pick dates like April Fools' Day or Columbus Day when you're probably not otherwise organizing.

tops for reduced glare. Be sure the opening under the desk is sufficient to accommodate a comfortable work chair or a wheelchair, if necessary.

L-shaped desks provide a more comprehensive workstation, allowing a greater volume of work to be accomplished at a single session. In addition to providing more storage space, the L-shaped surface is better designed for multi-tasking. It does, however, require more room.

Sliding chairs may be practical, but they can present problems for someone with poor balance. Be sure to match the type of chair to the abilities of the user.

A desk area requires dedicated task lighting. Some desks are equipped with their own lighting units. Recessed overhead lighting or a desktop lamp can also do the job. Be sure to position the lights to focus directly on the work area.

Arrange Drawers for Like Tasks

- Just like in the kitchen, arrange each desk drawer to hold items used for one project, like bill paying.

- Items used often should be kept handy.

- If space is tight, only keep enough supplies at the desk for short-term needs. Keep extra paper and envelopes in a nearby closet or cabinet.

Desks

- A kitchen desk may be a counter, with one drawer, a row of cubbyholes, and a phone. It's a great place to store bills, pay them, and make shopping lists.

- What used to be a letter-writing desk has turned into a computer station. Locate it out of the bedroom in a room for activity related to the use of the computer—whether business, relaxing, or investment tracking.

- Select the smallest desk to meet your needs. Have sufficient storage, but large surfaces tend to collect as many papers as are needed to cover them.

COMPUTERS
Several simple tools can make working at the computer easier

The computer is an essential part of a modern home. It is often used on a daily basis, so it is important to consider the elements and options that make its use most comfortable, easy, and safe.

Computer desks have a tray for the keyboard, low shelves to hold the computer, and spots for a printer or scanner. Arrange the desk for the way you intend to use the computer. The time you spend on the computer should be pain

free for doing repetitive movements.

Place the computer keyboard at a comfortable level. The user should have a straight arm from the elbow to the wrist. A wrist that is angled up will be uncomfortable and can lead to hand or wrist problems, so adjust the height of the keyboard to correct this problem.

Glare causes difficulty in seeing the screen, and it's also a leading cause of headaches and discomfort. To reduce this

Place Keyboard at Correct Height

- Computer desks have a pull-out shelf for placement of the keyboard.

- The placement should provide a level line from elbow to hands when typing.

- That straight ergonomic line can be achieved by a chair that can be raised or lowered.

- Adjust the height of the chair to minimize strain on wrist, arms, shoulders, and back.

Place Screen at Correct Level

- If agility and muscle function are already a problem, be careful that the computer monitor is at a correct height for the user. Too high or too low and neck strain can result.

- A computer monitor needs to be placed at the correct height for the individual user.

- Take computer work breaks every 30 minutes to flex and stretch.

irritation, consider adding a monitor filter. It fits easily over the computer monitor. Not only are you protected from the effects of glare, but the treated acrylic also helps prevent screen damage.

For enhanced screen visibility, purchase a monitor magnifier. This is a less expensive option than purchasing a new, larger monitor. Computer screen magnifiers can double the size of text on the screen. Some magnifiers also filter the glare and block harmful UV rays, making reading and working even more comfortable. They are installed quickly and easily. For very limited vision, check out devices that are available through associations for the blind.

If you are using bifocals, the monitor needs to be placed slightly lower than the traditional tabletop. An adjustable-height laptop table can be moved up and down to match your comfort level.

When purchasing a laptop, hook it up to a full-size desk monitor. Try out different keyboards to see which is most comfortable. Add an external mouse (or even a child's big ball mouse), which is simpler to use.

Collect Wires Out of the Way

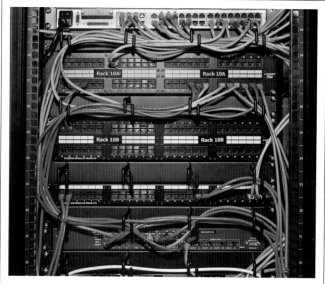

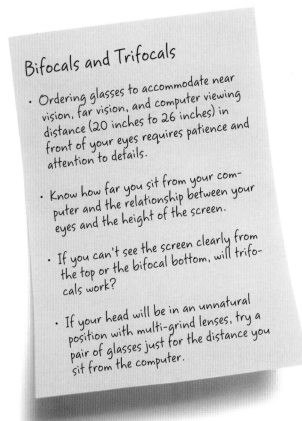

Bifocals and Trifocals

- Ordering glasses to accommodate near vision, far vision, and computer viewing distance (20 inches to 26 inches) in front of your eyes requires patience and attention to details.

- Know how far you sit from your computer and the relationship between your eyes and the height of the screen.

- If you can't see the screen clearly from the top or the bifocal bottom, will trifocals work?

- If your head will be in an unnatural position with multi-grind lenses, try a pair of glasses just for the distance you sit from the computer.

- Computers have many wires that need to be tamed, including electric cords, printer connectors, monitor cables, and wires to other computer accessories.

- An array of excess wires is not only chaotic, but dangerous.

- Rubber coils are inexpensive and work wonders for managing wayward wires.

- Plastic tubing can also tame many wires by gathering them together into one space.

LAPTOP TABLES

A handy, portable way to make tasks and hobbies more comfortable

Trays and rolling tables offer a comfortable, flexible option for eating, reading, or writing in bed or in a lounge chair.

Rolling laptop tables are designed to slide close to the sitter for comfortable reading and writing from any relaxed position. The base of the table, which moves on casters, slips under the chair or bed. The flat surface can be raised or lowered and even angled for personal preference. The adjustable height and angle allow for greater flexibility for working in any position. And the mobility makes it very versatile. Roll the table to the couch to enjoy a meal. Write comfortably while lying in bed. Pay bills from the comfort of your favorite upholstered chair.

As the name implies, laptop tables were originally engineered to hold laptop computers. Used for this function, computer work can be more relaxing and easier on the body. Simply angle the table for the most comfortable use.

Roll-up Tables

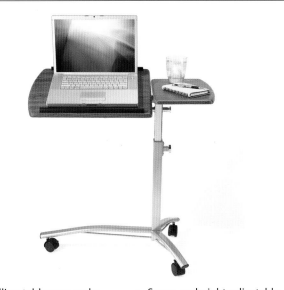

- Rolling tables can make working on a laptop comfortable—especially in an easy chair or in bed.

- Small roll-up tables are also ideal for eating dinner or snacking in front of the TV.

- Some are height-adjustable for extra versatility.

- Small and portable, these rolling tables are easy to maneuver and store when not in use.

Weighted, Portable Writing Lap Tables

- When reading or writing in a lounge chair or sofa, a portable lap table makes the task more comfortable.

- Some lap tables have hinged tops that open to hold papers, books, and notes.

- Reading in bed is less strenuous when a portable lap table is used as a supportive aid.

- Store pens, pencils, erasers, and dictionary inside to enjoy a daily crossword puzzle or Sudoku.

The solid flat surface keeps the computer off the body, eliminating usual laptop heat issues.

Legged trays, which are often also called laptop tables, can be used in bed or on a chair. These portable trays are usually lightweight, have folding legs, and can be moved from room to room for convenient use. They come in a variety of sizes and styles for individual use and taste. Choose one for your specific use: with a light for reading or a hidden storage section for pencils and papers.

Reading in bed is less tiresome when a portable tray is used.

Prop the book up on the table, nestle under the covers, and enjoy the book without tiring your arms.

Legged or Footed Trays

- Trays with foldable legs can be stored easily in a tall kitchen cabinet, a linen closet shelf, or under the bed.

- With the legs extended they straddle a lap, and rest on the bed or seat.

- These trays are useful for serving meals in bed.

- Footed trays are a more cost-effective and compact solution than roll-up tables.

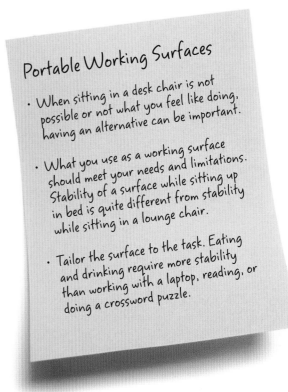

Portable Working Surfaces

- When sitting in a desk chair is not possible or not what you feel like doing, having an alternative can be important.

- What you use as a working surface should meet your needs and limitations. Stability of a surface while sitting up in bed is quite different from stability while sitting in a lounge chair.

- Tailor the surface to the task. Eating and drinking require more stability than working with a laptop, reading, or doing a crossword puzzle.

ORGANIZING PAPERWORK

Don't get buried by the paperwork

Organizing important papers and documents is one of the hardest organizational tasks because the amount of paper often becomes overwhelming. Papers need to be filed and stored in an orderly way so that they can be located and retrieved quickly when needed.

The first step in organizing papers is gathering them all in one area. Use a large box or bin to keep everything together in one space during the organizing process.

Next, sort through the papers and decide what is needed and what can be tossed. If there is no legal or financial reason to keep a paper, and the information on it can be found elsewhere when needed, throw the paper out. If possible, shred unwanted documents that contain identifying information so they cannot be retrieved from the trash. The more you get rid of, the easier the organizing will be.

Begin categorizing the remaining papers. Put like topics

Baskets for Organizing

- Decorative, inexpensive, and convenient, baskets can be used to hold a variety of odds and ends.

- Baskets are a simple solution for managing clutter and keeping commonly used items handy.

- Place baskets on shelves, tables, or desks where the stored items are used.

- The small size of baskets makes them portable and easy to transport throughout the house.

Digital Picture Frames

- Digital picture frames conveniently store and can display dozens of cherished photos as a continuous slide show. They have an on-off switch to save batteries.

- Photos need to be scanned and saved on a computer and then transferred to the frame via a provided cable.

- Replace bulky picture boxes with a sleek, fashionable digital frame that complements the room's décor.

- Pictures are effective in triggering memories, which is especially important for someone with dementia.

together so you can find what you need easily and quickly.

File papers in file cabinets or store them in attractive baskets or bins. Pretty storage pieces can be left out in the open so that paperwork is easily accessible.

Documents that need to be kept long-term but are not often accessed can be stored in files or bins in closets or attics.

Bulletin Board of Monthly Chores

- A monthly bulletin board calendar is useful for posting appointments, chores, and special occasions.

- Dry erase calendars allow for large writing, color-coded notes, and easy removal when tasks are completed.

- A common household calendar eliminates confusion and conflicts among family members.

- Place the bulletin board near the most commonly used door so it is seen whenever entering or exiting the house.

Memo Board with Important Numbers

- Keep a list of important telephone numbers—doctors, pharmacy, family members—on a memo board near the telephone.

- Choose a memo board with an attached pen so that it is always available when needed.

- Consider keeping a list of current medication and doses on the board.

BED HEIGHT
When it comes to beds, size does matter

For overall well-being, getting a good night's sleep is crucial. Since a big percentage of each day is spent in bed, it is vital to have a mattress that is not only comfortable to sleep in, but also easy to get in and out of.

For easy entry and exit, the top of the mattress should not be more than 22 inches from the floor. Higher beds are difficult to get into, and beds that are much lower to the ground can present problems for people trying to stand up. If family members can sit on the bed with feet resting on the floor, the bed is at a good height.

Eliminate all obstacles to a clear entrance and exit from the bed. There should be no sideboards or footboard to impede access or bang shins into. The floor space around the bed will also affect ease of access. Clear away all objects and furniture to create at least 5 feet of space all around. If a rug is desired to protect bare feet from a cold floor, be sure it is fringeless

Box Spring and Mattress

- Because a wooden bed frame may be difficult to see in the dark and can be easily bumped into, it is safer to put the mattress and box spring on a simple metal frame with the frame corners against the wall.

- This standard bed frame, sometimes called a Hollywood frame, is small and low and supports the bottom box spring.

- Eliminate the footboard for safety and to make it easier to sit on the side of the bed.

Height of Mattress

22"

- The height to the top of the mattress is dependent upon the thickness of the mattress, the depth of the box spring, and the height of the bed platform or frame.

- The correct bed height reduces strain on joints when getting in and out. Anyone with bad hips or knees will appreciate less bending.

- A bed height of 22 inches is a safe and comfortable rule of thumb.

and is anchored at the corners.

Adjustable beds, which can elevate head or feet to any position, help many people get a better night's sleep. They come in many models and sizes, and have optional features like heat and massage.

Adjustable Bed

- Adjustable beds elevate head and feet with the push of a button.

- They help people find more comfortable positions for reading and eating in bed.

- An adjustable bed can make sleep more restful.

- For someone who is paralyzed or weak and wants to remain at home, an adjustable bed can make it possible. They can be rented or purchased.

Alternative Seating

- Sitting on the bed to dress or put on socks and shoes may not always be comfortable or convenient.

- Space permitting, it is wise to have a chair in the bedroom.

- The chair should be low enough for bending to the floor to pick up shoes, but not so low that getting into and out of it is a challenge.

135

SHARING A BED OR USING TWINS

Proper space planning makes the transition from a king-size bed to twin beds easy and manageable

Making up twin beds is a breeze compared to the larger queen-size and king-size varieties. But when transitioning to twins, there are several practical considerations to keep in mind.

Although two twin beds take up approximately the same amount of floor space as one king-size bed, extra wall space is required to make the transition possible. Standard king-size beds measure 76 inches by 80 inches (California king-size beds are 72 inches by 84 inches) and twin beds measure 39 by 75 (extra-long twins are 39 by 80). With one large bed, the wall space only needs to accommodate the bed and ample walking room on either side; but with two beds, additional space

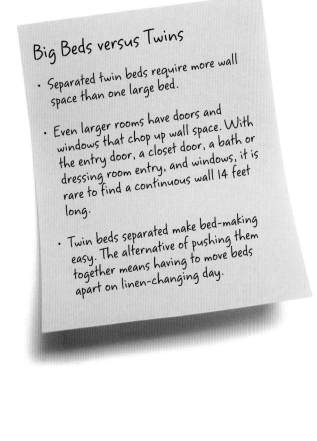

Big Beds versus Twins

- Separated twin beds require more wall space than one large bed.

- Even larger rooms have doors and windows that chop up wall space. With the entry door, a closet door, a bath or dressing room entry, and windows, it is rare to find a continuous wall 14 feet long.

- Twin beds separated make bed-making easy. The alternative of pushing them together means having to move beds apart on linen-changing day.

Twin Beds Next to Each Other

- If wall space does not permit separating twin beds, then putting them next to each other with walking space on each side is an alternative.

- If one person has trouble sleeping, separate mattresses can help.

- Although two beds together look like one bed—especially if made up with one bedspread—two mattresses allow for separate sleeping environments without the need for additional wall space.

is required between the beds as well. To have enough room for two beds, two nightstands, and ample walking space, be sure the wall is at least 13 to 14 feet wide. This allows for 29 to 30 inches of space on each side of both beds.

If the bedroom wall does not meet this requirement, there are other practical options. By placing the twin beds together with no space separating them, the benefit of two individual sleeping environments is achieved without the necessity of additional wall space. And replacing one bulky bed with two smaller ones means greater ease in changing sheets.

Another option is to replace the traditional larger-size bed with one that features separate controls for both sides. This solution allows each person to fix the angles to desired levels without disturbing the settings on the other side. Separate remote controls make adjusting the settings easy. Angles can be changed for sleeping, television viewing, and reading. Although the dual-control bed provides a smooth transition from a traditional bed, it does not provide greater ease in changing sheets.

Twin Beds Separated on a Wall

- If separated beds are the sleeping choice, a 13- to 14-foot wall is needed.

- With space between the twin beds, a single nightstand or table can be placed in the middle for joint use. This saves room and leaves more accessible space around the beds.

- Separate twins allow for the easiest bed making and mattress turning.

Sturdy Nightstand

- It is essential to have a sturdy nightstand or table next to the bed for accommodating often used and emergency items.

- Place a phone or emergency call monitor on the nightstand.

- The nightstand can also hold a radio, clock, and box of tissues for convenience.

- If there is no light switch near the bed, keep a lamp on the stand.

MATTRESSES
Once upon a mattress . . .

A bed is only as comfortable as its mattress. With all the options available (and more being added each day), choosing a mattress can be overwhelming. But sleeping on a comfortable mattress is crucial.

Regular, deep cycles of sleep are vitally important to physical, emotional, and mental well-being. A mattress that does not feel comfortable to you will prevent needed relaxation. Add an overlay or support pad, or purchase a new foam mattress, which adjusts to individual body shapes.

Mattresses run from firm to plush, and every level in between. The most important consideration is individual comfort. With all the literature and advice on what to buy, it often comes down to personal preference. If possible, test mattresses before you buy. Go to the store and lay in all the beds. Take your time.

The key to keeping a mattress clean and free from germs is

KNACK UNIVERSAL DESIGN

Non-flip Mattress

- Turning a mattress can be a daunting, if not impossible job for some people.

- If turning a mattress is recommended, follow the manufacturers' recommended schedule, and get help.

- Mattresses made of new foam material do not need turning.

- When in the market for a new mattress, consider the easier non-flip versions.

Weight of Mattress

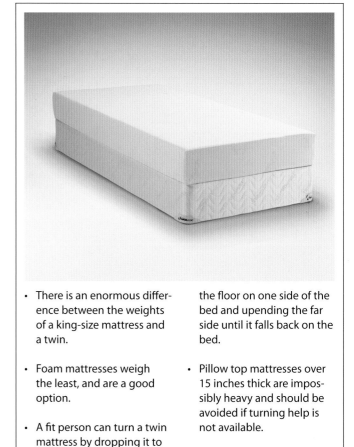

- There is an enormous difference between the weights of a king-size mattress and a twin.

- Foam mattresses weigh the least, and are a good option.

- A fit person can turn a twin mattress by dropping it to

- the floor on one side of the bed and upending the far side until it falls back on the bed.

- Pillow top mattresses over 15 inches thick are impossibly heavy and should be avoided if turning help is not available.

to protect it. Use a mattress protector made from cloth. This piece of fabric can be taken off and washed much more easily than cleaning the whole mattress. For those with allergies, encase the mattress in a dust mite cover.

Waffle Pads

- For people who have sensitive pressure points or spend a lot of time in bed, a waffle pad can make the surface more comfortable.

- Waffle pads should be placed over the mattress and under a mattress pad.

- Pads are a less expensive alternative to purchasing a new, softer mattress.

- They can also be used on a futon mattress to add a comfortable cushion.

Sitting Supports

- Consider a back wedge designed for comfortable reading, eating, or watching TV in bed.

- The bed support rests against the headboard, propping up and cradling the upper body.

- There are optional armrests to take the strain out of holding and reading a book.

- A bed rest is an inexpensive solution for comfortable sitting in bed.

BED TRANSFER SLINGS
An integral tool for caregivers supporting those in wheelchairs

Electric bed transfer slings are battery-powered, motorized mobile devices that are used to raise a resident from one surface and lower him or her onto another. They are often used to help move a person from the bed to his or her wheelchair and back, but can also be used to transfer from the wheelchair to any other surface, like a dining chair, sofa, bathtub, or toilet. These lifts can also hoist a person who has fallen to the floor.

Electric lifts are operated by pressing buttons on a mounted control or a handheld remote control. The remote option allows the caregiver to stay close and provide extra assurance to the person being lifted or lowered.

Transfer slings utilize a harness to support the patient as he or she is lifted. Most manufacturers have their own line of harnesses to be used with their lifts. A variety of styles are available to address the lifting needs of the caregiver and the

KNACK UNIVERSAL DESIGN

A Properly Installed Bed Sling

- In some cases, a bed transfer sling makes it possible for a person to transfer from bed to wheelchair.

- A ceiling mechanism moves along a track between the bed and the chair placed next to it.

- The sling is manipulated to slip under the patient and support him or her.

- The sling makes it possible for a wheelchair-bound person to be more independent.

Getting In and Out of Bed

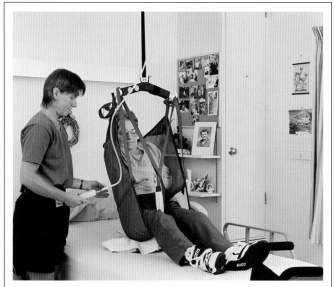

- With the push of a button, the transfer sling lifts the patient in it, out of the bed.

- It then moves along the track, carrying the person over to the wheelchair.

- Another button instructs the sling to lower the patient onto the wheelchair.

- This procedure can be reversed to return the person back into bed.

resident. Some slings support people in reclining or completely supine positions. Other slings are made for bathroom applications. There are also harnesses made to support a patient during walking training or therapy.

Using a transfer lift will reduce caregiver injuries while ensuring the dignity of the patient.

Easier for Caregivers

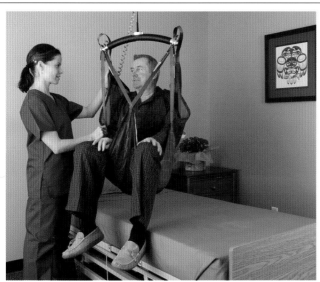

- When a patient has been safely transferred to the chair, the sling can be slipped out.

- When it is time to get back into bed, the procedure is reversed.

- The bed transfer sling eliminates possible back strain for caregivers who would otherwise have to lift and carry the patient.

- If a wheelchair-bound person wants to remain independent in his or her own home, a transfer sling can be a viable solution.

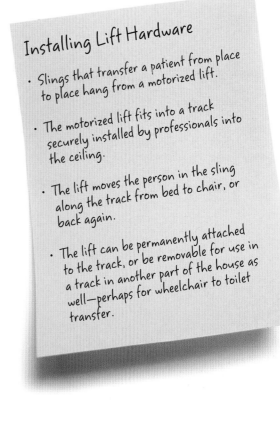

Installing Lift Hardware

- Slings that transfer a patient from place to place hang from a motorized lift.

- The motorized lift fits into a track securely installed by professionals into the ceiling.

- The lift moves the person in the sling along the track from bed to chair, or back again.

- The lift can be permanently attached to the track, or be removable for use in a track in another part of the house as well—perhaps for wheelchair to toilet transfer.

EMERGENCY PULL CORDS

A simple device offers peace of mind

Emergency pull cords provide residents with the ability to request assistance quickly and easily. When someone pulls on the cord, a wireless signal is sent to a central location, and emergency help is dispatched. The responder is able to identify the source of the signal and respond immediately.

Ideal locations for an emergency pull cord are near the bed, the toilet, and the shower. Pull cords are a safety feature for people who may have mild dementia or who are by

themselves in the home for any length of time.

An alternative to the pull cord is a wearable emergency call button. This is worn around the neck or on a bracelet and works like the pull cord, but it is more portable and requires no installation. The emergency call goes to a central desk in a senior community, or to an emergency response company if contracted privately from the home.

Family members can feel more secure knowing that their

Emergency Control System at Bedside

- Nursing homes, assisted living communities, and age-restricted neighborhoods may still have wall emergency pull cords.

- In private homes they are costly and unnecessary because wireless technology allows for less expensive portable systems.

- Wearable devices communicate through a master monitor, which should be kept by the bed.

- Unlike a portable phone, the monitor ONLY rings the emergency call center.

Emergency Control in Bathroom

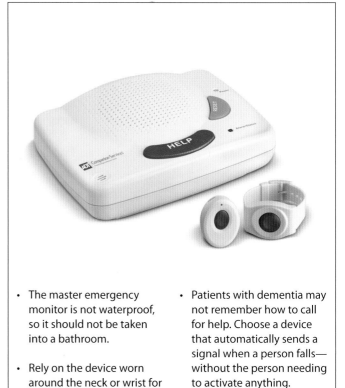

- The master emergency monitor is not waterproof, so it should not be taken into a bathroom.

- Rely on the device worn around the neck or wrist for bathroom emergencies.

- Patients with dementia may not remember how to call for help. Choose a device that automatically sends a signal when a person falls—without the person needing to activate anything.

relatives have the capability of calling for help, even in the middle of the night. One of the biggest fears of family members is that their loved ones will be helpless in an emergency and will have to wait many hours before someone discovers their plight and comes to their aid. The emergency call button or pull cord can alleviate these fears and enable older residents to live independently with greater confidence and security.

An emergency call button enables residents to generate an emergency signal even when they are unable to dial the telephone. Physical disabilities or sudden medical emergencies could render a person incapable of placing a call. The wearable button is always reachable, even after a fall, and requires much less effort than using a telephone. It can summon the aid of emergency personnel and lifesaving equipment within minutes.

Emergency Lock Box

- When a residential emergency device is activated, the call center will dispatch paramedics.

- If the door is locked and no one answers, they will break in.

- A break-in can be avoided by providing an accessible lock box, which can be opened by emergency personnel when needed.

- By entering a passcode, the lock box is opened, revealing the hidden key.

Bedroom Emergencies

- An emergency module, call button, or device that rings to dispatch central is important when accidents or medical emergencies happen.

- Unlike a telephone, only one button has to be pushed. If nothing is said to the dispatcher, help is still sent immediately.

- Select an emergency call provider with a recommended reputation. They need to be a large enough company to handle the generated call volume quickly and efficiently.

143

LIGHT CONTROLS

The placement and type of light controls can add to a relaxing bedroom environment

Lighting requirements are higher for older eyes. Since the bedroom is used during darker hours, lighting control is a matter of safety.

Light switches should be located within easy reach of the bedroom door so that lights can be turned on before entering the dark room.

It is also important to install light controls near the bed for safety and convenience. If a resident wakes in the dark, the light can be turned on before he or she gets up. It is also handy to be able to shut off the lights at night from the bed, instead of having to walk across the room and return to bed in the dark.

Light Switch at Bedside

- A bedside light control is necessary for turning on a light before getting out of bed, and turning off the light without getting up.

- It can be a switch on a wall or in an accessible cord to a lamp.

- For safety and convenience, put light controls on both sides of a double bed.

- A light-sensing night-light is a safe aid in the bedroom; it can be plugged into any outlet, and it lights up automatically when the room dims.

Bed Reading Light

- A reading light can be installed on a headboard or on the wall above. It should have a shade or cover to direct the light downward toward the pillow.

- The focused light allows one person to read in bed while the other sleeps.

- Reading lights cast a soft glow and can act as a night-light when needed.

- A light installed on the headboard is easy to find in the middle of the night if a little illumination is necessary.

Eliminate the need for standing, reaching, or uncomfortable stretching by positioning light controls within easy access of all seating areas in the bedroom. If no light switch is nearby, place a table or floor lamp close to the bed or chair. Touch-on/touch-off lamps are easy to operate.

Replace standard light switches with simpler rocker switches. These light controls are easy to operate, even for arthritic hands.

Illuminated switch plates eliminate the need for fumbling around in the dark while looking for the light control.

BEDROOMS

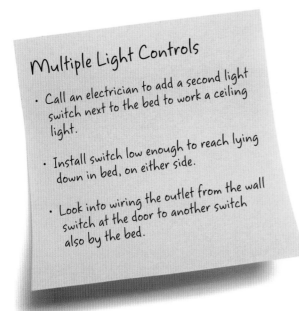

Multiple Light Controls

- Call an electrician to add a second light switch next to the bed to work a ceiling light.

- Install switch low enough to reach lying down in bed, on either side.

- Look into wiring the outlet from the wall switch at the door to another switch also by the bed.

Dimmer Switches

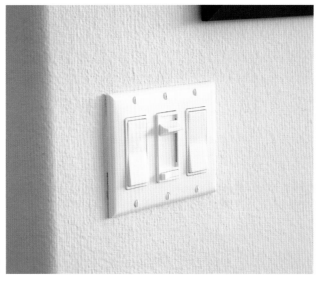

- Traditional light switches can be replaced with dimmer switches.

- Dimmer switches allow many lighting intensities and moods without changing the bulbs.

- Some dimmer switches are able to "hold" the most recent setting when turned off, and return to the same level of brightness when turned back on.

- Dimmers work by gradual changes, so it is possible to set the light from very dim to full power, and anywhere in between.

145

CLOSETS

A well-designed closet makes choosing and storing outfits more stress free

Storing clothes in a universal design home is organized and intuitive. Clothing and accessories are placed where they are easy to see and reach.

Rods and shelves mounted at comfortable levels accommodate those with limited reach. Adjustable open shelving is a good option. Place shelves where they are convenient, and keep the most often used items at mid-body level.

Hang closet rods at a height that is comfortable. This usually means lowering the rod. An option is hooking an add-on rod to the existing fixture. This rod then hangs at a lower height.

Look also for hinged rods that rest high out of the way, but can be easily pulled down to access clothing.

Portable Closet Lights

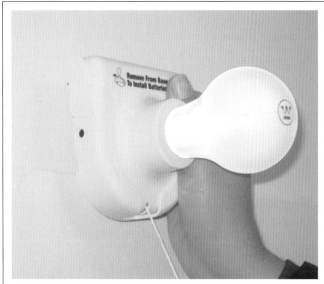

- Smaller closets often have no internal lighting, relying on light from the hall or room in which they are located.

- Since poor vision requires the best possible light, look for portable, battery-powered lights to install in small closets.

- When they burn out, just replace the batteries.

- Some portable lights have adhesive backs so they are a snap to install.

Organizing Compartments

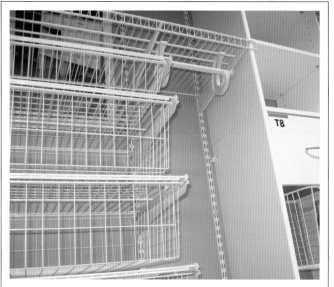

- Closet organizers create safe, convenient, stress-free spaces.

- Look in organizing and hardware stores for baskets, cubbies, and shelf dividers to keep your accessories organized and at an accessible height.

- Wire shelving kits are inexpensive and come in varying sizes, complete with brackets and hardware.

- Buy what you think you need, and if you find you need more, additional units can be added.

A closet system can integrate cabinets, rods of varying levels, and even a cherished dresser. A pull-out shelf can be installed for resting accessories. Cubbies will store shoes, scarves, and handbags.

If you have a large closet—at least 4½ by 6 feet—consider a high-tech motorized clothing carousel. Push a button, and your clothes come to you.

On shallow wall closets, doors can be removed for easier view of all its contents.

Storing Accessories

- The more convenient and organized storage is, the easier it is to function within a home.

- Some accessories lend themselves to basket storage, like scarves, gloves, and soft hats.

- Other accessories are best organized on hooks, like ties, belts, and purses with handles.

- Place like accessories together. This may encourage a forgetful person to put items away and find them quickly.

Lower Clothes Rod

- Clothes rods are commonly hung 5 feet off the floor.

- The standard height is too high for short people, anyone bent over, and those in wheelchairs.

- A lower rod can be installed to make everyday clothes more accessible.

- An adjustable metal rod can be hung from the existing clothes rod to create additional hanging space at a lower, more convenient height.

DRAWERS & SHELVES

Create easy access to clothing and accessories by placing drawers and shelves conveniently

An ideal closet combines open shelving, sliding drawers, and hang bars at varying levels.

Wall-mounted shelves and drawers are the most secure. Bending and reaching can be avoided if all the shelves are placed between waist and eye level. Install drawers at the same level or lower. Pulling outs a drawer allows one to see items more easily than bending to look on a low shelf.

Organize a closet without major remodeling by purchasing shelves and baskets that hook onto existing shelves and hang beneath them.

Make sure all closet drawer slides are working smoothly and that they have safety stops so that they do not pull out

Easy Grip Drawer Pulls

- Since many items of clothing may be stored in closets as opposed to bedroom furniture, appropriate closet drawers and shelving come in handy.

- Closet doors and drawers need to have easy-to-grip pulls. Replace hardware with U-shaped grips that can be operated simply.

- Drawers and storage baskets should glide easily and have glide locks that keep them from pulling all the way out.

Shelves Eye-level to Waist

- Plenty of shelf space is a great convenience in any home, provided it is within reach and accessible without too much physical effort.

- To minimize bending and reaching, store frequently used items on shelves below eye level and above the hips.

- With multiple residents, the ideal height of shelves can differ from person to person. Choose a height that is most convenient for all members of the household.

- Store heavier closet items within easy reach at mid-body height, even if these items are used infrequently.

and fall to the floor. Replace hardware with easy-grip drawer pulls.

Keep all drawers and shelves organized. There are organizing tools for every type of clothing and accessory. Organizers are a cost-effective and practical solution to keeping the closet clutter free, and safe.

Get Shoes Off the Floor

- Except for daily-worn shoes and slippers, store all shoes off the floor.

- Shoes stored on the floor become a jumbled mess and require bending and sorting to recover.

- A jumble of shoes also makes it hard to clean in the closet, and can be a tripping hazard when sorting through hanging garments.

- Store shoes in a hanging bag, shoe cubbies, or a floor stand designed for stowing shoes.

Rarely Used Items

- Rarely used or seasonal items can be stored less conveniently out of easy reach.

- Store infrequently used items in closed boxes or plastic bags to safeguard them from dust and dirt.

- High shelves are ideal for storing lighter items that only need to be taken down once in a while. Heavy items are best stored low for later access.

LINENS

Arrange towels and bedding by use and store them where they are needed

Linens are used in bedrooms and bathrooms, yet that is not always where home linen closets are. If you're lucky enough to have a linen closet in each bathroom, then, of course, that is where you keep towels. And hopefully there is a closet in each bedroom for that room's sheets and bedding.

Over time closets can get jammed with towels, blankets, and sheets held onto long after they are needed or used. Organizing your closets, and getting rid of all unused and unneeded towels, sheets, and comforters will make finding whatever you are looking for easier. A less cluttered closet is easier to arrange and organize.

Ideally a linen closet should be kept cool and dry. If yours is

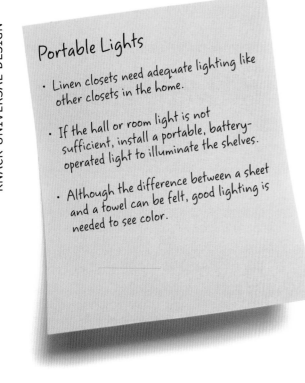

Portable Lights

- Linen closets need adequate lighting like other closets in the home.

- If the hall or room light is not sufficient, install a portable, battery-operated light to illuminate the shelves.

- Although the difference between a sheet and a towel can be felt, good lighting is needed to see color.

Keep Towels Handy for Use

- Linens do not have to be kept behind closed doors.

- Inexpensive cubbies can be added to a spare bathroom wall for easily accessible towels.

- When a linen closet is located elsewhere, keep extra towels in plain sight in the bathroom.

- If a linen closet has doors, be sure they have easy-to-open grips, since they are often opened with a stack of linens in one arm.

in a bathroom, try replacing the shelves with ventilated wire shelving for increased airflow between the linens. Or run an exhaust fan when you shower or bath.

If your home has one main linen closet, consider making towels more convenient by storing some of them on shelves or in wall-mounted cubbyholes in the bathroom. This will make them more convenient to retrieve.

Store bed sheets near or in each bedroom so they are also convenient for frequent retrieval and storage. Seasonal bedding, like quilts and summer blankets, can be stored in the main closet and retrieved when they are needed. If it isn't possible because of lack of storage space to keep linens close to where they are used, organize the one main linen closet by function. Separate bedding by bed size and arrange towels according to which bathroom they go in.

If you organize linens and find sheets and towels that you no longer use, the Red Cross collects linens after every flood and earthquake disaster. Many other charities also accept donations for redistribution.

Organize and Sort Linens

- Keep linens stored as close to where they will be used as possible.

- If there is no convenient cabinet in a bathroom for towels, add wire racks, tubes, or cubbyholes to hold them.

- Space above towel racks or toilets can support the storage devices. Be sure they are installed out of the way of your head.

- Bed linens can be stored on a closet shelf.

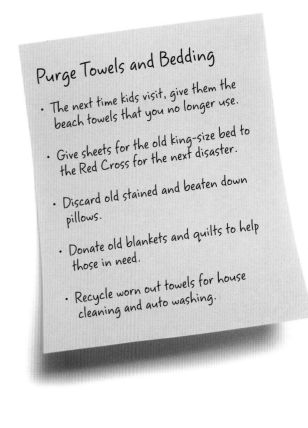

Purge Towels and Bedding

- The next time kids visit, give them the beach towels that you no longer use.

- Give sheets for the old king-size bed to the Red Cross for the next disaster.

- Discard old stained and beaten down pillows.

- Donate old blankets and quilts to help those in need.

- Recycle worn out towels for house cleaning and auto washing.

COLLECTIBLES
Organize and display a lifetime of memories

While many things in the home need to be stored out of sight, collectibles should be left out in the open for daily visual enjoyment.

Organize and sort through what you have collected. You may find that you have more collectibles than you imagined. Purge things that are no longer meaningful. Toss those pieces, or plan to give them to family members who share those memories. Group remaining items into categories, then sort them by date, style, special trip or event, etc.

Arrange groups of collectibles then decide what can be displayed and what should be saved out of sight. Then decide what lends itself to shelves, frames, or shadow boxes. Collectibles make a bigger impact when presented together than if they are scattered around the home randomly. Assembling collectibles grouped by the events they remind you of is a lovely idea.

Display Collectibles in Groups

- A side table is a perfect place to display small collectibles.

- Group and display like items together so that they create a vignette.

- Displaying cherished collectibles in plain view will add happy memories to daily life.

- Collections can be helpful reminders for those with dementia, who may relate to pictorial aids. Group collectibles by past events to trigger specific memories.

Put Them Up High

- High spaces can be reserved for beautiful collections that are enjoyed by viewing and not touching.

- In small rooms, think vertically to find space for displaying collectibles.

- Consider displaying collections on bookshelves, individually hung wall shelves, or wall-mounted shadow boxes.

- Some items will look terrific hung right on the wall. Display them like you would any other artwork.

The happy memories they evoke make a home warmer. Placing collections or groupings of photos and collectibles in plain view may also help to trigger recall for those with dementia or memory problems.

If your treasured pieces are delicate, place them on higher shelves or areas that are less likely to be bumped. If shelf space is sparse, mount shadow boxes high up on the wall. Since most collectibles are intended to be viewed and not touched, they can remain safely unreachable but enjoyed.

Display Familiar Photos Prominently

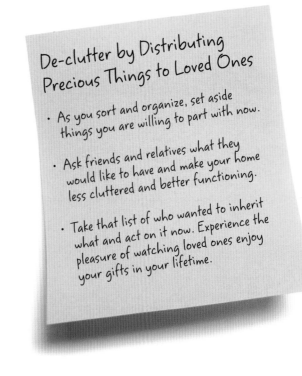

De-clutter by Distributing Precious Things to Loved Ones

- As you sort and organize, set aside things you are willing to part with now.

- Ask friends and relatives what they would like to have and make your home less cluttered and better functioning.

- Take that list of who wanted to inherit what and act on it now. Experience the pleasure of watching loved ones enjoy your gifts in your lifetime.

- Photos can serve as memory triggers to help orient those with dementia.

- Photos from the past, logically grouped and displayed, can spark identification for people suffering memory loss.

- Placement of displays can serve as homing aids. Put collections of photos outside a bedroom door or inside the room on a far wall to draw a person into the space.

PHOTOGRAPHS
Organize photos for storage or attractive display

How delightful it is to look through photos of family, friends, and past events. But a collection of photos gathered over a lifetime can take up a lot of space. If not organized, photos can become clutter. And if not displayed well, they cannot be truly enjoyed.

Sort through photos and arrange them into categories, purging any that are not needed. You may want to create a special pile or box to place photos that you want to give to others.

Going through old photos can be fun when done with other family members, especially grandchildren, who can learn about family history through the photos. Other relatives may also enjoy reminiscing with you over past photographs.

Choose the most special photos to display in the home. An arrangement of family photos or pictures from a memorable past event will look beautiful and add enormous joy to a home when grouped together and hung on a wall. Have

Label All Photos

- Photos worth saving are worth labeling and either scanning or putting in albums.

- Give grandchildren a sense of family. Recruit them to help you organize, label, and catalogue all your photos.

- They might love to scan them and save them to a disc.

- This educates them about their relatives, even the ones who are gone, and helps you organize.

Place Photos on Walls

- Mount photos on walls so they are out of the way and less likely to get knocked into and broken.

- Frames and picture mattes can coordinate with or add a splash of drama to the décor.

- Arrange photos at eye level on the wall so they can be seen easily from all areas in the room.

- Since pictures are for viewing and do not need to be physically accessible, placement can be above shoulder height.

each grouping mounted in similar frames with the same color matting.

Other photos that you just can't bear to part with can be arranged in photo albums. Label each album with a category and store the books on accessible shelves. Books can be pulled out and enjoyed whenever the desire strikes.

Put Photos in Digital Frame

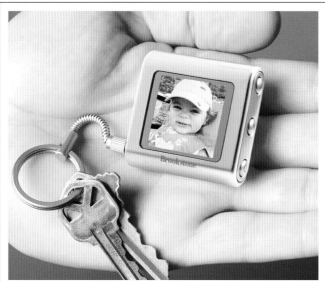

- A digital photo key chain stores many photos in a compact, portable accessory.

- Those with poor vision may not see the tiny photos clearly but still may enjoy knowing the family is "in their pocket."

- Once photos are scanned and saved as digital images, they can be viewed on the computer, distributed through e-mail, or grouped together and printed as a collage.

- Digital frames also come as large as 10" x 12".

Old Family Photos

- Photos are a non-verbal way to trigger memories.

- Dementia patients retain the ability to identify with photos for some time after other cognition skills may fade.

- Using photos of a childhood home or people known long ago can help them recognize and remember.

- Use collections of such photos to help them navigate down a hall and locate their bedroom.

MEMORABILIA

Evoke pleasant memories by displaying cherished mementos around the home

Memorabilia—often referred to as souvenirs, mementos, or keepsakes—are objects that are treasured and valued for their connections to past events or travels. The goal of memorabilia is to bring back the pleasant memories.

If memorabilia are to do their job of evoking happy memories, they need to be openly displayed. Pieces stored away and hidden cannot fulfill their duties, so have fun decorating your home with your keepsakes. Put items on shelves, hang pieces on the wall, or place a special memento near the bed so it can be seen morning and night.

Toss or give away pieces that no longer hold any meaning. While memorabilia can trigger pleasurable thoughts, too

Control Clutter for Safety

- Review collected and saved belongings to separate memorabilia from clutter. Toss items that do not have sentimental or practical value.

- Items that are no longer functional or do not relate to something worth remembering can be classified as clutter.

- Sorting and storing like items together in baskets can help keep them neat and all in one place. It is easier to find things when items are categorized into separate baskets.

Place Items Wisely to Trigger Memories

- Collectibles add warmth to a home and reflect the personal style of the homeowner.

- To keep interior walkways, closets, and shelves manageable, develop a strategy for eliminating clutter and retaining only cherished or useful items.

- Items that generate fond thoughts of past activities brighten the home and keep old memories alive.

- Add cheer to any room by incorporating collectibles into the décor. Unique items from the past spark special memories and are great conversation pieces.

much just becomes clutter. Clutter leads to safety hazards in the home, including potential tripping and fires. If there is no more room for displaying keepsakes neatly and artfully, it is time to get rid of some.

Discussing mementos with the younger generation can be a delight. Kids will learn more about you and the family history in a fun way. Tell stories of where each piece was found and why it is meaningful to you. You may even want to gift an item to a grandchild or other relative so the memory can live on.

Photo Memories

- Organizing and labeling photos is a good memory exercise.

- Share organization and creation of a photo album with a grandchild since their fingers are more agile. At the same time they get to learn about their relatives, many of whom they may not have met.

- Photos allow people to share personal memories with each other.

Unclutter Your Home

- Memorabilia can add comfort and warmth to any home. But clutter can be a safety concern, or can cause confusion in dementia patients.

- De-clutter by storing or getting rid of things saved from a life you no longer lead.

- Purge the attic and basement of things you don't care about and organize things others will want to inherit.

- Leave close at hand only what you want to see or refer to regularly.

HALLWAYS

Inspect the hallway and make adjustments for safety

Because hallways usually do not have windows they can be darker than other rooms in the home. Some simple modifications can create a safer passageway to get you from place to place in your home.

Make sure your hall flooring is even and made from anti-skid material. Flooring between the hall and adjacent rooms should be level. The thresholds between those rooms and the hallway should be flush with the floors in both spaces.

Provide good contrast in transitions. Contrasting colors on the wall and doorjambs help everyone—especially those with poor vision—find his or her way into rooms. Because colors are not as easy to distinguish at night, you might install horizontal and vertical lighting around the doorjamb. This will provide a helpful cue if a family member needs to get around in the middle of the night.

During the day, keep the doors along the hallway opened.

Ambient Lighting

- Because hallways rarely have windows, they can be dark, even during the day.

- Any doors off of the hallway should be kept opened to allow room light to stream into the hallway.

- Clerestory windows, sky-lights, and Solatubes can be installed to bring daylight to a hallway.

Distinct Flooring

- Flooring patterns can help a person distinguish the length of a hallway and the location of adjacent doorways.

- If an area rug or runner is used in the hall, anchor the corners with special rug tape to reduce the chance of slipping or tripping.

- With wall-to-wall carpet, install carpet insets that break up the pattern and distinguish doorways coming into the hall.

- The same technique can be used with wood or vinyl flooring surfaces.

This adds ambient light to an otherwise dark hall. If needed, install additional lights in the ceiling or on the wall to keep the lighting uniform. Lights that are too far apart can cause patterns of light that can be confusing and disorienting.

Choose light switches that are large and easy to use. An inexpensive option is an illuminated light switch, which shines in the dark. If remodeling, move your switches lower on the wall so that everyone can reach them without stretching.

ZOOM

Enhance or embellish a hallway with pictures and collectibles. But be sure they will not be in the way of traffic flow. Consider having a carpenter add niches between the studs so precious things can be displayed to enrich passage down the hall.

Night-lights

- If it is not economically feasible to add track lights, wall sconces, or recessed lighting in a dark hallway, consider plugging night-lights into hall outlets to help illuminate the way.

- To save power use night-lights with on/off switches.

- If the hall gets enough light during the day, save power by using sensor night-lights that only illuminate when the light is dim.

Dual Light Controls

- All hallways and stairwells should have light controls at both ends.

- If they do not, an electrician can add switches as needed.

- At stairwell top and bottom landings, have illuminated switch plates installed so they are visible and reachable before embarking on the stairs.

CHAIR RAILS & BANISTERS
Add safety to areas that hold the greatest possibility for accidents

Banisters and chair rails can be beautiful architectural elements in a home. With the myriad materials, shapes, colors, and styles available, a banister or chair rail could add drama and splendor to the décor. But the function should be considered as well.

Stairs—a common location for accidents—can be made safer with the right banisters. The most important part of a banister to consider is the handrail. Choose a rounded

wooden rail about 2 to 3 inches wide for the most comfortable hand grip.

Ensure that the banister is installed far enough from the wall. The hand must be able to fit around and grasp the whole handrail, so that it can support and pull the body up while ascending the stairs.

You don't have to give up beauty for safety. If you love the look of wrought iron or stainless steel, use that material for

Molded Chair Rails

- It is often possible to install a helpful aid in the home that looks like a purely decorative element.

- A chair rail installed on the wall down a hallway will not only add architectural beauty, but can be used to support a person

with mobility or balance challenges.

- Select chair rail molding that is at least 2 inches thick—which is enough depth for grabbing or resting a hand upon.

Banister Rails

- When choosing a banister, avoid flat sharp edges and instead opt for one that is rounded.

- A rounded wood rail installed securely into wall studs will be most comfortable to grip.

- Metal banisters can be cold to the touch and angular or sharp.

- A wooden banister rail can be fitted over an existing metal one without the need to remove the original.

the spindles of the banister. As long as the handrail is made from a rounded material that is comfortable to grasp and easy to hold onto, the rest of the railing can be decorative. Just ensure that the banister is installed into wall studs and that the end result is sturdy.

It's a good idea to install banisters on both sides of the stairway. If one arm is stronger than the other, one banister side may be used going up, and the other going down.

Walking down a long hallway can be tiring, and since there are usually no pieces of furniture to provide support, installing a chair rail is a safe idea. The traditional use of chair rails is to protect walls from chairs as they are moved out from a table, but many people install chair railing simply to add a dramatic accent to a space. A deep molding installed down a hallway will appear to be completely decorative, while it can be used for leaning and supporting an unsteady person traveling down the hall.

Banister Height

- Banisters can be like breathtaking artwork and add beauty to a home, but the main purpose of the railing is to ensure safety for people going up and down the stairs.

- Typical banister rails are installed 31 inches above the stairs.

- The height of the railing can be adjusted to ensure comfort for members of the household.

- If a banister is too high or too low, it is more difficult to lean on when ascending or descending.

Adding a Banister in a Narrow Stairwell

- Many narrow residential stairways do not have banisters on both sides because the walls are deemed close enough for safety.

- When climbing or descending the narrow stairs is a challenge, a banister can be added.

- When installing a banister, be sure it is spaced far enough from the wall for fingers to grip around it.

- Have a professional secure the new banister into wall studs.

ILLUMINATED LIGHT SWITCHES

Illumination guides the way for safe passage up and down stairs and through hallways

Even with 20-20 vision, finding one's way through a darkened hallway searching for a light switch is a daunting task. Instead of stumbling through the dark or feeling along the wall to turn on the lights, use a low-energy, illuminated light switch to increase safety and save time.

Illuminated light switches provide a soft, welcoming light,

even when the switch is in the off position. This is a cost-effective solution to poorly lit or dark stairs and hallways. In some homes, a hall or other light is kept on at all times to ensure well-lit passageways. By simply replacing the traditional switch with an illuminated type, the area will be adequately lit at a fraction of the cost of a regular light. In

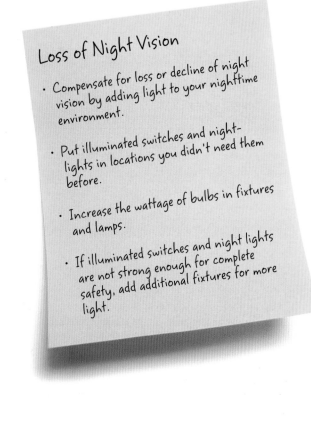

Loss of Night Vision

- Compensate for loss or decline of night vision by adding light to your nighttime environment.

- Put illuminated switches and night-lights in locations you didn't need them before.

- Increase the wattage of bulbs in fixtures and lamps.

- If illuminated switches and night lights are not strong enough for complete safety, add additional fixtures for more light.

Illuminated down the Hall

- An illuminated light switch allows you to find a control to turn on the light in the dark.

- In a hallway, the switch can act as an orientation point and allow you to find your way in the dark.

- An illuminated switch remains on day and night without consuming a lot of electricity.

- If a switch does not emit enough light, install motion sensors so a stronger light will go on when needed.

addition, the illuminated light switch is not as bright as a standard light, which means it is less likely to disturb the sleep of people in nearby rooms.

No special light bulbs are required, and the installation of the illuminated light switch is relatively easy to perform. Illuminated light switches are available in a number of styles including toggle switches, rocker switches, and dimmers—all of which can be purchased in various colors and styles to complement the décor in the hallway.

A variation of the illuminated light switch is the motion sensor night-light. This device provides the same benefit of lighting darkened hallways and stairs, but it also has the added feature of turning off when it is not needed. The sensor detects movement in the darkness and automatically turns on the night-light. It turns off when exposed to light or when a predetermined amount of time has lapsed after motion has stopped.

Light-sensor Night-lights

- Light sensitive night-lights turn on when the overall lighting in the area becomes dim.

- These night-lights can be plugged into any outlet, where they turn on only when ambient light is insufficient.

- When there is sufficient light in the room—as the sun streams through the windows or the lamps are turned on—the night-light shuts off, thereby conserving energy and reducing electric bills.

Illuminated Dimmer Switches

- The latest innovations in light controls make them even more functional and convenient.

- Illuminated dimmer switches are easier to locate in the dark especially from across the room.

- With an illuminated control, visually impaired individuals have a better chance of finding the switch to turn on the lights or change the light's intensity.

- An illuminated dimmer switch functions like a traditional dimmer.

ELEVATORS

Residential elevators can be incorporated into most existing homes and in some staircases

A residential elevator is an effective solution for many older or physically challenged people who have trouble negotiating stairs.

Residential elevators can be installed in stairwells as a movable platform that can hold a wheelchair attached on runners or tracks on each side of the stairwell or as free-standing

elevators—similar to the elevators we are familiar with in commercial businesses.

The decision regarding which type of lift is best should be based upon the mobility of the person to use it, and stairwell and other home space constraints. It may be worth it to get evaluations and quotes for more than one type of elevator

Stairwell Lifts

- Sometimes a house is most easily adapted to accommodate someone in a wheelchair with installation of an elevator that spans the entire width of the stairwell.

- When parked at the top or bottom of the stairs, this elevator lift allows free access to walk by and go up or down.

- It uses only the stairwell space in the home to transfer a wheelchair-bound person from level to level.

Two-level Elevators

- Elevators can be installed between two floors without disturbing the foundation or slab base. This makes them considerably cheaper than a three-story elevator, which does need to be counter-sunk below the first level.

- The landings at the top and bottom of the staircase may need to be large enough to allow a wheelchair to move away from the elevator doors.

- They can be small enough to hold just one person with or without a wheelchair.

or lift, in the same way that one would get several quotes for any major home expenditure.

The less expensive elevator will be one that requires the least amount of retrofitting of space on every floor affected by the elevator.

When choosing a traditional elevator, consider the vertical space it will occupy, the "cab" size (the interior compartment), the door, and where it faces on each level. Unlike an elevator install when a building is constructed, one added after the fact may be visible on the outside from three or even four exterior sides. That means consider the décor, not just of the inside of the elevator, but of the outside as well.

There is a huge difference in cost for an elevator that goes up and down between two floors, and one that serves three floors. The latter must be countersunk below the floor level for support, which means the labor involved is much more costly.

Inside the elevator consider the interior floor and wall finish, lighting, and the location of the interior controls. Will the buttons be pushed by a seated person, or one who is standing?

Larger Elevators

- Elevators that hold several people need to be located carefully to work with the floor plan.

- Adequate space is needed on both floors, so the elevator may need to be located away from the stairs.

- Sometimes the most viable solution is to build an elevator on the exterior of the house—though it is actually accessible only from inside.

First Things First

- Done wisely, an elevator can add value to a house.

- Making life easier for one resident should not disturb the pathways for others.

- Get competitive bids and listen to the different ideas presented.

- Only one type of lift or elevator will be best for you and your home.

STAIRWAY HELPERS

Banisters, seat lifts, and ramps make climbing stairs easier and safer

Staircases are among the greatest challenges for older people living in multistory homes. Fortunately, there are a broad range of aids and devices that facilitate ascending and descending staircases.

Properly installed seat lifts alleviate the burden of negotiating staircases. Seat lifts are installed on a sturdy railing using a heavy-duty aluminum track. The standard capacity for a seat lift is usually 300 pounds, although some manufacturers make seats that can accommodate up to 400 pounds. For comfort and safety, most seat lifts feature soft stops and starts so there are no sudden, jarring motions. Seat belts and remote controls are necessities for safe operation.

Chair Lifts

- Stairwell chair lifts allow a person to get upstairs in a seated position.

- They are much less costly to install than a full elevator, but they don't work for all stairs.

- Chair lifts operate by moving along a continuous railing from one floor to the next. Landings can interfere.

- Some landings can be spanned with a continuous railing, but if a stairway changes directions, a stair lift can be difficult to install.

Banisters

- A stairway banister must be securely mounted into wall studs for safety.

- When there is only one usable banister in a stairway, it may be necessary to add another one along a solid wall.

- Be sure there is sufficient space between the banister and the wall for someone to get their hand around it and get a good grip.

- The banister diameter should be comfortable for the user to grip.

Other features on seat lifts include footrests, call-send controls, obstruction sensors, padded seats, fold-up arms, flip-up seats, and rechargeable batteries. An important option is the swivel seat. When riders reach the top of the stairs, swivel seats enable them to maneuver the chair so they are facing away from the staircase. This makes disembarking from the unit safer and less troublesome. Wheelchair-bound individuals will need assistance getting on and off seat lifts.

For individuals who are more mobile, railings may provide all the support they need. When designing or renovating residential railings, consider safety first. Install handrails along every flight of stairs in the home, ensuring they are comfortable enough for an easy, sturdy grip.

If a home features small level changes and short staircases, ramps can be installed to span the steps, or one side of the stairs. Ramps should also feature sturdy handrails for stability. Make sure the slope of the ramp is not too steep, and that there are adequate landings at the top and bottom of each ramp.

Ramps for Small Flights

- A ramp can be added to one or to a short series of steps for greater accessibility.

- The ramp can span the entire width of the steps or just a portion.

- If a ramp will be used for a wheelchair, it should be at least 36 inches wide.

- Make sure there is enough room in front of the bottom stair so the ramp is not too steep. Making the ramp longer will reduce its slope.

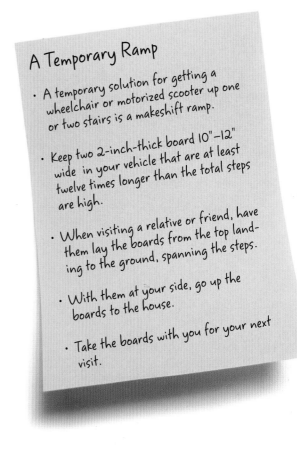

A Temporary Ramp

- A temporary solution for getting a wheelchair or motorized scooter up one or two stairs is a makeshift ramp.

- Keep two 2-inch-thick board 10"–12" wide in your vehicle that are at least twelve times longer than the total steps are high.

- When visiting a relative or friend, have them lay the boards from the top landing to the ground, spanning the steps.

- With them at your side, go up the boards to the house.

- Take the boards with you for your next visit.

167

THE AGING EYE

Choosing colors involves personal taste but safety should be a factor as well

When selecting colors for rooms in your home, think first about safety and then the mood you want to create. Your next consideration should be the visual cues that your color choices provide. Awareness of color values will help you make choices that create a safer and more comfortable living environment.

As people get older, the ability to distinguish between pale colors diminishes. Because of this, spatial distinctions become more difficult. If a door is painted in a similar color to the wall, it can be difficult to identify as such. The same is true for furniture and flooring. If a sofa color is close to the hue of the floor and does not have legs lifting it off the floor,

Monochrome Interior Blurred

- Even if it is well lit, a monochromatic room can be a blur to someone with poor vision.

- In spite of different textures, a beige carpet is still indistinguishable from an ecru painted wall.

- Unfortunately, the use of monochromatic patterned fabrics is lost on someone with poor vision.

- Plan ahead when decorating, and make color decisions that allow you to age in place comfortably.

Monochrome Interior with Yellow Overlay

- The aging eye may see a yellow cast over everything.

- Light shades and faded colors are overwhelmed by the yellow cast and become indistinguishable from each other.

- Deep shades are less affected by yellowing, as are tones of blues and greens..

its edges may be hard to see.

To create a safer home, use contrast to highlight differences. The contrast must be in colors that the older eye can easily differentiate. How is color perception changed? All colors tend to be less intense, and others may have a yellower cast. Lilac can turn to puce for example and be hard to distinguish against grey. Greens can look yellower, so green against yellow may be harder to distinguish.

Warmer colors are easier to tell apart. Bright reds, yellows, and oranges are good choices because the eye retains its ability to see these colors. The more highly saturated the color, the better. Fortunately, these warm colors not only are more visible, but when used well will help create a cheerful environment.

Color has also been shown to alleviate simple ailments. Red stimulates appetite and increases circulation. Orange raises energy levels. Yellow releases serotonin in the brain and causes optimism.

Monochrome Interior with Central Vision Clear

- The same room will look different to people with different eye issues.

- Age-related macular degeneration (ARMD) causes central vision loss. Glaucoma can cause loss of peripheral vision.

- Declining peripheral vision can be accommodated if the head can turn freely, but with age that, too, becomes more difficult.

- Help those with impaired vision by planning interiors with distinctive vertical and horizontal planes.

Blurred Interior with Good Contrast

- To help the visually impaired distinguish between rooms, create contrasts in flooring color.

- Even in familiar spaces, strong color contrasts will help make navigating more comfortable and stress free.

- Those with dementia, such as Alzheimer's, may have difficulty recognizing a room and have to find their way using color cues.

THE EFFECTS OF YELLOWING
When colors aren't what they used to be

The lens of the eye may become more yellow and opaque with age. This can affect color perception and make color contrasts harder to notice. The eye grows less sensitive to subtle differences in shades, and it can become difficult to notice where an object ends and its background begins.

The yellowing of the eye also reduces illumination because the lens becomes less transparent. As it grows more opaque, less light can enter the eye, and, thus, color perception is further affected. This necessitates stronger colors and greater contrasts between colors in the home for safety.

When the eye lens allows less light to get to the retina, dark blue or red may appear even darker. It can be hard to tell the

KNACK UNIVERSAL DESIGN

Color Wheel

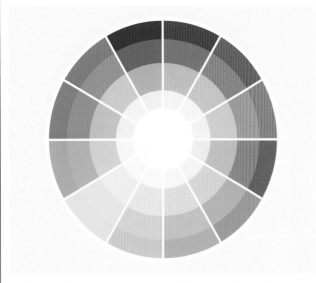

Color Wheel with Yellow Overlay

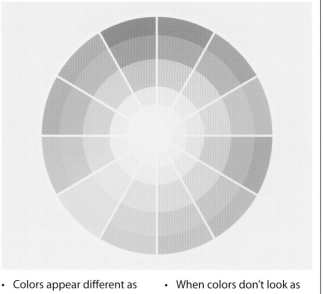

- Choose the colors you like best to decorate your home. You might love blue, but then you need to make a choice between light and dark blue, or grayed tones versus clear tones.

- People have preferences

- for deep colors or light ones and tend to decorate accordingly.

- Colors do not continue to appear to us in the same way throughout our life. Changes in our eyes can make a difference.

- Colors appear different as the eye ages.

- The most common change is that colors appear to be tinged with yellow.

- When colors don't look as pleasing as they used to, replace fabrics and paint walls in more vibrant colors, which are less affected by vision yellowing.

- Some color combinations will be easier to distinguish than others.

difference between them and black. The aging eye often has trouble discriminating between colors that differ mainly in their blue content, like red and purple. Consider this when choosing contrasting colors for the home. For example, red and green will make a stronger visual contrast than red and purple. Light shades may change even more dramatically with less light or a yellow cast over them.

Keep in mind that white objects start to appear more yellow. A soft yellow will not be a strong contrast to white.

Even when colors are bold and strongly contrasted, good lighting is still needed. Bright lighting will help to make things in the home more distinguishable.

Good Contrast Interior

- Use colors and textures that create contrast between walls, furniture, and floors.

- Contrast the color of window coverings with the adjacent walls to help the visually impaired identify a window.

- Floor-length window dressings should contrast the floor color as well.

- To reduce the likelihood of bumps and bruises, furniture should be clearly distinguishable from floor surfaces.

Good Contrast Interior with Yellow Overlay

- Deep colors contrasted with light hues help distinguish elements in a room, even for someone with poor vision.

- The clouding effect of cataracts and the gradual yellowing of vision have less effect on deep, saturated colors.

- Mixing light and deep colors can maximize the eye's ability to evaluate the size of a space and recognize the arrangement of furniture.

CONTRASTING WALLS & FLOORS

Use color to help the eye distinguish varying levels, obstructions, and dangers

Many accidents in the home are caused by a failure to see obstructions or dangers. A cause of mishaps is not clearly seeing the edge where a wall meets the floor or something poorly placed in the path of traffic flow. In the former case, the use of contrasting colors can lessen the chances for accidents.

Make sure that there is a clear, distinct contrast between the floor and the walls. If the floor is dark, paint the walls in a light color or cover them with wallpaper that gives an overall hue of being light colored. Remember that slight differences in hue will not be enough of a contrast for safety, especially in dim light. Anyone with visual challenges will need to see a

KNACK UNIVERSAL DESIGN

Contrasting Baseboard

- When the shade of the floor and wall are similar, it can be hard to tell where one ends and the other begins.

- This can be exacerbated by poor depth perception, blurry vision, or inadequate lighting.

- Painting the baseboard in a bold, contrasting color is an inexpensive way to address the problem.

Light Walls and Rug with Dark Flooring

- A light, monochromatic decorating scheme can still be distinguishable if the flooring is dark.

- An accent rug that is similar in shade to the walls is still clearly separated from the wall because of the dark floor border.

- The contrast flooring acts as a visual clue that the floor is meeting the wall.

- Any rugs should have a non-slip pad beneath, and ends should be anchored with tape.

strong color contrast in order to distinguish where the floor ends and the wall begins.

Beware of glossy flooring and walls. Glare and reflections from the flooring can obscure the contrasting colors, visually blurring the floor and walls into each other. Glare from high gloss paint—often used in the kitchen and bathroom—can do the same. Glare may also cause other reactions in vision, making it harder to see in general. A floor with a matte finish—or carpeting, which offers no glare—is safest. For kitchen and bathroom walls use semi-gloss paint or washable wallpaper.

Baseboards should also be considered to create wall/floor delineation. If the floor is dark, a similarly colored baseboard may be confused with the floor. Match it to the wall.

Dark Floors and Light Walls

- Contrast wall and floor colors to make a space definable for those with poor vision.

- Dark floors and light walls may be more natural for orienting someone who tends to get disoriented.

- When shopping for flooring, put samples on the floor and view them while standing up straight for an accurate view of the installed final look.

- Darkly painted walls will suck up light, making the room darker.

Accent Wall with Lighter Carpet

- Painting one wall in a contrasting color will create drama and add decorative interest to a room.

- An accent wall at the far end of a room helps to define the room's boundaries.

- It can be an orientation aid for a confused person or a person with poor vision.

- For a room with a pitched roof, an accent wall can change the scale of the room making it appear to have more volume.

MAKING EDGES DISTINCT

Make sure edges in the home are visually distinguished from surroundings

As people age, the stiffening of the eye lens reduces the ability for the two eyes to converge on an object. This can affect the perception of distance and depth. Because of this, it becomes more difficult to recognize edges and varying levels. More mishaps can occur if objects cannot be differentiated from their surroundings.

Contrasted colors create clearer visibility between surfaces and give spatial differentiation. Deliberately using distinct colors can create visual appeal while reducing the potential for accidents.

Consider all of the edges in your home. Wherever something needs to be distinguished from its surroundings or

Contrast Counter with Floor

- Countertop color should contrast with the surrounding floor, and the color difference needs to be noticeable from a standing position.

- Be wary of patterned flooring that appears to have color in the small samples; when installed and viewed from a standing position, it can appear faded and monochromatic.

- When evaluating counter and floor colors, look at the counter sample 18 inches from your eye, with the flooring pattern about 3 feet below it. You want to see clear contrast.

Level Change within House

- Because split-level homes are fraught with dangerous level changes, modifications are needed to add safety.

- Consider installing a different flooring type on the stairs to make them distinguishable from flat floors.

- Alternatively, mark stairs clearly with tape, a paint strip, or a change in tile color at the edge of the top and bottom step.

- Be sure stairs are well illuminated day and night.

from another abutting item, contrast should be employed.

To reduce the chances of having things slip to the floor, tops of counters and tables should be contrasted with the color on the floor below. This will make the edges more visually apparent. The side edges can also be addressed to make the whole surface more visible.

Furniture is safer when its color contrasts with the floor surrounding it. Sofas and chairs that are being placed on carpet need to contrast with the floor. Legs under sofas help by creating a shadow area on the carpet at the furniture edge.

If colors are too similar, consider highlighting the edges of certain pieces with contrasting trim.

Don't forget the edges of each step. If it is difficult to distinguish one step from the next highlight the edges with a strong contrasting color. This is especially important in poorly lit stairwells.

If there is a slight level change or a difference in texture, make the edge visibly distinct. Or consider adding a bevel to make the transition more gradual.

Stair Edges

- The width of the stairwell should be clearly visible, especially if a stairwell is circular or curves irregularly.

- If carpeting the stairs in a color that blends with the walls, consider leaving a contrasting surface visible on the edges to emphasize the turns in the stair directions.

- Installing contrasting hard wood or tile edges will make the steps easier to see and navigate.

- A wood surface can be sanded and painted for a less expensive, yet equally effective option.

Single-step Hall to Living Room

- Small level changes in a home are the most dangerous.

- A step down between a hall and living room should be clearly distinguishable by a change in flooring.

- If the flooring type is the same, make sure the color is distinct.

- If people repeatedly trip here, consider ramping the transition.

COMBINING PATTERNS
Create visual interest, but be safe

The aging eye can have a hard time distinguishing between similar colors, and the use of well chosen patterns can help.

If you are choosing any of your furniture in a similar hue to the flooring it is going on, make sure it has a bold pattern so it can be easily set apart from the floor.

Avoid busy patterns because they can confuse the eye. Plaids sometimes are subtle in their coloring and can appear to be one color. If selecting a plaid, pick one with strong contrasting colors. The use of several small patterns close together in one space, even if they are color coordinated, can create a confusing environment for some people with poor vision or dementia.

If you want to mix patterns, consider mixing a small pattern with a much larger one. The eye can then distinguish between the two patterns and the areas or furniture they cover. For room harmony, have them share some colors in

Making Furniture Distinctive

- Patterned fabrics can present a predominant hue when seen from across the room.

- That color hue will determine how distinctive the upholstered piece will look against the room's flooring or wall.

- Wood furniture and wooden chair legs can be distinctive when set on carpeting. If against hardwood floors or in a wood-paneled room, the shade of the wood has to make it distinctive.

Making Floor Levels Distinctive

- From the top of the stairs, one should be able to clearly see down to the level floor below.

- A change in flooring at the bottom will help accomplish that.

- A small area rug at the bottom of the stairs, securely anchored with tape, can also do the trick.

- Bright stairwell lighting, along with sufficient lights at top and bottom, also helps make descending the stairs safe.

common. If wallpaper is used, note how it appears from across the room. Consider its overall depth of color and pattern. Is it clearly a separate surface from the floor?

Wall-to-wall carpeting is best in solid or tweed colors. If bold patterns are wanted on the floor, place rugs on top of the carpet or hardwood flooring. Use bold rugs sparingly and in careful contrast with other flooring and furniture colors. They should be free of fringes and beveled at the edges to minimize transitions.

Creating visual interest by combining floor patterns is a great idea. But since area rugs, carpeting, and other textured treatments can be dangerous for people with mobility challenges, it is best to simulate the look with safer flooring options.

Avoid Busy Patterns

- Anyone with blurry vision or dementia may be bothered by busy patterns.

- Combining different patterns or using several colored tiles in a small space may create a busy or dizzying feeling.

- If unsure, a good rule of thumb is to use only one pattern in a small space.

Avoid Busy Patterns on Furniture

- If an elaborate fabric pattern is chosen for a large piece of furniture, avoid repeating it on other pieces.

- Choose solid colors from the pattern for other pieces in the room.

- Natural stone surfaces can sometimes present themselves as busy patterns.

- The folds in drapery panels and swags create a visual pattern, so be selective when choosing a drape fabric; otherwise the combining effect can be too busy.

MINIMIZING LINEAR ELEMENTS

Remove psychological barriers to promote freedom of movement within the home

It is helpful to know how the decorated environment can visually and psychologically impact members of the family.

In some areas of the home, it is ideal to use linear patterns to guide people to move in a desired direction. The use of a carpet runner or contrasting flooring down the hall is a good example. This type of directional contrast is not often used

deliberately in the home; yet inadvertently, linear elements are used without awareness of their effects on some people.

Some people with dementia may see lines and linear elements as an uncrossable barrier. This may be experienced when there is a definite linear pattern in the flooring or when a long narrow rug overlays a tile or wood floor with a contrast

Stair Hazards: Stairs without Risers

- Floating stairs, or ones that have no risers between the treads, can be scary for anyone with a fear of heights.

- Poor balance or poor vision can also cause a person to feel trepidation on this type of staircase.

- If stairs in this location cannot be avoided, replacing them with continuous stairs and risers could be necessary.

Linear Signals in Carpeting

- Some people with dementia reach a point when they will not cross a line.

- Flooring patterns that may be pleasing to others can be a debilitating obstacle for them.

- Although it is desirable to delineate a room with a

strong flooring pattern, be aware that this might create a barrier for some household members.

- The barrier signal can come from a strong border, an area rug against a contrasting floor, or a tile pattern.

178

color. If someone sees the edge of the carpet as an uncrossable obstacle, he or she may feel compelled to keep moving down the center of the hall and be unable to step off. This can pose a host of issues that would negatively impact the lives of family members.

Consider if the decisions you make for decorating or ease of upkeep reasons will have other impacts on family members. Linear elements that can be used to lead people in proper, safe directions may be a comforting thing. Create any linear element, border, or edge only after wise consideration.

ZOOM

Linear Elements: Besides concerns regarding linear patterns that might be created by rugs in hallways, remember that wheelchairs and motorized scooters also have difficulty with hallway rugs. Be sure edges of rugs are secured with special rug tape and only use rugs without fringes.

Checkerboard Patterns

- Checkerboard patterns may be created with tiles or found in a rug design.

- If the pattern is strong, it can be disturbing to some people, who may then be reluctant to venture into the space.

- To make the space more user-friendly, consider changing the floor.

Tiles in Lines

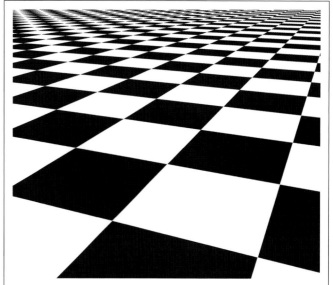

- Be aware that any lines—straight or curved—may become obstructions for a person with dementia.

- Some patients with dementia will not cross a line or will continue moving in the linear direction. If that is the appropriate direction through the space, lines can be effective.

- If a flooring pattern becomes a problem, consider covering it with something workable.

PATIO DOORS

A patio door lets in sunlight while creating easy access to the outside

For bringing in natural light or a view of a pretty backyard, bigger windows are better. Large sliding glass patio doors let in light and views, and have the added practical value of offering easy access to the outdoors with ample space for wheelchairs to pass through.

But access is only easy if the doors are simple to open. Many sliding doors are heavy and difficult to move. This could be due to the model of door, or it could be that the wheels or rollers simply need maintenance and a little oil. If your existing doors present a challenge for you, there are several options for improvement.

Try maintenance first. Sometimes just vacuuming around

Slider Doors

- Slider patio doors are available with wood, vinyl, or aluminum frames, with wood being the best insulator.

- Along with an easy-to-grip handle, good door rollers will help the door slide smoothly.

- Select a U-shaped handle that fingers can easily wrap around.

- Exterior slider doors need easy-to-manipulate locks.

Slider Screens

- Sliding glass doors include a screen that slides in its own exterior track.

- Screen locks are often hard to turn and manipulate, but there are screens available with easier locks.

- If the security of a locked screen is not necessary, consider keeping the latch in the open position permanently, so no one ever locks himself or herself out.

the door track will make the door glide more smoothly. The track area can also be cleaned with a soapy solution, or a candle can be rubbed over it to make it run smoother. A handyman can remove the door to see if the rollers need to be replaced.

If the door still won't slide easily, replacing it may be the way to go. There are new patio doors with convenient features like smooth gliding and easier to use locks and handles.

An alternative is to replace sliding patio doors with French doors, which open and close like standard exterior doors. It is easier to get good grippable hardware for French doors.

You can also add an automatic system, which operates the door by remote control. The remote can be portable or mounted on the wall.

Screens add convenience to your patio door. They allow air circulation while keeping out unwanted pests. Choose a screen with heavy-duty rollers, an easy-to-grasp lock, and a smooth glide for easy operation.

French Doors

- French doors, which are usually more costly than sliding doors, can replace patio door openings for a different look and function.

- French doors can open wider than standard sliding doors, giving greater access if needed.

- Choose traditional levered door handles and easy-to-use locks, similar to the other exterior doors.

Retractable Screens

- A retractable screen, installed on the outside of French and sliding patio doors, is completely hidden when opened.

- The opened screen allows for a completely unobstructed view through the glass door.

- Because they are designed to snap into rollers when released, retractable screens may not be a good choice for arthritic fingers or weak hands and wrists.

CUSTOM WINDOWS

Choose specialty windows for function and beauty

Windows come in many shapes and operate in many different ways. Custom windows will add personalization, function, character and beauty to a home.

Casement, or crank-out, windows are windows that are hinged on the side and swing out. Because casements can open fully, they offer very good ventilation. When closed, casement windows have a very tight fit, creating added protection from the elements.

While casement windows are generally easy to open and close, the cranks can be difficult to operate for anyone with hand challenges. Make sure the handles are easy to grip and smooth to turn. If not, fit them with a rubber cover that creates a larger, softer grip for cranking.

Arch windows add a pretty architectural element to a room, while allowing extra sunlight to stream in. The arch top is usually stationary so it won't open for air. Like clerestory

Gripping Small Latches

- New windows can offer many benefits. They have easy-to-grip locking mechanisms.

- New glides make windows simpler to open and close without much effort. Replacing old locks can make the windows easier to lock and unlock.

- Replacing old windows with double- or triple-pane windows will also add energy efficiency.

Crank-out Windows

- Crank-out windows open fully, allowing maximum airflow.

- They can be installed to open to the left or right.

- Handles on crank-out windows are easy to grasp.

- The lever locks take some force to open and close, but are also easy to grasp.

windows which are also high on a wall near the ceiling, they may allow very intense light in at certain times of the day or season. When decorating an arched or clerestory windows, select window coverings that highlight their uniqueness, but provide glare control when needed.

Flip windows are a good option for easy window cleaning. They come with vertical or horizontal turning ability, depending upon shape. These windows flip 180°, so washing both sides can be done from the interior of the home.

For extra personalization, other special custom-shaped windows are available. Round windows, extra large rectangles or squares, and angle-topped windows can bring drama and pizzazz to a home. They can be used by themselves or in combination with other windows for endless possibilities.

Flip Windows

- Windows that present danger when opened should be fitted with guards that limit how wide they open.

- Some windows can be secured on the bottom and opened from the top.

- When someone has dementia, safe window conditions should be addressed.

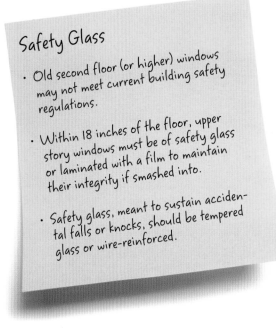

Safety Glass

- Old second floor (or higher) windows may not meet current building safety regulations.

- Within 18 inches of the floor, upper story windows must be of safety glass or laminated with a film to maintain their integrity if smashed into.

- Safety glass, meant to sustain accidental falls or knocks, should be tempered glass or wire-reinforced.

183

SLIDING WINDOWS
Windows that slide side to side

Standard widows in most homes are ones that slide, either up and down or side to side. Originally up and down windows had wood frames, but development of other materials means there are other options. Wood, however, is still an excellent insulator. Aluminum frames are generally less expensive and are not as good at insulating. The advent of vinyl, now available in a variety of colors means good insulation for the frame, without the trouble of painting.

Windows that slide sideways can also be purchased in aluminum or vinyl frames.

The design of the home and the age in which it was built determine the type of windows it has. Replace windows to update things, or to get the benefit of greater insulation than old single-paned windows offer.

If insulation is a concern—as it is in climates with cold winters and/or hot summers—replace windows with double-

Locks on Vertical Sliding Windows

- Old wooden-framed windows often have hard-to-operate locks.

- Even in good condition, a traditional window latch can be hard to grasp and turn.

- In addition to having awkward locks, older windows may not be energy efficient.

- Replacing old windows with new double-pane windows will reduce heating and cooling bills and keep the interior temperature more comfortable.

Locks on Horizontal Sliding Windows/Doors

- Sliding metal-framed windows can be hard to unlock and slide open.

- Look into replacement locks that are more user-friendly.

- If necessary replace with windows that come with easier to operate locks.

- Replacement windows that better insulate the home can be installed right in the existing window space.

pane ones, improving the insulation quality. In severe weather climates, triple-pane windows can be installed

Wooden windows that slide up and down do so with ropes as guides and supports. Their lock is generally a small device that you rotate from side to side. If fingers are not agile enough to work the lock, find out from the manufacturer if a different, larger, easier-to-manipulate lock can be installed.

Sideways sliding windows move in their channel and generally have up and down slide locks. If these locks are hard to manipulate, again, ask the manufacturer, or a handyman if they can be replaced with ones that are easier to grasp and move.

All windows should be cleaned and serviced to slide opened and closed easily to reduce the chances of muscle strain or injury.

Double- or Triple-pane Advantages

- Multi-pane windows offer maximum insulation from extreme outside temperatures.

- With new multi-pane windows, energy costs are reduced.

- When replacing windows, consider ones with blinds installed between the panes. Since they are dust-free, they are perfect for those with allergies.

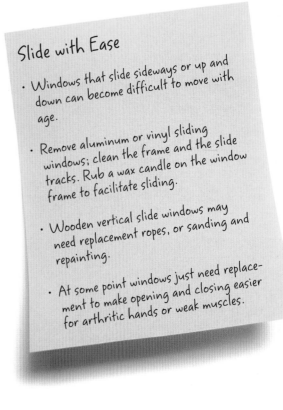

Slide with Ease

- Windows that slide sideways or up and down can become difficult to move with age.

- Remove aluminum or vinyl sliding windows; clean the frame and the slide tracks. Rub a wax candle on the window frame to facilitate sliding.

- Wooden vertical slide windows may need replacement ropes, or sanding and repainting.

- At some point windows just need replacement to make opening and closing easier for arthritic hands or weak muscles.

185

WINDOW COVERINGS
The finishing touch to a beautiful room can be practical as well

Window treatments provide the perfect combination of function and beauty—if you choose the right ones. Though the unlimited variety of options can be overwhelming, your selection becomes much easier if you first answer a few questions.

What are the main reasons for covering this window? Do you need privacy? Light control? Sound absorption? Added beauty or softness? There are window coverings for every need. When you identify your specific needs, you can eliminate the treatments that *won't* work. This gives you a much more manageable group of options.

Next decide what style or mood you are creating. Windows are a part of the whole room's design scheme, so if the space is already decorated, you will want the window coverings to harmonize with the overall style already in place. If you haven't decorated yet, think about the mood you want to create.

Shutters

- Horizontal blinds can be louvered to direct the light away from or toward specific areas as desired.

- Blinds can be louvered opened at various angles or pulled up completely for an unobstructed view.

- Note that the color of a closed blind will look different when opened.

- The strength and amount of sun entering a window should determine the blind material chosen: Too much strong sun will fade interior surface colors.

Window Shades

- The old roller or Roman shade has graduated to a shade that can close and open from the top down or the bottom up.

- Select a style and fabric to fit your window exposure and lifestyle.

- Covering the window only at the bottom can provide bedroom privacy in a ground floor room, while letting in daylight.

- Some window covering fabrics are gossamer and block the glare of the sun, without keeping out all the light.

Lastly, of course, you want to consider ease of use. If there is anyone in your home who has arthritis or hand gripping issues, choose a treatment that can be operated easily. Shutters are a great choice because the tilt rod is simple to push up and down with a wrist or forearm. Also, most horizontal blinds have a cord tilt option to louver, or angle, the slats, which is much easier to operate than a thin twist rod.

Ask for extra long controls so that all family members can reach and maneuver the window coverings without stretching. But for safety, make sure to keep cords off the floor.

Because most cords get longer when the blind or shade is pulled up, it is important to install a "cord cleat" so that you can wrap the cord and keep it from becoming a tripping or choking danger. Cord cleats are small and easily installed with one screw.

Vertical Blinds

- Vertical blinds are commonly used on sliding doors because of their ability to slide to the side to allow access.

- They are available in unlimited colors, textures, sizes, and materials.

- Vertical blinds can be custom-made to fit any window or door.

- The vertical slats can be tilted to provide privacy, while letting in sufficient light to illuminate the room.

Curtains

- Treat floor-length window dressings the same as walls when choosing colors; curtains need to contrast with the floor for easy visibility.

- When choosing a fabric for a window treatment, consider the overall look, rather than the individual colors in the pattern or fabric.

- Fabric treatments can be used alone or in addition to blinds and shades to enhance and complete the look and meet lighting needs.

LIGHT & GLARE
When light becomes too much

Sunlight is necessary for our overall well-being, but it has to be controlled or it will cause problems in the home. Sun makes a room too hot in the summer and greatly raises air conditioning bills. It also damages furnishings and flooring. And when it shines right in your face or on the television, it can be uncomfortable and annoying.

Window treatments are the solution. There are window coverings that are specially designed to cut down on glare

and heat. Cellular shades, also known as honeycombs, provide insulation and are extremely energy efficient. They are available in a broad spectrum of colors and materials, and can be custom shaped to fit any window.

Wood blinds and shutters are good choices for light control because they allow you to angle the sun as it comes through the window. At certain times of the day, you may want to focus the light up and away from the television. You can keep

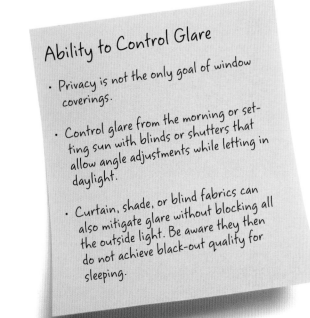

Ability to Control Glare

- Privacy is not the only goal of window coverings.

- Control glare from the morning or setting sun with blinds or shutters that allow angle adjustments while letting in daylight.

- Curtain, shade, or blind fabrics can also mitigate glare without blocking all the outside light. Be aware they then do not achieve black-out quality for sleeping.

In-pane Blinds

- By law, replacement windows must be insulated, which means they have to be double- or triple-paned.

- The space between the glass allows for mullions to be inserted creating an interesting architectural look.

- Horizontal blinds can also be inserted between the glass. Controls to raise, lower, and tilt the blinds are user-friendly.

- Having blinds or mullions placed between the panes makes window cleaning easier.

the room bright by allowing the sun in, but just face it away from expensive furnishings. This flexibility is important for comfort.

Many window coverings have a "top-down" option. The control mechanism draws the shade open from the top instead of pulling it open from the bottom. "Top-down, bottom-up" window fashions offer you the ability to operate the shade in any direction to meet all your light control and privacy needs and are the ultimate in versatility.

If you love natural light but still want to control the glare, sheer draperies are another choice. Sheer fabrics, which come in unlimited patterns and colors, filter the light, cutting down on bothersome glare and giving the room a soft glow.

Up or Down Window Coverings

- The three main functional reasons for covering windows are privacy, light control, and insulation.

- Double and triple cellular shades are ideal for providing added insulation.

- Privacy and light control can be achieved with most blinds and shades, provided they are not made from sheer materials.

- If privacy is needed, but sunlight is still desired, a shade that opens from the top is the ideal solution.

Glare Control Window Coverings

- Sunlight is helpful to people with poor vision, but glare can be very distracting. The right window treatment will cut the glare while allowing maximum sunlight.

- Sheer fabric drapery panels cut down on disturbing glare, but still let in light.

- Horizontal and vertical blinds in honeycomb configuration can allow total room illumination while eliminating glare. Vertical or horizontal slat blinds can be tilted to direct the glare away from certain areas.

REMOTE CONTROLS

Operate almost anything in the house with the touch of a button

Remote controls are available for more than just televisions. You can enjoy the convenience of operating your window treatments, turning on and off lights, controlling your thermostat, and even locking up your home—all from the comfort of your couch or bed.

Motorized operating systems on window treatments offer wonderful flexibility and simplicity. They eliminate the need for dangerous and unsightly cords and make privacy and light control as simple as pressing a button.

There are several power options for window treatment remote controls. The simplest, least expensive version is a battery-powered control. The blind or shade has a battery pack hidden in the headrail, and a handheld, battery-powered, wireless unit operates the window treatment.

Motorized window treatments can also be powered by a hard-wired system that is installed in the walls of the home.

Curtain Walls

- Remote controls can open or close curtains with the push of a button.

- A single remote or wall switch can open, close, and adjust groups of window treatments in several rooms.

- Remote controls eliminate the need for cords, which can be unsightly, unsafe, and sometimes awkward to operate.

- Poor mobility or arthritis no longer needs to be an obstacle to opening or closing the drapes.

Outside Window Coverings

- Roller shutters installed on the outside of large windows help control glare, but can be opened with a remote control button when an unobstructed view is desired.

- Outside installation allows for a cleaner aesthetic inside.

- Remote control operation eliminates the need for a manual crank; a simple push of a button moves the shutter down or up.

Operation of these window coverings is via a wall switch or a handheld remote control. Although these motorized treatments can be installed in an existing home, pre-wiring during the building phase makes it much easier.

The two basic types of remote control systems are infrared and radio frequency. With an infrared system, the handheld transmitter must be pointed directly at the individual window treatment to operate it. A radio frequency operated window covering can be controlled by the transmitter from virtually anywhere in the house.

Although it is simplest to purchase window coverings with the motors already installed, older blinds, shades, and draperies can be retrofitted to make their operation more convenient. Contact a local window coverings professional for all the remote control options.

For those with mobility and vision challenges, remote controls are essential for independence. They provide solutions to many common tasks that would otherwise be impossible to perform.

Remote Controls

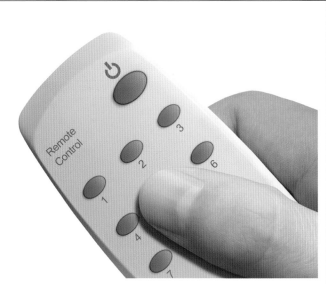

- Remote control is not always a retrofit for an existing device. It may require installing a new drape or shade.

- An electrician can install remote controls on existing lights, however.

- Balance the luxury and convenience of remote controls with importance of exercising muscles daily.

- Continuing to walk and use your arms and hands as much as you can is good daily exercise.

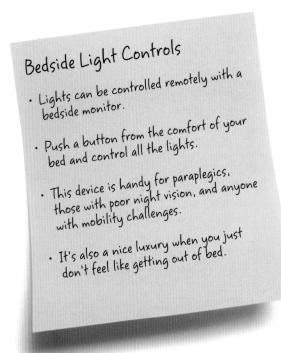

Bedside Light Controls

- Lights can be controlled remotely with a bedside monitor.

- Push a button from the comfort of your bed and control all the lights.

- This device is handy for paraplegics, those with poor night vision, and anyone with mobility challenges.

- It's also a nice luxury when you just don't feel like getting out of bed.

SKYLIGHTS
When the light comes from above

The need for ample lighting cannot be taken lightly. Because our eyes take in less light as we grow older, it becomes harder to see colors, edges, and changes in levels. This can make even our own living environment challenging. Additional lighting will alleviate many of the daily struggles.

The best light of all, of course, is natural lighting. Skylights open up your home and let the sunshine in. They add warmth and cut down on the need for artificial light.

If you are thinking of adding a skylight to your home, you have many options. Material, shape, operation, and size are just some of the choices you need to make. You want the skylight to be beautiful and add drama to your home, but it must meet your functional needs as well.

If you choose a ventilating skylight, make sure it is motorized. You don't want to be messing with cranks or poles, which can be a struggle to use and are often cumbersome to

Kitchen Skylights

- Kitchens are used both day and night and require sufficient lighting for safety and comfort.

- Many kitchens receive insufficient sunlight. Due to upper cabinets, refrigerators, and stove hoods, windows can be lacking.

- With less sunlight, artificial light is used more often.

- If it is possible, add a skylight above diffused light fixtures so during the day there is natural daylight and in the evening artificial light comes from the same direction.

Stairwell Skylights

- A skylight installed in the stairwell adds safety, warmth, and beauty by increasing the amount of sunlight cast onto the steps.

- Good, natural light from above makes seeing the steps easier.

- Consult a licensed con-

tractor to determine if a skylight can be installed in the stairwell.

- A window installed high on a side wall is another option.

- As with all remodeling projects, obtain all necessary building permits.

store. For peace of mind, add the sensor option, which closes the window when it rains.

Fixed skylights add light to a room without ventilation. They come with or without blinds inserted. If your skylight does not have a covering already installed, you can have pleated shades, honeycombs, or mini-blinds custom-fitted for light and heat control. You will want these shades motorized, as well.

Opening Skylights

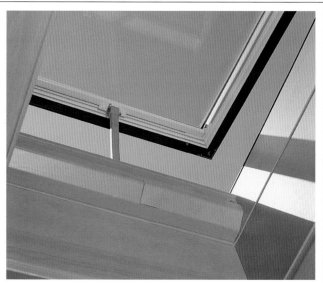

- When adding or replacing a skylight, consider one that opens for ventilation.

- Ventilating skylights release the hot air that naturally accumulates near the ceiling, creating a fresher, healthier environment.

- Venting skylights can be opened with a manual crank, pole, or chain. This can be difficult even for an agile person with good vision, so opt for remote control operation.

- Skylights that run on an electric motor use only negligible electricity.

Solatubes

- A Solatube is a cylinder that runs down from the roof into a room's ceiling, allowing sunlight to enter the room.

- Unlike a traditional skylight, its small size—about a foot in diameter—fits between roof joists.

- Through the use of optic glass, it throws light into the room far beyond what one would expect from such a small window.

- From inside the room, a Solatube looks like a light fixture.

AMBIENT LIGHTING
Overall light in a room is as important as task lighting

There are different types of lighting to consider as we light our homes, beginning with overall room illumination, known as ambient lighting.

General lighting needs to fill each room completely, revealing everything—walls and corners, furnishings, any possible obstacles. When more light is needed, many homeowners make the mistake of thinking that they just need more lights in the ceiling. But for the safest, most comfortable illumination, light needs to come into the room from all directions. Use recessed lights, chandeliers, wall fixtures, and perimeter cove lights.

Avoid bare light bulbs because the direct glare can decrease the ability to see clearly. Add translucent shades or covers that diffuse the light. Paint your ceiling in a light color to reflect the light back into the room, and consider adding a wall mirror for greater light reflection.

Overall Room Illumination

- Natural daylight is best for illuminating the home.

- In condominiums and apartments where there are windows on only one or two sides, relying on natural sunlight—even during daylight hours—may be impossible.

- Adding extra artificial lighting is necessary in darker homes.

- When selecting an orientation for new living quarters, pay attention to the exposure. South- and west-facing windows get good light more hours of the day.

Kitchen Ceiling Lighting

- Ceiling lighting is important in the kitchen even if windows or skylights allow sunlight to stream in.

- In winter, daylight may be gone by the time dinner is prepared—or certainly when the remains of the meal are cleared away.

- Central ceiling lighting should illuminate all the major appliances and counters in the kitchen to make them clearly recognizable and to make kitchen tasks easy and safe.

Glossy floors and countertops will also increase the glare because they don't reflect evenly. While working in the kitchen, you may feel like a light is shining up from the counter right into your eyes, making tasks very difficult.

Windows provide terrific ambient lighting. If you need privacy but don't want to sacrifice the natural light, you can cover the window with a top-down shade. These window treatments cover the window just where you need it, while still allowing sunlight to stream in at the top.

Pay special attention to areas in your home where there are no windows. Dark hallways, dim stairways, and other poorly lit areas can become very dangerous. Add sufficient ambient lighting to all of these spaces. Create balanced illumination by adding various lighting that comes from several directions to avoid hazardous shadows.

To take the most advantage of the light you have, paint your walls and ceilings in light colors using an eggshell finish.

Hallway Lighting

- With diminishing visual acuity, the need for better artificial lighting increases.

- Hallways often have to rely on artificial ambient light.

- Dimmer switches can adjust the light as needed at different hours.

- Make sure there is a switch at each end of the hallway for turning lights on and off.

Bedroom Lighting

- A bedroom may be graced with adequate windows to provide all the daylight needed for getting around.

- Proper furniture placement can even help to provide adequate sunlight for tasks like reading and sewing.

- Dressing areas in bedrooms may require unique lighting for comfortable performance of tasks even during the day.

- Nighttime lighting needs to provide overall illumination for safety, as well as specific lighting for tasks.

RECESSED LIGHTS
A flexible, inexpensive lighting choice for any room

Do you need to add more light to your home? Recessed lights are very popular due to their relatively low installation and material cost and ease of use. They are a quick way to add general overall, ambient lighting, specific task lighting, or even lighting used to accent your treasured artwork.

Recessed lights should be spaced properly on the ceiling to create even, overall light below. A professional electrician will know the proper spacing for the size of the recessed cans

installed. Usually the recommended distance is 4 to 6 feet apart, but it will be a function of the height of the ceiling. The wall color or finish will also be a factor.

If task lighting is needed, install a recessed ceiling light above a reading chair. On the other hand, if lights are already installed, place your furniture to best take advantage of the available light. You might increase the wattage in a canister, but do so only after knowing the designated safe maximum

Ambient Lighting

- Recessed lighting spaced throughout the ceiling will illuminate the room more evenly than a central ceiling fixture.

- This leads to less shadows and dark corners.

- Recessed canister lighting accepts halogen floodlights or compact fluorescent bulbs. Both are considered energy efficient.

- Select the amount of cans and the bulb wattage for each fixture based on the personal needs of the household.

Task Lighting

- Recessed fixtures installed over specific areas can provide sufficient illumination for performing tasks, without the need for a lamp.

- Install a recessed light over the bed for nighttime reading, over a desk where bills are paid, or over a bookcase.

- Use cool-color compact fluorescent bulbs in recessed fixtures for task lighting.

- The bulb strength needed depends on the user's vision and how far the light fixture is from the task.

wattage for that fixture. The chair used for reading should be set slightly in front of a light stream.

Some recessed lights have dropped, adjustable cans so the light can be directed to highlight a special piece on the wall. If artwork is moved, the light can be aimed differently without the need for installing or purchasing a new fixture. Other cans are specifically designed to be wall washers and shine only on the wall adjacent and below them.

Decorative trim is available to surround each recessed light. Trim runs from simple to extravagant and can be painted to match the décor of the room. A single ceiling fixture or chandelier dictates where furniture pieces must be placed, but the general overall lighting created by recessed lights allows for greater flexibility in furniture arrangement.

Over Dining Areas

- Although a chandelier makes a design statement, well-located recessed lighting will generally do a better job of casting light on all diners.

- A dimmer switch allows more flexibility with ceiling lighting. Dim or raise illumination levels to any degree for mood and effect.

- Recessed lighting can also be specifically placed to illuminate other features in the room, such as a buffet or artwork.

Energy Efficient Bulbs

- Halogen floods are specified for indoor or outdoor use. They generate a lot of heat so should be used in open canisters. Great for task illumination, they also provide good ambient lighting.

- LED bulbs will screw into most fixtures. Although more expensive, they emit a soft white light for good overall illumination without glare.

- Compact fluorescent bulbs are relatively inexpensive and long lasting. They are safest when used in open-style fixtures.

TASK LIGHTING

Specific chores and tasks require specialized, focused lighting

After tackling the ambient lighting in your home, you will want to supplement it with task lighting that meets your specific needs.

Task lighting provides needed illumination for home activities. Reading, cooking, sewing, bathing, game playing, and even conversing all need targeted light.

Think about where your activities occur, and place extra lights in those areas. Whenever possible, if a task is always done in the same area, such as cooking and food preparation, add the lights permanently and out of the way. If a task could move around the room with furniture rearranging, the task lighting source might do well to also be movable. Floor or hanging lamps and table lamps fit into this category.

Be careful of the direction in which the light is cast. When writing at a desk, see that the light comes from the opposite side of your writing hand to avoid working in your own

Stove Lighting

- An overhead stove light is important for all cooks regardless of their vision.

- Many hood lights have controls on them. If the on/off button is difficult to manage, have an electrician add a wall switch as a second control.

- If additional light is needed, purchase an inexpensive, portable under-counter light fixture. Plug it into an existing outlet and attach where needed.

Counter Task Lighting

- Lighting is important in the kitchen to perform tasks safely and comfortably. Because overhead lighting can cause shadows and create dark spots, additional illumination is needed.

- Lights installed on the underside of upper cabinets can provide sufficient, shadow-free lighting for counter tasks.

- Choose fixtures that accept LED or compact fluorescent bulbs if possible because they cast soft white light. Most counters are shiny and reflective. Soft-light bulbs minimize glare.

shadow. If light comes from the side or from over your shoulder be careful your head doesn't cast a shadow over the knitting or book it's meant to illuminate.

Task lighting over your stove and sink needs to be in front of you rather than behind, so you will not block the light needed for safe cooking with your shoulders and head.

The amount of wattage or lumens you need may change with age or eye degeneration. Your eye professional may be able to help you determine what strength bulbs you need. Never place more wattage in a fixture than is recommended by the manufacturer. This may mean permanent fixtures will need to be replaced to accept more wattage. Moveable light sources may also need replacing or supplementing with a second fixture.

Reading Lights

- To illuminate an area for comfortable reading, place a floor or table lamp with a bright bulb near a chair.

- Position the lamp behind your left shoulder if you are right-handed, and behind your right shoulder if you are left-handed, so your hand and arm don't cast a shadow on the book as you read.

- When installing overhead ceiling lights, plan one for over the location of a lounge chair.

Desk Illumination

- For safety, avoid tabletop lamps, and instead opt for a desk lamp that attaches to the desk edge.

- Overhead lighting is a convenient alternative because it doesn't get in the way of paperwork. It can do an excellent job of illuminating the desk task area and opened drawers.

- Position the desk so overhead light is not directly overhead but off to one side to avoid the shadow of a head in the middle of paperwork.

SENSORS ON LIGHTS

Lights go on as you approach, providing illumination, safety, and comfort

Years ago, it was considered a rich man's luxury to have lights that went on and off as the homeowner moved about the house. Now it is much more commonplace, and motion sensors on lights are an important part of a universal design home.

A motion sensor on the front door light is important. As you approach the front of your house, the light goes on like a beacon leading you safely down the path to your door. It also works to warn unwanted visitors away. For added convenience, aim one light directly on the doorknob and lock area. You will be able to get in much quicker and with less frustration.

Patio Lights

- Motion sensor patio lights are a safety feature that can be added to any outdoor connection.

- Sensors trigger the lights to go on as someone walks onto the patio without anyone having to flip a switch.

- Lights on sensors also go on if an unwanted trespasser enters the patio, alerting residents to an intruder. This shock to the prowler may be enough to frighten him away.

Front and Back Door Lights

- Fixtures that illuminate exterior doors can be replaced with ones that instantly turn themselves on when they sense movement.

- The inside switch is left on all the time, but the light will only go on when the movement sensor tells it to.

- When lights at the front door go on as you approach, you can find and insert your keys easily.

- Light sensors alert residents that someone is at the door.

Inside the home, light sensors can aid your trips to the bathroom and kitchen in the middle of the night. The motion sensors should not only turn on the lights in those rooms, but in the hallways and stairwells leading to them as well.

Think about where automatic lights would help you around the house. Do you often walk into a dark room and fumble around for the light switch? Add a motion sensor to the lights in that room. There are also fixtures that turn themselves on automatically when it gets dark. They are available in styles for outside entries and over garage doors.

Remember that the sensor needs to be placed in the area where you want to sense motion. This area should precede the area where the light goes on so that you can see your way there.

In Stair Wells

- When there is not a handy light switch at each end of the stairs, installing a fixture with a motion sensor is a safety precaution.

- Light sensors properly placed in stairwells cause lights to go on whenever a person goes to ascend or descend.

- Motion sensor fixtures in stairwells are also a must for those with a memory disorder. They may not remember to manually turn on the light, but it will turn itself on with their approach.

Checklist of Motion Sensor Locations

- For security, put motion sensor fixtures on outside lights. When bulbs burn out replace them promptly.

- Where hallways and stairs are close to each other, a motion sensor fixture adds safety.

- Attics and basements with dark corners are likely places for trips and bangs unless a motion sensor light illuminates them before anything happens.

201

SWITCHES & SWITCH PLATES
For safety and convenience, don't neglect these details

Two of the most overlooked components in traditional interior design are switches and switch plates. These neglected features are usually upstaged by more prominent aspects of the home, but they need attention too! Universal design gives them the consideration they need.

Selecting appropriate switches and switch plates will provide added safety and comfort while reducing the risk of danger and injury. Let's take a closer look at the options and

issues associated with switches so that you can make the best decisions for your home.

Light switches should be installed lower than standard height to provide greater accessibility—especially for people in wheelchairs. Replace existing switches with larger rocker-style switches; they require less physical effort to operate, and they are easier to see, especially if illuminated internally. For even greater simplicity, you can install touch-on/touch-

Safety Electrical Plugs

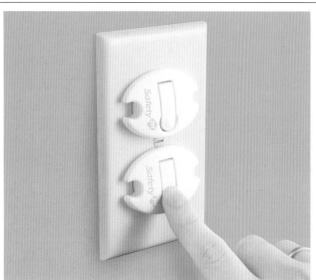

- Childproof safety plugs, traditionally used to keep babies safe, should be used in the home if there is someone with dementia.

- Avoid plastic plugs that are placed directly into the outlet. Although they are effective in covering the dangerous opening,

- they are difficult to remove when needed.

- Look instead for spring-loaded outlet covers. The shield is moved to the side to insert a plug, and automatically blocks the open socket when the plug is removed.

Illuminated Light Switches

- Illuminated switch plates offer a continuous glow, making them useful for navigating around the house at night.

- They are also helpful for going down a dark hall or flight of stairs.

- Instead of groping around in the dark, find an illuminated switch easily so lights can be turned on.

- Illuminated switch plates are useful for attic and cellar lights.

- Plastic illuminated plates come in pure white and off-white to match other plates.

off switch plates. You will avoid the hassle of searching for light switches if you change your switch plates to illuminated ones. They have a small internal light that is on all the time but consumes only a small amount of electricity.

An alternative is to strategically set certain areas of your home on timers. This can provide ample lighting in hallways, bathrooms, and kitchens in the middle of the night. Timers on lights are also great for creating the illusion that someone is home. And if your lights are connected to timers, you won't have to worry about walking throughout the house if you forget to turn off a light when you leave a room.

Let's not forget about switch and outlet covers. Be sure to choose colors that contrast with the wall so they are easier to see. For safety, use childproof plugs to protect children and people with dementia from unsafe tampering.

Illuminated Dimmer Switches

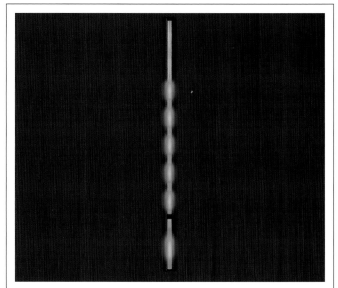

- When navigating and performing tasks, strong light is needed by those with poor vision. Sometimes a softer light is desired for relaxation.

- By installing illuminated dimmer switches, residents have the benefit of controlling the intensity of the light. Illumination can be transitioned from bright task lighting to a romantic or relaxing mood with the sliding of a dial.

- Because they are illuminated, the switches can be located easily, even when the light is off or set to dim.

Lights on Timers

- Lights that are used every day during specific hours can be set to go on automatically.

- Timers are available in switch plates with multiple preset buttons and options.

- Less elaborate, portable timers are plugged into the wall, and a lamp or appliance is plugged into them.

- Settings control when the light or appliance goes on and off on a twenty-four-hour cycle.

THERMOSTATS

Get a programmable one, so you can set it and forget it

Temperature control is important in any household, but especially for family members of advanced age or with medical issues. Thermostats have gone through many transformations and improvements over the years, becoming more practical and user-friendly with technological enhancements. People who are still using older-style thermostats can benefit by upgrading to an energy-efficient, cost-effective, programmable unit. It works even with your old furnace or

air conditioner. To maximize safety and comfort for all family members, follow these recommendations regarding thermostats:

Programmable thermostats are helpful because they can be set once and then forgotten. In addition to their ease of use, they save energy and provide greater safety. By programming the thermostat to remain at a desired temperature, there are no worries about making the house too hot

Programmable Thermostat

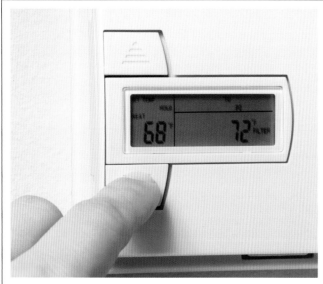

- Hire an electrician or heating professional to replace any standard thermostat with a programmable thermostat.

- They take digital savvy to program, but once done, they require no further concern.

- Programmable thermostats turn the air conditioner or furnace on and off on schedule.

- They can be set for multiple temperatures in a twenty-four-hour span: morning, daytime, evening, night.

Program It for Heat

- Besides ease of function, programmable thermostats benefit the home by saving energy.

- Set the thermostat to automatically lower the heat after everyone is asleep. Heat can also be programmed to turn down during the daytime hours

- when no one is home.

- Arrive home to warmth because the heat goes back on automatically.

- If circumstances change and people are home unexpectedly, the program can be overridden with the touch of a button.

or too cold. Although it is possible to purchase a unit that controls only heat or air conditioning, most thermostats can perform both functions.

Because they work digitally, thermostats may need to be programmed by a friend or relative if the resident is not computer literate.

Many programmable thermostats are available with large-screen touch displays. People with visual impairments will appreciate the greater visibility of the numbers and the ease of programming that these models provide.

Another important factor to consider is the height at which the thermostat is installed. To ensure convenience for all family members, place the thermostat on the wall at a height where users can see the digital read-out straight on. The thermostat should also be easily accessible and not surrounded by pieces of furniture.

Some thermostats are equipped with sensors to measure the outdoor temperature. This added feature makes it easier for household residents to prepare for the elements without having to first venture outside to check the weather.

Program Differently for Cooling

- A programmable thermostat allows you to set a regular schedule for the air conditioner to go on and off automatically.

- To minimize energy costs, set the air conditioner temperature higher during times of the day when no one is home.

- If the day temperature is too hot for comfortable sleeping, set a lower one for night.

- At any time, the program can be overridden to change the temperature. The thermostat then goes back to its regular schedule.

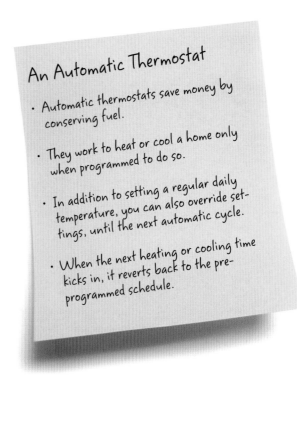

An Automatic Thermostat

- Automatic thermostats save money by conserving fuel.

- They work to heat or cool a home only when programmed to do so.

- In addition to setting a regular daily temperature, you can also override settings, until the next automatic cycle.

- When the next heating or cooling time kicks in, it reverts back to the pre-programmed schedule.

205

SMOKE & GAS DETECTORS

Two essential early warning devices that save lives and provide peace of mind

By law all newer homes have installed alarms already. If your home lacks them, portable smoke alarms are inexpensive, easy to install, and provide early detection that can mean the difference between life and death.

Battery-powered smoke alarms can be installed with a screwdriver or a self-stick adhesive. Check installation instructions, as each manufacturer has separate directions. Units that are hard-wired into the electrical system will need an electrician to perform the installation. Smoke alarms are usually required by law at the top of stairs and outside bedrooms.

Smoke alarms fall into two main categories: ionization and photoelectric. Ionization alarms are designed to quickly detect

Portable Smoke Detectors

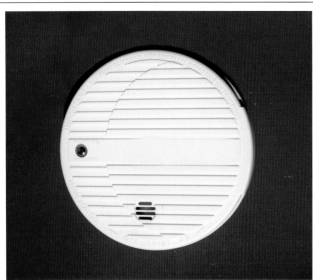

- Portable smoke detectors should be added to any home that does not have hard-wired smoke detectors.

- It is imperative that portable smoke detectors be mounted on the ceiling outside every bedroom and at the top of all stairways.

- Don't forget the top of attic and cellar stairways.

- Portable smoke detectors that run on batteries need to be checked and batteries should be replaced approximately every six months.

Hard-wired Smoke Detectors

- Hard-wired smoke detectors are required by law in all new homes, condominiums, and apartments. When an older building is sold, code may require their addition.

- Hard-wired units differ from portable detectors because they are wired into the home's electric grid for power, and, thus, do not need batteries.

- Although there are no batteries that need to be replaced, hard-wired smoke detectors should be checked and tested periodically.

fast-moving fires, and photoelectric alarms are better at sensing smoldering fires. Since both types of fires are potentially fatal, it is best to use both styles in the home. There are also dual sensor alarms that function as both ionization and photoelectric types in a single device. For people with hearing disabilities, units are available that feature flashing lights.

Replace batteries in portable alarms every six months to a year. When the smoke alarm makes a chirping noise, the battery should be replaced immediately. All smoke alarms should be tested on a monthly basis. It is recommended that smoke alarm units be replaced every eight to ten years.

A gas detector should also be installed when a sense of smell has declined. Early detection can significantly reduce the chance of a fire or explosion. Some units are relatively easy to install; others require a professional electrician. Detectors should be placed near the sources of gas. Some gas detectors require calibration to work properly. And like battery-operated smoke detectors, sensors can wear out over time. Check the instructions to determine the life of a gas detector.

Gas Detectors

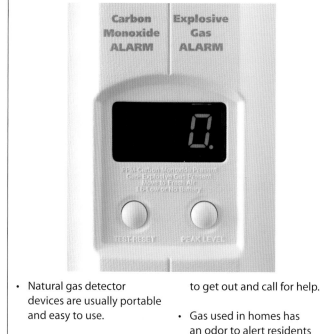

- Natural gas detector devices are usually portable and easy to use.

- Place a gas detector in the kitchen, near the gas water heater, and near a gas dryer as safety precautions.

- If there is a gas leak, the detector will alert residents to get out and call for help.

- Gas used in homes has an odor to alert residents to a leak, but noses lose their acuity with age and shouldn't be relied upon to detect all dangers.

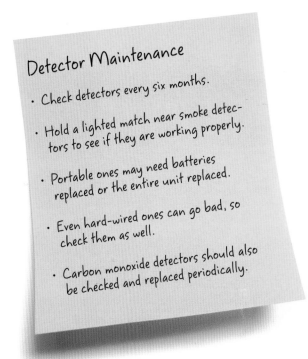

Detector Maintenance

- Check detectors every six months.

- Hold a lighted match near smoke detectors to see if they are working properly.

- Portable ones may need batteries replaced or the entire unit replaced.

- Even hard-wired ones can go bad, so check them as well.

- Carbon monoxide detectors should also be checked and replaced periodically.

HOME SECURITY

Enjoy security and peace of mind with a professionally installed and monitored alarm system

Residential security systems detect attempted or actual entry into the home by monitoring the opening of doors and windows. Systems with built-in sensors are also capable of detecting movement inside the home. Outdoor security systems are available to identify movement on the grounds surrounding the home, including the driveway, to offer

protection for vehicles that are not garaged.

When the system detects a breach of security, it can set off a number of events including a piercing siren or alarm sound, flashing lights, and communication to a monitoring agency or police department. The noise and lights are designed to alert the homeowner and neighbors of a break-in, draw

Windows Wired

- With most home security systems, the first floor windows are wired with sensors.

- Make sure the technicians are aware of windows that are usually kept open when the family is home or away.

- Ask the installers for specific instructions on how to activate and deactivate the system.

- In some two-story homes, upstairs windows may need to be wired to the security system as well.

Doors Secured

- Security systems provide protection for homeowners, especially for elder or those who live alone.

- All exterior doors should be part of the security alarm network. This includes interior garage doors and walkout basement doors.

- Security systems operate using motion sensors. They have different settings for when family members are home and when they are out of the house.

- The alarm should always be activated when the house is empty.

attention to the home, and scare off the intruder. The security company relays the address to the police department for immediate response.

Due to the many types of systems and options available, it is wise to consult a security professional to perform an assessment of the home and grounds. This way, vulnerable areas can be addressed and sensors can be placed at strategic locations within and outside the home.

The security system is only as good as the monitoring company whose service you hire.

If you have a wearable emergency call button, the alarm should ring to the same monitoring company as your home security.

Control Module

- The main control module is generally installed near the front door. Secondary units can be placed in a closet or by other commonly used doors.

- All occupants of the house should know the codes for system activation and deactivation. Residents should also learn the stress code for emergencies.

- People with dementia may have difficulty remembering the codes. Be sure the alarm monitoring company is aware of the situation.

Finding a Monitoring Company

- An emergency call button and the control module are only as good as the monitoring company they connect to.

- Use a company recommended by people whose judgment you trust. Why not ask a neighbor who they use?

- The security company may do emergency health monitoring as well as home security. If you have both, you want them to be with the same provider.

- The provider doesn't have to be local but does have to relay your call for help to your local ambulance and paramedic service quickly.

GARAGE DOOR OPENERS

Enjoy the comfort and safety of automatic access to a secure garage

Electronic garage door openers are a necessary convenience for most homeowners. They eliminate the need for lifting heavy doors, and make coming home in the rain or the dark much quicker and more comfortable.

The safety of a garage door opener adds to its convenience. When coming home alone at night, there is no need to get out of a running car and fumble in the dark to open the door. With a single push of a remote control button from the comfort of the car, the door opens. The car can then pull into the well-lit garage, where exiting the vehicle is more secure.

An electronic garage door opener can be added to most existing garage doors. There are several types of drive systems available that use different lifting mechanisms. A powerful screw drive system moves along a threaded steel rod. It has few moving parts and requires the least amount of maintenance. A chain drive system uses a metal chain to move the

Garage Door Opener

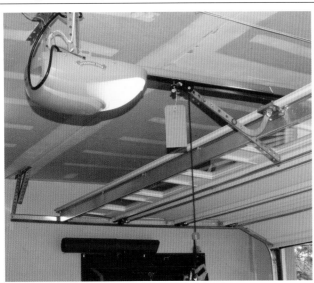

- An electric garage door opener allows remote operation of the door with the press of a button.

- The garage can be opened or closed from the car or a button on the garage wall near the door into the house.

- Newer electric garage doors are equipped with an electric eye that warns if there is an obstruction. The closing door immediately reverses direction.

- Older electric doors only stop if they make contact with an object.

In-car Opener Device

- To operate electric garage doors, a small remote control device is kept in the car. The button is pushed to open or close the door.

- The remote control device is battery operated so every few years it will need a battery replacement.

- The device comes with a clip for attaching to the windshield visor.

- If security is a concern, keep the remote control in the glove compartment.

door up and down along its tracks. This is the most common and usually least expensive system. A computer-controlled drive mechanism takes the least amount of space, leaving more room for ceiling storage.

If the electronic mechanism fails or there is a power failure, a release lever allows the garage door to be operated manually.

Outside Control Device

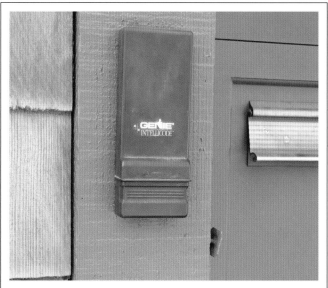

- An exterior control usually accompanies electric garage door openers. The control is often installed on the outside garage doorjamb.

- This can be a keyed device that works like any door lock. Insert and turn the key, and the garage door opens.

- Another kind of exterior module is a battery operated, programmable keypad. The garage opens or closes when the correct numbers are entered into the pad.

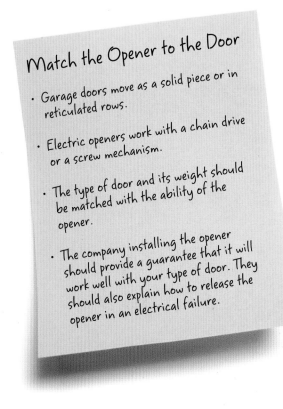

Match the Opener to the Door

- Garage doors move as a solid piece or in reticulated rows.

- Electric openers work with a chain drive or a screw mechanism.

- The type of door and its weight should be matched with the ability of the opener.

- The company installing the opener should provide a guarantee that it will work well with your type of door. They should also explain how to release the opener in an electrical failure.

OTHER ELEMENTS

211

ORGANIZING FOR TRAVEL
Make traveling more convenient with a few simple tips and gadgets

Traveling requires organization, especially when people get older or need assistance. More items need to be taken on trips, so additional systems should be put in place.

Many gadgets are available to make traveling more convenient. Portable versions of items used at home can be brought along. Foldable shower seats, smaller hair blowers, and adjustable folding walking canes are just some of the tools available to help make a retreat location feel like home.

To organize all the medicines and cosmetics needed, purchase a hanging toiletry bag with many pockets. This can be rolled up and taken on a plane if items will be needed during that part of the trip. It can also be hung on the back of a car seat during road trips.

If a trip will require walking, bring along a money belt or small purse that hangs around the neck and fits under the shirt. These are lighter, more compact, and much easier to

Back of Car Seat Organizers

- For people who require medication or mobility devices, taking a car trip requires organization. If there is no formal rest area along the way, be prepared for contingencies.

- A car organizer is perfect for people with medical issues. It contains many convenient compartments and hangs on the back of the front seat.

- Car organizers can hold a wide array of items to make traveling easier and more comfortable.

Package of Small Plastic Bottles

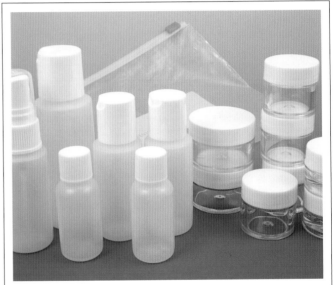

- Plane travel is burdensome for most people, but for those with medical issues, it is even more complicated.

- If it is necessary to carry liquid containers on board that exceed the allowable limit, bring a doctor's prescription to security.

- Bring a collection of small plastic bottles for non-prescription liquids you need to carry on the plane. Never decant any prescription medication into another bottle.

- Bottles of varying sizes and shapes can be bought at most drugstores.

carry than a traditional wallet or pocketbook. They are also safer because they are hidden from view.

For easiest travel, bring clothing in one color scheme so that everything mixes and matches.

Make sure to arrange for any out-of-town medical procedures—like dialysis or oxygen refills—well ahead of time.

Hanging Toiletry Organizer

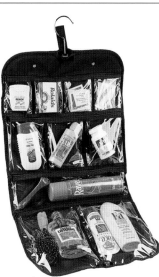

- Old age, infirmities, and ailments can make traveling light a challenge.

- A hangable toiletry organizer makes traveling easier and more comfortable. Always carry it aboard the plane with you. Remember to pack liquids separate for check-in.

- Use the organizer to hold medications and other important supplies.

- Include items that are used on a daily basis or in emergencies. Since organizers have limited space, prioritize supplies according to need and frequency.

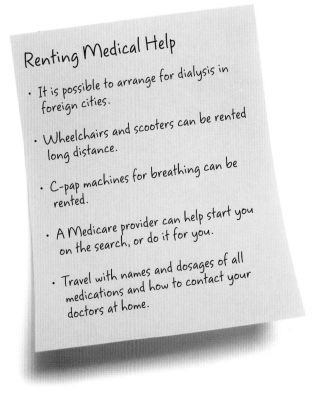

Renting Medical Help

- It is possible to arrange for dialysis in foreign cities.

- Wheelchairs and scooters can be rented long distance.

- C-pap machines for breathing can be rented.

- A Medicare provider can help start you on the search, or do it for you.

- Travel with names and dosages of all medications and how to contact your doctors at home.

213

ADAPTED TELEPHONES
New devices and services make calling quicker and easier

Traditional telephones present many challenges for anyone with limited sight, hearing challenges, or joint issues. But there are specialty telephones that solve any issue.

For those with minor hearing challenges, a phone with adjustable volume or a loudspeaker may be sufficient. When more aid is needed, look into TTY phone services. This special service for deaf and hearing-impaired people transcribes voice messages into print. The printed message is then transmitted to a device in the recipient's home. If seeing is also a challenge, the message can be printed in large type.

Portable phones make talking more comfortable because the speaker can sit or move wherever he or she wants without being restricted by wires. The downside is that these phones can be misplaced. If purchasing a portable phone, make sure there is a button on the base that will ring the missing phone so it can be easily located.

Speaker Phone

- Speaker phones amplify callers' voices, which can facilitate conversation for hearing-impaired individuals.

- Many modern telephones are equipped with speakers that can be activated by pressing a button.

- Using a speaker phone eliminates the need for holding the telephone to the ear. This can make conversing by telephone more relaxing.

- Some hearing aids beep if placed against a telephone. This is avoided by using speaker phones.

Large Button Phones

- Large button phones with big letters and numbers are a huge help to people with poor vision.

- They are often available free of charge from phone service providers. They are also available for purchase where other phones are sold or in office and electronic stores. An Internet search will provide a large variety of available large-button phones.

- Large buttons are not only easier to see, but also simpler and less painful on hands with fine motor skill challenges.

For visual and dexterity challenges, choose a phone with large number buttons. They are much easier to see and less of an ordeal to press.

When remembering phone numbers becomes more difficult, memory buttons are a savior. Store phone numbers in the phone one time, then whenever someone needs to be called, simply press the button labeled with his or her name.

TTY/Large Print

- TTY is a telephone service for deaf and hearing-impaired individuals. It transcribes voice messages into print, and then transmits the messages to a device in a recipient's home.

- It is now possible to get a machine that prints in large type, making it easier for people with poor vision to use the device.

- Human relay operators are intermediaries and interpret telephone messages between deaf and hearing individuals.

Help from Unexpected Sources

- Through federal, county, local, or independent non-profits, help can be available for retrofitting a home to accommodate handicaps.

- Some 700 area agencies on aging receive federal money to keep track of all the agencies providing services in their area.

- Service providers offer free or discounted items to encourage use of their services (e.g., free large-button telephones).

- Home sharing agencies match those with homes and space with those seeking discounted rent and willing to help out with cleaning, gardening, etc.

GARDEN LIGHTING

Add safety to the garden while enhancing the mood and creating architectural beauty

Spending time on the patio and in the garden can be a delight. Garden lighting allows you to enjoy the outdoors after dark.

Outdoor lights can be functional or aesthetic. The right combination will provide needed light for safety and enjoyment and beautifully enhance the garden area.

On patios and decks with steps, place lighting on vertical posts and recessed in the stair risers. This will allow you to navigate around the patio safely. Direct lights toward gates and door entries for secure entrance and egress. All walkways should be well illuminated so that walking is easy and comfortable.

Make Patios Safe to Use after Dark

- Install adequate lighting on the patio to ensure safety and optimize enjoyment.

- Upgrade the wattage if lights don't produce enough illumination for clarity and comfort. Halogen bulbs can be purchased specifically for outdoor use.

- Ensure all areas of the patio are sufficiently lit. Install lighting around potential hazards including uneven surfaces, steps, and surrounding ground.

- Motion sensor fixtures ensure lights are always on when people are present.

Going Green with Yard Lighting

- Solar lights are a cost-effective way to illuminate walkways and paths at night. They are more economical than hard-wired lights, although they may provide a weaker glow.

- Solar cell lights are self-contained units. The solar cell on the top collects and stores the sun's rays. When the sun sets, the unit emits light until the cell is depleted.

- After a sunny day, the units have enough capacity to last several hours before needing to be recharged by the sun.

Motion sensor lights are a good choice for patios and walkways. They light up as someone approaches, making the area safer to traverse while dissuading unwanted trespassers. Use them in all areas where potential intruders could lurk.

Economically place solar lights along walkways. They don't require any hard wiring. If a stronger, more reliable light is desired, have a professional install hard-wired lights along the path.

For architectural effect, place low-voltage outdoor lights under trees to create shadows and texture.

MAKE IT EASY

Ambient and Task Lighting: To create general illumination for comfortable and safe gardening at any time of the day, install floodlights high in trees or above the patio directed only on the area you wish to illuminate. Use several lights and overlap the light streams to soften potential shadows and create uniform lighting in recreation and activity areas.

Lights Only When You Need Them

- Outdoor light fixtures can work from sensors or from a wall switch inside the house.

- Sensors can be motion or light sensitive. Light sensor fixtures turn lights on when the sun sets.

- Both types of sensor units are ideal for front doors, patios, and the front of garages.

- Sensor lighting also enhances landscaping when directed on a tree or special group of plantings in a garden, illuminating it after dark.

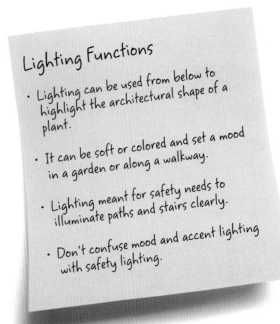

Lighting Functions

- Lighting can be used from below to highlight the architectural shape of a plant.

- It can be soft or colored and set a mood in a garden or along a walkway.

- Lighting meant for safety needs to illuminate paths and stairs clearly.

- Don't confuse mood and accent lighting with safety lighting.

LANDSCAPING & GARDENING

217

SOFTSCAPE VS. HARDSCAPE
The right balance creates beauty and accessibility

Inside the home, flooring can be arranged to ensure that movement is safe and effortless. The outside "flooring" is more challenging to arrange, but it is necessary to plan for safe garden accessibility. For a safe, enjoyable gardening environment, there needs to be a combination of softscaping and hardscaping.

A softscape is the horticultural, or living, elements of the landscape design. Flowers, vegetables, grass, and shrubs all make up the softscape. Softscapes should be complemented by hardscape design elements, like stone walls, brick walkways, wooden decks, and patios. These features not only add variety and beauty to a garden, but also provide safe ways for gardeners to get around. Balancing the softscape and hardscape in a garden creates beauty and balance.

For wheelchairs and walkers, walks and pathways should be created from concrete or pavers. Although packed dirt,

It's Easier to Move on Paving

- When designing a walkway, select lightly textured material for greater traction, especially when wet.

- Create a level walkway, with no height differences between corners, individual pavers, or pavement sections.

- Install walkways that are at least 36 inches wide to accommodate walkers and wheelchairs.

- Even if it isn't needed now, a wide, level walkway is ideal for comfortable aging in place.

When You Don't Want to Mow

- For a low-maintenance garden, ground cover can be a colorful addition; it requires less water than grass.

- Most ground cover has an uneven, spongy surface. Exercise caution when walking on ground cover. It is not recommended for wheelchairs or people with difficulty walking.

- To use ground cover between pavers, choose a compact, low-growing variety such as Irish or Scottish moss. Clip or mow it to keep it low.

gravel, and bark chip are all sturdier than natural grass or dirt, they are still too soft for wheelchair use and can cause accidents for those using walkers.

Pavers and bricks used for walkways and patios must be placed close together and packed securely in sand or concrete to reduce unevenness. Any flooring that is not even will be dangerous for people who shuffle, use canes, or are simply unsteady.

Install walkways and access routes between plantings so that flowers and trees can be enjoyed from all angles. An evening stroll through the garden can be delightful, especially if it is done on a safe surface.

Along the same lines, be sure to plant interesting, beautiful, fragrant flowers and trees around walkways and patios to make traveling through the garden—or simply resting in the yard—a feast for the senses.

The Luxury of a Lawn

- Grass is a universal favorite choice for gardens. Many people enjoy gazing across the expanse of a lush, green lawn.

- Grass is not an appropriate surface for individuals who have difficulty walking or those who use wheelchairs or walkers. For added safety, install a pathway through the lawn to traverse from one side to another.

- For access to planter beds around the garden's periphery, leave a hard-packed dirt path.

No-Mow Lawns

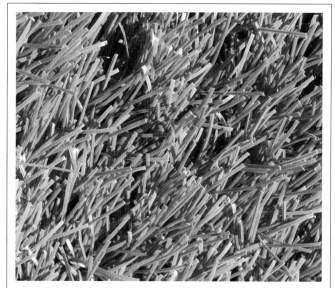

- Artificial grass is becoming more popular and has the appearance of an authentic, well-maintained lawn.

- Although it is expensive to purchase and install, artificial grass is low maintenance and provides long-term savings by eliminating the need for watering, fertilizing, edging, and mowing.

- Because artificial grass acts like a carpet, people in wheelchairs find it relatively easy to glide over it.

- The area is leveled before artificial grass is installed, so the danger of tripping is minimized.

219

LEVELS & TOPOGRAPHY

Managing levels in the backyard makes gardening safer and more enjoyable

Slopes, curves, and angles add beauty and character to a backyard, but they can also make gardening more difficult and potentially dangerous. Gardening is easiest when the yard is perfectly level and flat, but very few homes are situated on this type of property.

All yards are required to be sloped so they can drain easily.

Even if these differences in levels are slight, they may still pose risks and inconveniences when it comes to gardening. There are several ways a homeowner can minimize the negative impact that grade changes cause in the backyard. For example, by building a patio, a more level area can be attained. This is helpful for people with mobility challenges,

Slopes

- All gardens have some degree of slope so excess water can drain effectively.

- Lawns are designed to slope away from the house and toward a street or drainage area.

- Small properties with close-by neighbors may even have swales to take drainage to the street.

- Properties with steep slopes can be hard to navigate on unsteady legs or in a wheelchair.

Terraced Yards

- Consider adding a terrace to a sloping yard to compensate for the elevation change. Be sure there is still enough of a slope to properly drain rainwater.

- Use terrace edges to create raised planters for easy gardening from the lower ground.

- A raised bed eliminates bending and can be easily tended from a wheelchair.

- Level changes can make the view across a yard more varied and interesting.

especially those in wheelchairs.

Decks can do wonders to level off slopes. Even steep elevations can be evened out by building a deck to compensate for the changes in height. Landscape architects are brilliant at designing practical and aesthetically pleasing solutions to eliminate hazards and meet the requirements of homeowners.

Bending to tend beds might be difficult, but with the aid of a professional, the property can be re-graded to create terraces that can be used for flowers and vegetables. Terraces or elevated beds make some gardening tasks much easier and more accessible.

Bedding areas can be installed in areas of the yard that are more accessible and conducive to gardening. Making minor additions or adjustments in the natural landscape sometimes resolves physical challenges brought upon by varying levels. If you seek creative solutions, topography won't get in the way of enjoying the rewards of a vegetable or flower garden.

Decks with Planks Close Together

- Areas with large changes in elevation can be made usable by installing a wooden deck. Decks provide large functional areas to enhance enjoyment of a backyard.

- Decks are built on elevated posts of varying heights to ensure that they are level.

- Install wooden deck planks without spaces to minimize the risk of canes, walkers, and high heels getting caught.

- Wooden decks may require yearly maintenance to preserve their finish.

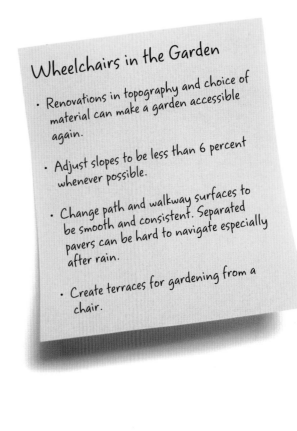

Wheelchairs in the Garden

- Renovations in topography and choice of material can make a garden accessible again.

- Adjust slopes to be less than 6 percent whenever possible.

- Change path and walkway surfaces to be smooth and consistent. Separated pavers can be hard to navigate especially after rain.

- Create terraces for gardening from a chair.

GARDENING WITH ARTHRITIS
Don't let arthritis get in the way of your hobbies

The pain of arthritis can take away the joy of gardening. But with some creativity, special gardening tools, and a bit of planning, gardening can be made easier.

Know your limitations. If bending and sitting low for long periods of time become too difficult on your joints, plan the garden with a raised flowerbed. Keep a bench nearby for comfortable sitting.

Plan to garden during the times of day when you feel your best. To get your body ready for gardening activities, warm up your joints and muscles by taking a walk and stretching first. The extra preparation will make for a much more enjoyable gardening experience.

There are many specially adapted tools available that make gardening easier for people with arthritis. Choose lightweight tools with thick, padded handles. Ergonomically angled garden trowels keep the hand and wrist in a natural position

Good Grip Tools

- Padded tools with large handles make gardening easier for people with arthritic hands. Several manufacturers make these tools, so choose one that has a comfortable grip.

- Instead of bending over using a small hand shovel, consider starting with a long-handled shovel or transplanting spade. When the soil is loosened, change to the hand tool.

- Allow natural body weight to help in gardening tasks. This alleviates some of the handwork.

Knee Pads for Gardening

- Kneeling can be uncomfortable, so consider using knee pads if gardening tasks require working at ground level.

- Store-bought knee pads are worn around the knees so they do not need to be lifted from place to place around the garden.

- Makeshift knee pads can be created from several folded towels, but they are not waterproof and need to be moved for each new task.

while digging. Long-reach hoes and forks allow for gardening without stooping. Tools with enlarged handles require less hand strength.

Add arm support cuffs to small digging instruments. This takes the strain off the hand, allowing the arm's strength to be used.

To make kneeling and rising gentler on the joints, use a kneeler with sidebars and wear knee pads.

Long-handled Digging Tools

- Long-handled garden tools allow body weight to assist in the garden work, alleviating strain on the back and hands.

- A transplanting spade or long-handled shovel can replace a hand shovel for turning soil or digging holes. Switch to the hand-held tool when a firm grip is not needed to move dirt.

- A long rake or cultivator is easier on the back and hands than a handheld hoe.

Power Edger

- Power tools are now available for most tasks in the garden. Power edgers make lawn maintenance much less strenuous.

- Electric-powered edgers provide continuous energy, but can only go as far as the cord will allow. Gas-powered edgers are not limited to a specific distance, but they do need to be refilled.

- A power edger requires a sturdy grip.

- Keep the blade away from the body, and avoid getting close to healthy plants and flowers.

LANDSCAPING & GARDENING

223

PRACTICAL MOBILITY SOLUTIONS

No need to give up hobbies when there are solutions

Mobility challenges may cause gardening to be difficult, but by making a few adaptations, gardening enjoyment can continue.

Be sure all pathways are level and easy to navigate and wide enough for you and your tools.

If digging, lifting, and bending is a challenge, purchase adaptive, gardening tools. Most garden implements offer lightweight alternatives. Long handles allow for digging and weeding without bending over.

For an easily accessible garden, add a raised garden bed two or three feet above ground level. It can become a choice flower or herb garden with less bending required. Keep the bed no more than 3 or 4 feet wide so it can be reached from either side. This is the same idea as creating terraces in a sloped lawn and using the terrace top as a raised planter bed.

Automatic Sprinkler

- In regions where rain does not fall regularly, gardens need water to remain healthy.

- An automatic sprinkler is a good solution for people with physical limitations or memory difficulties, or with other things to do with their time.

- Sprinkler heads connect to a central electric control, which can be manually operated or programmed for automatic use.

- The control can be programmed to water the lawn as often and for as long as necessary.

Flex Hose Lines for Pots on Timer

Water lines fit right into pot

- For people with difficulty remembering, physical limitations, or busy travel schedules, watering flowerpots with a timed watering system solve this problem.

- Automatic watering systems can be connected to ⅛-inch to ¼-inch tubing. The tubing is attached to a special sprinkler head that feeds water to pots as far away as the tubing will reach.

- This is a great option for balcony and porch pots not exposed to rainfall.

Automate as many of the gardening chores as you can. Automatic sprinklers and drip irrigation can help in arid regions. Automate watering flower pots outside.

Consider purchasing a rolling garden vehicle that is small enough to wheel through a garden path and strong enough to carry garden supplies. A lightweight wheelbarrel with sturdy handles is perfect. Devise a way to hang things on a wheelchair or on a cart to make transporting equipment easier.

Window boxes are an easy, fun way to enjoy gardening without any of the major difficulties. There is a large selection of sizes and styles available at garden centers and nurseries.

Raised Planter Bed Gardening

- When leveling a slope, create a raised bed by using the excess dirt as fill behind a wooden support.

- If creating a raised bed from scratch, use potting soil to fill the bed. This provides a healthier growing environment.

- A raised bed eliminates the need for kneeling or squatting when working.

- A 24- to 30-inch high bed is comfortably accessible from a wheelchair.

Use Carpenter's Apron

- Carrying tools, fertilizer, gloves, and plants is hard on arthritic hands. It can also be a burden on a person prone to lose track of tools.

- A carpenter's apron can hold common gardening items. It is made of sturdy material and has many pockets around its hem.

- Garden tools can be stored in the apron, which can be hung on a hook in the garage or garden room ready for the next use.

GARDENING ALTERNATIVES

When outdoor gardening presents challenges, consider more convenient options that provide similar enjoyment

The lack of appropriate space or the right outdoor tools does not mean you can't enjoy gardening. Indoor and container gardening provide the same opportunities for fulfillment.

Elevated, portable garden beds are easily accessible from a wheelchair and are much more comfortable for anyone who has trouble kneeling or stooping for long periods of time. Some portable gardens are designed for the indoors. Some are even on wheels, so they can be moved around as desired.

Window boxes are traditionally used to bring color and life to the exterior of windows, but they can also be hung on the interior of the window or placed on a wide sill to add pizzazz

Gardening in Pots

- People with limited mobility or small outdoor spaces can still enjoy the pleasures of gardening.

- Many plants can be grown successfully in pots with proper watering and use of fertilizer. A wide range of options is available for people who enjoy gardening in pots.

- Dwarf fruit trees and other interesting plantings can be purchased at many nurseries. Some flourish quite well in pots.

Indoor Gardens

- For those who are homebound, indoor container gardening can be a way to enjoy an old hobby.

- Place plants throughout the home where there is appropriate sunlight to sustain them.

- Indoor plants need a safe place for excess water to collect. A saucer is perfect for this task.

- Large indoor pots can be placed on plastic trays with wheels so they are mobile.

to any area. It is quick and easy to take care of plants and flowers in window boxes. When using them on the inside, choose materials that coordinate with the décor and will not leak on the flooring. Window planters come in many shapes and sizes, and are available in wrought iron, wood, vinyl, copper, bronze, and aluminum.

Tending to an indoor herb garden is not only enjoyable, but appetizing, as well. Cooks can add their homegrown flavors to daily meals, saving money and creating a sense of fulfillment. Herb gardens can run from simple—a small pot or two

on the windowsill—to extravagant, an entire garden of herbs outside the patio window.

A flowerpot can be a miniature garden. Since pots can be placed wherever is convenient, and plants can be found to match the light provided, nurturing the tiny gardens can be pleasing.

Consider indoor gardening so you can continue to enjoy your cherished hobby.

Interior Plant Lights

- Plants can be maintained indoors in pots or planters without sunlight if special plant lights are used.

- Plant lights can be turned on daily to simulate the sunshine that the plants are not getting.

- To minimize utility costs, occasionally move the plants to a window to reduce the need for plant lights.

- Lights can be put on an automatic timer to save energy and ensure sufficient light when required.

A Place to Work

- Ideally, every gardener should have a garden room with a sink and a counter.

- Gardeners need to create a counter space where they can re-pot plants or set up a flat of seedlings.

- Work counters should be 32 to 40 inches high. If creating a separate counter is not feasible, a patio pass-through window or a workbench in the garage will suffice.

RESOURCE DIRECTORY

Chapter 1: Life Cycles

About-Dementia.com
www.About-Dementia.com

Alzheimer's Association
www.alz.org/index.asp

American Academy of Audiology
www.audiology.org

American Foundation for the Blind
www.afb.org

Arthritis Foundation
www.arthritis.org

Disability Systems
www.disabilitysystems.com

ForgettingThePill.com
www.forgettingthepill.com

Good Grips
www.oxo.com

Google
www.Google.com

National Multiple Sclerosis Society
www.nationalmssociety.org

Oreck
www.oreck.com

***Seniorresource*.com/Aging in Place**
www.SeniorResource.com/ageinpl.htm

Walking Equipment
www.walkingequipment.com

Chapter 2: Entries & Doorways

Andersen
www.andersenwindows.com

Chamberlain
www.liftmaster.com

Disability Systems
www.disabilitysystems.com

Genie
www.geniecompany.com

H.I.S.
www.thehis.com

Jeld Wen Windows & Doors
www.jeld.wen.com

R&R Mobility Vans & Lifts, Inc.
www.rrvan.com

Schlage
http://consumer.schlage.com

VMI
www.vantageminivans.com/

Chapter 3: Flooring Treatment

3-M Rug tape
http://multimedia.3m.com

Bane – Clene Systems
www.baneclene.com

Chilewich
www.chilewich.com

RESOURCES

GelPro
www.gelpro.com

J.C. Penney
www.4.jcpenney.com

MatsMatsMats.com
www.matsmatsmats.com

Chapter 4: Kitchen Work Surfaces

Formica Group
www.formica.com

Franke
www.frankekitchensinks.com

Home Depot
www.homedepot.com

KitchenAid
www.kitchenaid.com

KitchenWorks
www.kitchenworks.com

Kohler
www.us.kohler.com/onlinecatalog/

Staron Surfaces
www.staron.com

Thomasville
www.ThomasvilleCabinetry.com

Viking
www.viking.com

Chapter 5: Kitchen Storage

Amerock
www.amerock.com

The Container Store
www.containerstore.com

HomeCrest Cabinetry
www.homecrestcab.com

International Association of Certified Home Inspectors
www.nachi.org

Online Organizing
www.onlineorganizing.com

Organize.com
www.organize.com

Pot Racks Online
www.pot-racks-online.com

Safety1st
www.safety1st.com

Stacks and Stacks
www.stacksandstacks.com

Storables
www.storables.com

Thomasville
www.ThomasvilleCabinetry.com

TotSafe.com
www.totsafe.com

U.S Consumer Product Safety Commission
www.cpsc.gov

Chapter 6: Kitchen Appliances

Frigidaire
www.frigidaire.com/default.aspx

General Electric
www.geappliances.com

KitchenAid
www.kitchenaid.com

Sears
www.sears.com

Silestone by Cosentino
www.silestoneusa.com/index/

Chapter 7: Arthritis Hand Aids

Arthritis Foundation
http://community.arthritis.org

Brookstone
www.brookstone.com

The Container Store
www.containerstore.com

EZoff
www.jaropener.com

Good Grips
www.oxo.com

Kohler Company
www.kohler.com

Sunbeam
www.sunbeam.com

Wise Choices
www.wise4living.com/khcarpet/electric-broom.htm

Chapter 8: Bathroom Fixtures

The Alzheimer's Store
www.alzstore.com

American Standard
www.americanstandard-us.com

Amerock
www.amerock.com

Clarity/Ameriphone
www.clarityproducts.com

Corian
www.corian.com

Kohler Company
www.kohler.com

Nexternal
http://store.nexternal.com

Pioneer Security
www.pioneeremergency.com

TOTO
www.performancetoilets.com

Chapter 9: Tubs & Showers

AmBath
www.ambath.com

Amazon.com
www.amazon.com

American Standard
www.americanstandard-us.com

Cherryville, North Carolina
www.cherryville.com

Independent Living USA, LLC
www.usatubs.com

Kohler Company
www.kohler.com

Moen Incorporated
www.moen.com

Safety Tubs
www.safetytubs.com

YES I CAN
YesICan.com

Chapter 10: Living & Dining Rooms

About.com
http://interiordec.about.com/od/lightingbasics/

American Foundation for the Blind
www.afb.org

Dixieline ProBuild
www.dixieline.com

KidSmartLiving
www.kidsmartliving.com/fursecandsaf.html

Safety1st
www.safety1st.com

TotSafe.com
www.totsafe.com

Chapter 11: Home Office & Den

Brookstone
www.brookstone.com

The Container Store
www.containerstore.com

Cost Plus World Market
www.worldmarket.com

Frys Electronics
www.frys.com

Ikea
www.ikea.com

KidSmartLiving
www.kidsmartliving.com/fursecandsaf.html

Staples, Inc.
www.staples.com

Chapter 12: Bedrooms

Angel Accessibility Solutions
www.angelsolutions.com/index.cfm

Bed Bath & Beyond
www.bedbathandbeyond.com

Cost Plus World Market
www.costplus.com

PHC-online
www.phc-online.com

Pioneer Security
www.pioneeremergency.com/medical-alert.shtml

TempurPedic
www.tempurpedic.com

Chapter 13: Storage & Organizing

Aaron Brothers
www.aaronbrothers.com

Brookstone
www.brookstone.com

The Container Store
www.containerstore.com

Home Depot
www.homedepot.com

Chapter 14: Halls & Stairs

About.com: Interior Decorating
http://interiordec.about.com/od/lightingbasics/a/Grecessedlights.html

AmeriGlide Stair Lifts
www.ameriglide.com

Disability Systems
www.disabilitysystems.com

Econol Lift Corp.
Cedar Falls, IA; 319-277-4777

Inclinator
www.inclinator.com/

Lowe's
http://www.lowes.com/lowes/lkn?action=howTo&p=Repair/RepElecSwtch.html

Lutron Electronics
www.lutron.com

San Diego Elevator, Inc.
760-268-0826

Sunset
http://search.sunset.com/

eMedicineHealth
www.emedicinehealth.com

50+ Housing Council of the National Association of Home Builders
www.nahb.com

J.C. Penney
www.4.jcpenney.com

Macular Degeneration Foundation
www.eyesights.org

Pantone, Inc.
www.pantone.com

Chapter 15: Color Considerations

Alzheimer's Association
www.alz.org

American Foundation for the Blind
www.afb.org

ECO House
www.ecohaus.com

Chapter 16: Windows & Treatments

Bravo Screens
www.bravoscreens.com

General Electric
www.ge.com

Home Depot
www.homedepot.com

RESOURCES

Hunter Douglass
www.hunterdouglass.com

Milgard Windows
www.milgard.com

Quality Solar Screens
www.qualitysolarscreen.com/faq.html

Pella
http://web.pella.com/products/DoorStyles

Solatube
www.solatube.com

Chapter 17: Lighting

Home Depot
www.homedepot.com

Lighting Orient Lighting Solutions
www.ledlightsorient.com

Pacific Sales
www.pacificsales.com

Safety1st
www.safety1st.com

TotSafe.com
www.totsafe.com

Chapter 18: Other Elements

American Foundation for the Blind
www.afb.org

The Container Store
www.containerstore.com

CVS Pharmacy
www.cvs.com

Genie Company
www.geniecompany.com

Home Depot
www.homedepot.com

OnlinePhoneStore.com
http://specialneeds.onlinephonestore.com

Panasonic Corporation
www.panasonic.com

Pioneer Emergency
www.pioneeremergency.com

Sears
www.sears.com

Travel Smith Inc.
www.travelsmith.com

Chapter 19: Landscaping & Gardening

Brookstone
www.brookstone.com

Good Grip Tools
www.oxo.com

Home Depot
www.homedepot.com

Indoor Plant Lighting
http://retirees.uwaterloo.ca/~jerry/orchids/light.html

Sunset Magazine
www.sunset.com

Yard Lover
www.yardlover.com

GLOSSARY

Agility: Ability to move easily, smoothly, and/or quickly. Usually refers to ambulation but may be used in reference to hand ability or dexterity.

Alzheimer's Disease: A disease that causes progressive brain dysfunction. It is one of the most common causes of decreased brain function. Alzheimer's dementia is a progressive mental deterioration that is more common as people reach late age and is associated with memory loss, language problems, and personality changes.

Ambient Lighting: Lighting in a room or area in general, versus spot or targeting lighting for tasks. Often refers to light cast from windows and skylights, although it can refer to general ceiling illumination for a large area.

Arthritis: A group of diseases that involve inflammation or damage to joints of the body making movement of affected parts difficult.

Banister Rail: A rail supported by posts secured to stairs or attached to a stairwell wall that follows the edge of a stairwell. It is a safety feature, although can be quite decorative.

Bed Transfer Slings: A fabric sling suspended from a movable device attached to the ceiling beams that enables someone supported in the sling to be moved, mechanically, from a wheelchair or side chair into a bed. Getting into and out of the sling requires human effort.

Bifocals/Trifocals: Eyeglass lenses made in two or three parts by different grindings. The top portion is for distance focusing and the bottom is for close focusing such as reading. In trifocals the middle grind accommodates mid-distance focusing.

Bullnose (in reference to countertop edging): A rounded convex edge that forms the edge of a counter top.

Cadillac Toilet: Refers to any toilet that offers fancy trappings beyond the normal flushing and carrying away the waste, i.e., some toilets double as a bidet, cleaning the user, and eliminating the need for the use of toilet paper.

Cans: Ceiling installed canisters that are electrical fixtures and hold a flood type bulb, Halogen or LED.

Ceiling Floods: Interior flood lights (bulbs) used in specific canisters that are recessed into the ceiling into the space between floors. They can hold bulbs meant to provide ambient light or spot targeted, task lighting.

Chair Rail: Originally a molding strip installed on a wall at the height of a chair back preventing the chair from being moved back into the wall. It can be used as a design element to separate the finish of the lower wall from the upper wall.

Corian (Countertops): A E. I. du Pont de Nemours trademarked product made of a synthetic composite that is relatively impervious to stains. Sometimes used to define a type of synthetic countertop material that may be similarly durable, but of a different patent.

Dementia: A mental condition from any one of a variety of causes marked by functional loss, memory loss, and at least one other brain impairment, such as language or visual-spatial orientation problems.

Easy Chair: A chair in which to lounge or relax.

Edge Seat (in reference to showers): A tub edge that is wide and flat enough for someone to sit upon it at least temporarily while transferring into or out of the tub/shower.

Emergency Call Buttons: Buttons, whether worn or device mounted, that connect through hard wire or airwaves transmission to a central location that responds or sets response in motion.

Ergonomic Design: Maximization of interface between worker and equipment or environment for efficiency and ease of use.

Flip Windows: Windows that do not slide up and down or sideways but rather flip on an axis from inside to outside. They facilitate cleaning of both sides of the glass from inside, and can be set at an angle to provide 100 percent exposure to the outside air since 50 percent of them are not a fixed pane.

Fluorescent Lighting: Bulbs common in industrial and commercial settings, kitchens, and bathrooms. They have been adapted from their original shape of long and cylindrical to be able to fit in normally incandescent fixtures. They consume considerably less electricity for the amount of light emitted than incandescent bulbs, at economic prices. They generally require an open fixture.

Formica (Countertops): A composite, patented material of the Formica Corporation, used for countertops for more that 30 years. It is relatively inexpensive, but may be subject to cuts and stains on its surface.

Galley Kitchens: Kitchens that are long and narrow with cabinets and appliances along both sides, reminiscent of what one would expect in a boat's kitchen.

Good Grip: A brand of tools for the home or garden with padded handles and ergonomic engineering manufactured by OXO International, Ltd.

Grab Bar: A securely mounted bar that has space between it and the wall behind to be grasped firmly. It is used alongside a toilet or inside or next to a tub or shower to facilitate safe sitting, standing, and stepping.

Handicap: A disability that distinguishes one from the population "norm."

Hardscapes: Outside surfaces that are firm for walking, i.e., paving, stones, wooden decks.

LED Bulbs: Offer great longevity and their solid composition (unlike a filament incandescent bulb) makes them less breakable. They are still relatively expensive for the amount of light emitted.

Levers (in reference to door handles, etc.): Door openers that do not have to be gripped firmly to open the door latch; they require a downward pressure, not the torque required for a door "knob."

Linear Elements (reference found in color considerations chapter): Design or color elements that run in straight lines, versus circular or random patterns, or solids.

Lock Box: A box that hangs on an exterior door handle that has designated, limited access (i.e., the fire department, or the Real Estate multiple listing association) within which a house key is kept.

Mobility: The quality of moving about freely.

Monitor Magnifier: A magnified glass that specifically fits in front of a computer screen to enlarge images beyond the capability of the program being viewed.

Parkinson's Disease: One of several motor system disorders caused by the loss of dopamine-producing brain cells. It manifests itself in tremors, stiffness, slowness of movements, and falls. Parkinson's disease can be associated with dementia or depression.

Portable Call Buttons: See Emergency Call Buttons above. When worn on a bracelet or around the neck as a necklace, it is "portable."

Pre-fab Fiberglass Showers: One piece pre-formed shower stalls of a fiberglass material. They are installed as a seamless unit in a space plumbed for their faucet and drain openings.

Pull Cords (in reference to emergencies in bathrooms): An emergency button may be difficult to reach in a shower or alongside a bed, but a cord hanging from the central control provides a wider range of access.

Recessed Lighting: Lighting installed above the level of the ceiling.

Retractable Screens: Screens that roll to one side into a tube. They are used with floor-to-ceiling slider glass doors so that when the door is closed and the screen not needed, no screen is visible. When the door is opened the screen unrolls as it is pulled across the opening and fastened to remain stretched across the opening.

Safety Glass: Sandwiches a thin layer of flexible clear plastic film between pieces of glass that holds the glass in place should it be impacted. The film can also stretch with the glass sticking to it, making it quite difficult to penetrate laminated safety glass. Some residential window placements are dictated to require safety glass.

Sculpted Pile: Carpeting with the pile or nap "carved" at varying heights into an all-over pattern that presents a sculpted appearance.

Silestone (Countertops): A man-made composite of, among other things, ground quartz suggesting the look of marble or granite. It is durable and stain resistant and does not require periodic sealing.

Sliders (doors, screens): Refers to sliding glass doors that are floor to above head height (or almost to the ceiling) and usually provide access to a patios or balconies. May refer to the type of large screen that covers the same area as the large glass sliding doors.

Softscapes: Garden areas that are planted or dirt.

Solatube: A trademarked tube installed from the ceiling to the roof above. A prism inside the tube intensifies the light coming inside to much more than you would normally get from a 12" diameter skylight.

Stairwell Lift: A specific kind of elevator or lift that spans the width of a staircase. When at the top or bottom, its platform can be walked upon to access the stairs.

Task Lighting: Light that focuses on a spot or area to illuminate it while a task is being performed, i.e., reading, food preparation.

Track Lighting: Lighting fixtures installed on a track, and movable along that track. It is usually installed on ceilings, but some can be placed on a vertical surface. It can be wired into an outlet through the internal walls, or can have a cord to plug into an outlet.

Traffic Flow: The expected path people take when moving through a space or room.

Transfer Board (in reference to showers/wheelchair needs): A laminated board made for supporting the weight of someone who needs to scoot along on his or her bottom to get from a chair outside the tub or shower onto a seat inside the tub or shower.

Triangle Work Space (in reference to kitchen design): The spacing of sink, stove, and refrigerator is believed to be most efficient if placed as points of a triangle.

TTY Phone Services: A TeleTypwriter that converts voice to printed word and vice versa used in the home of the hearing or speech impaired.

Universal Design: Design that makes areas and devices universally accessible and usable. It means the environment is barrier free or that it uses assistive technology.

Waffle Pads (in reference to beds/mattresses): Foam pads that are made in a regular pattern of high and low spots—thicker and thinner spaces. They are used to relieve pressure on body part because as you shift different parts rest on the high spots.

Wall-mounted (ovens, faucets, etc.): Appliances that are mounted into a vertical surface instead of a horizontal one, or in the case of ovens, in a free-standing stove.

Wheelchair Accessible: An area that presents no barriers to wheeled transport: i.e., level, or a ramp that spans the stairs at a shallow angle. The area provides sufficient area for the wheelchair to rotate freely without hitting walls, doors, or furniture.

PHOTO CREDITS

Chapter 1: Life Cycles

vii (left): Photographed by Mark Davidson at Sun City Shadow Hills by Del Webb

vii (right): © Christopher Nuzzaco | Dreamstime.com

2 (left): Courtesy of Oxo

3 (left): Photographed by Mark Davidson at Sun City Shadow Hills by Del Webb

4 (left): © Joggie Botma | Dreamstime.com

4 (right): Photographed by Mark Davidson at Sun City Shadow Hills by Del Webb

5 (left): Photographed by Mark Davidson at Sun City Shadow Hills by Del Webb

7 (left): © Erwin Wodicka | Shutterstock

8 (left): © Alon-o | Dreamstime.com

8 (right): © Tmcnem | Dreamstime.com

9 (right): Courtesy of www.rollaramp.com

10 (left): © Marilyn Zelinsky-Syarto

Chapter 2: Entries & Doorways

12 (left): Photographed by Mark Davidson at Sun City Shadow Hills by Del Webb

12 (right): Photographed by Mark Davidson at Sun City Shadow Hills by Del Webb

13 (left): © Galushko Sergey | Shutterstock

13 (right): Anna Adesanya

15 (right): Photographed by Mark Davidson at Sun City Shadow Hills by Del Webb

18 (left): Photographed by Mark Davidson at Sun City Shadow Hills by Del Webb

18 (right): Photographed by Mark Davidson at Sun City Shadow Hills by Del Webb

19 (left): Photographed by Mark Davidson at Sun City Shadow Hills by Del Webb

19 (right): © Kingjon | Dreamstime.com

21 (left): Photographed by Mark Davidson at Sun City Shadow Hills by Del Webb

21 (right): Photographed by Mark Davidson at Sun City Shadow Hills by Del Webb

22 (left): © Shawn_tsk | Dreamstime.com

22 (right): © Shawn_tsk | Dreamstime.com

23 (right): Photographed by Mark Davidson at Sun City Shadow Hills by Del Webb

Chapter 3: Flooring Treatments

24 (left): Photographed by Mark Davidson at Sun City Shadow Hills by Del Webb

24 (right): Photographed by Mark Davidson at Sun City Shadow Hills by Del Webb

25 (left): © pics721 | Shutterstock

25 (right): Photographed by Mark Davidson at Sun City Shadow Hills by Del Webb

26 (left): Photographed by Mark Davidson at Sun City Shadow Hills by Del Webb

26 (right): Courtesy of Merida Meridan

27 (left): Photographed by Mark Davidson at Sun City Shadow Hills by Del Webb

27 (right): Courtesy of Green Building Supply

28 (left): Photographed by Mark Davidson at Sun City Shadow Hills by Del Webb

28 (right): © Majaphoto | Dreamstime.com

29 (left): © Barbara Krueger. Photographed at home of Mr. & Mrs. Horace Dietrich.

30 (left): Photographed by Mark Davidson at Sun City Shadow Hills by Del Webb

31 (right): Photographed by Mark Davidson at Sun City Shadow Hills by Del Webb

32 (left): Courtesy of GelPro

32 (right): Courtesy of Victor Schrager for Chilewich

33 (left): Courtesy of Green Building Supply

33 (right): © Britishbeef | Dreamstime.com

34 (left): Courtesy of FibreWorks

34 (right): Courtesy of Expanko Inc.

35 (left): Courtesy of Expanko Inc.

35 (right): © Dragan Trifunovic | Dreamstime.com

Chapter 4: Kitchen Work Surfaces

36 (left): © Crodenberg | Dreamstime.com

36 (right): Photo Courtesy of Thomasville Cabinetry

37 (left): © Soniak | Dreamstime.com

38 (left): © RazoomGame | Shutterstock

38 (right): Courtesy of Formica Group

39 (left): Photo Courtesy of Thomasville Cabinetry

40 (right): Courtesy of Kohler Co.

41 (left): Courtesy of Kohler Co.

41 (right): Courtesy of Kohler Co.

42 (left): © Lisa Turay | Dreamstime.com

42 (right): © Barbara Krueger

44 (left): Photo Courtesy of Thomasville Cabinetry

45 (left): © Marzanna Syncerz | Dreamstime.com

46 (left): Courtesy of Kohler Co.

46 (right): Courtesy of Kohler Co.

47 (left): Courtesy of Kohler Co.

47 (right): Courtesy of Kitchen Aid

Chapter 5: Kitchen Storage

48 (right): Courtesy of The Container Store

49 (left): Courtesy of Diamond Cabinets

49 (right): Courtesy of The Container Store

50 (left): © Wollwerth | Dreamstime.com

50 (right): Courtesy of Diamond Cabinets

51 (left): Courtesy of Diamond Cabinets

51 (right): Photo Courtesy of Thomasville Cabinetry

52 (left): Courtesy of The Container Store
52 (right): © Barbara Krueger
53 (left): © Barbara Krueger
53 (right): Photo Courtesy of Thomasville Cabinetry
54 (left): Photographed by Mark Davidson at Sun City Shadow Hills by Del Webb
54 (right): Courtesy of Crown Point Cabinetry
55 (left): Courtesy of HomeCrest Cabinetry
55 (right): Courtesy of Amerock
56 (right): Photo Courtesy of Thomasville Cabinetry
57 (left): Courtesy of Diamon
57 (right): © Barbara Krueger. Photographed at home of Drs. Krueger and Rodgers
58 (right): © Dorel Juvenile Group 2008. All Rights Reserved.
59 (left): © Milkos | Dreamstime.com
59 (right): © Foment | Dreamstime.com

Chapter 6: Kitchen Appliances
60 (left): Courtesy of Frigidaire
60 (right): Photographed by Mark Davidson at Sun City Shadow Hills by Del Webb
61 (left): © Ranguita | Dreamstime.com
62 (right): Photographed by Mark Davidson at Sun City Shadow Hills by Del Webb
63 (left): © Flashkralove | Dreamstime.com
63 (right): Photographed by Mark Davidson at Sun City Shadow Hills by Del Webb
64 (right): Courtesy of Viking
65 (left): Courtesy of Wolf Appliances
66 (right): © Anthony Berenyi | Dreamstime.com
67 (left): © Ginger Monteleone | Dreamstime.com
68 (left): Photographed by Mark Davidson at Sun City Shadow Hills by Del Webb
68 (right): Courtesy of Maytag
69 (left): Courtesy of GE

69 (right): © photos.com
70 (right): © John Keith | Dreamstime.com
71 (left): Photographed by Mark Davidson at Sun City Shadow Hills by Del Webb
71 (right): Photographed by Mark Davidson at Sun City Shadow Hills by Del Webb

Chapter 7: Arthritis Hand Aids
72 (left): Photographed by Mark Davidson at Sun City Shadow Hills by Del Webb
73 (right): © Marilyn Zelinsky-Syarto
74 (right): Photographed by Mark Davidson at Sun City Shadow Hills by Del Webb
75 (left): © Newphotoservice | Dreamstime.com
76 (left): © Batman2000 | Dreamstime.com
76 (right): © William Casey | Dreamstime.com
77 (left): © Shutterstock
77 (right): © Serghei Starus | Shutterstock
78 (left): Courtesy of Oxo
78 (right): © Barbara Krueger
79 (left): Courtesy of Oxo
79 (right): © Enruta | Dreamstime.com
80 (left): © Shariff Che' Lah | Dreamstime.com
80 (right): © Krzysztof Chrystowski | Dreamstime.com
81 (left): © Brookstone's Rechargeable Wine Opener
81 (right): Courtesy of Bed Bath & Beyond
82 (left): © Mark Stout | Dreamstime.com
82 (right): © Xphantom | Dreamstime.com
83 (right): © Borislav Gnjidic | Shutterstock

Chapter 8: Bathroom Fixtures
84 (left): © Borislav Gnjidic | Shutterstock
84 (right): Photographed by Mark Davidson at Sun City Shadow Hills by Del Webb
85 (left): Photographed by Mark Davidson at Sun City Shadow Hills by Del Webb

85 (right): Photographed by Mark Davidson at Sun City Shadow Hills by Del Webb
86 (left): Photographed by Mark Davidson at Sun City Shadow Hills by Del Webb
86 (right): Photographed by Mark Davidson at Sun City Shadow Hills by Del Webb
87 (left): Photographed by Mark Davidson at Sun City Shadow Hills by Del Webb
87 (right): Device courtesy of Ageless Design, Inc./The Alzheimer's Store. Photo © Mishoo | Dreamstime.com
88 (left): Photographed by Mark Davidson at Sun City Shadow Hills by Del Webb
88 (right): Photographed by Mark Davidson at Sun City Shadow Hills by Del Webb
89 (right): © Jorgeantonio | Dreamstime.com
90 (left): © Sorsillo | Dreamstime.com
90 (right): Courtesy of Kohler Co.
91 (left): © Baloncici | Dreamstime.com
91 (right): Mark Davidson
92 (right): JACLO's Luxury Grab Bar Collection
94 (right): © Cruphoto | Dreamstime.com
95 (right): Courtesy of Clarity

Chapter 9: Tubs & Showers
96 (left): Courtesy of Safety Tubs
97 (left): Courtesy of American Standard Brands
97 (right): © Aleksandar Kamasi | Dreamstime.com
98 (left): © Teresa Azevedo | Shutterstock
98 (right): Courtesy of Kohler Co.
99 (left): Courtesy of Moen Incorporated
99 (right): Photographed by Mark Davidson at Sun City Shadow Hills by Del Webb
100 (left): © Lisafx | Dreamstime.com
100 (right): © Barbara Krueger. Photographed at home of Mr. & Mrs. Jay Krueger.
101 (left): Courtesy of Kohler Co.

102 (left): Photographed by Mark Davidson at Sun City Shadow Hills by Del Webb

102 (right): © terekhov igor | Shutterstock

103 (left): Photographed by Mark Davidson at Sun City Shadow Hills by Del Webb

103 (right): Courtesy of Kohler Co.

104 (left): © Ilfede | Dreamstime.com

105 (left): Courtesy of American Standard Brands

105 (right): © Ioana Drutu | Shutterstock

106 (left): Courtesy of Kohler Co.

106 (right): Photographed by Mark Davidson at Sun City Shadow Hills by Del Webb

107 (left): © Sebastian Czapnik | Dreamstime.com

107 (right): © John Wollwerth | Shutterstock.com

Chapter 10: Living & Dining Rooms

108 (left): Photographed by Mark Davidson at Sun City Shadow Hills by Del Webb

108 (right): Photographed by Mark Davidson at Sun City Shadow Hills by Del Webb

109 (left): Photographed by Mark Davidson at Sun City Shadow Hills by Del Webb

109 (right): Photographed by Mark Davidson at Sun City Shadow Hills by Del Webb

110 (left): Photographed by Mark Davidson at Sun City Shadow Hills by Del Webb

110 (right): Photographed by Mark Davidson at Sun City Shadow Hills by Del Webb

111 (left): Photographed by Mark Davidson at Sun City Shadow Hills by Del Webb

111 (right): Photographed by Mark Davidson at Sun City Shadow Hills by Del Webb

112 (left): Courtesy of LEE Industries

112 (right): Courtesy of Cisco Brothers Corp.

113 (left): Courtesy of LEE Industries

114 (left): Photographed by Mark Davidson at Sun City Shadow Hills by Del Webb

114 (right): © Corel Juvenile Group 2008. All Rights reserved.

115 (left): Photographed by Mark Davidson at Sun City Shadow Hills by Del Webb

115 (right): Photographed by Mark Davidson at Sun City Shadow Hills by Del Webb

116 (left): © Zheng Bin | Dreamstime.com

116 (right): © Krzyssagit | Dreamstime.com

117 (left): © Andrey Butenko | Dreamstime.com

117 (right): Photographed by Mark Davidson at Sun City Shadow Hills by Del Webb

118 (left): Photographed by Mark Davidson at Sun City Shadow Hills by Del Webb

118 (right): Photographed by Mark Davidson at Sun City Shadow Hills by Del Webb

119 (right): Photographed by Mark Davidson at Sun City Shadow Hills by Del Webb

120 (left): Photographed by Mark Davidson at Sun City Shadow Hills by Del Webb

120 (right): Photographed by Mark Davidson at Sun City Shadow Hills by Del Webb

121 (left): Photographed by Mark Davidson at Sun City Shadow Hills by Del Webb

Chapter 11: Home Office & Den

124 (left): Photographed by Mark Davidson at Sun City Shadow Hills by Del Webb

124 (right): Courtesy of Stacks and Stacks

125 (left): © Nicholas Moore | Jupiter Images

125 (right): © William Casey | Shutterstock

126 (left): Courtesy of Stacks and Stacks

126 (right): © Jostein Hauge | Dreamstime.com

129 (right): © Amy Walters | Shutterstock

130 (left): Courtesy of Brookstone

130 (right): Courtesy of Brookstone

131 (left): Courtesy of Stacks and Stacks

132 (left): Courtesy of Home Decorators

132 (right): Courtesy of Brookstone

133 (left): © Miflippo/dreamstime.com

Chapter 12: Bedrooms

135 (left): Courtesy of TempurPedic

138 (left): © Macdaddy | Dreamstime.com

138 (right): Courtesy of TempurPedic

139 (left): Courtesy of Bed Bath & Beyond

139 (right): © Marilyn Zelinsky-Syarto

140 (left): Courtesy of Angel Accessibility Solutions

140 (right): Courtesy of Angel Accessibility Solutions

141 (left): Courtesy of Angel Accessibility Solutions

142 (left): Courtesy of ADT Security

142 (right): Courtesy of ADT Security

143 (left): © Anne Kitzman | Shutterstock

144 (right): © Peolsen | Dreamstime.com

Chapter 13: Storage & Organizing

146 (left): © Marilyn Zelinsky-Syarto

146 (right): © Stephen R. Syarto

147 (left): Courtesy of Organize It

147 (right): Courtesy of Organize.com

148 (left): Courtesy of Kohler Co.

148 (right): Photographed by Mark Davidson at Sun City Shadow Hills by Del Webb

149 (left): Courtesy of Stacks and Stacks

150 (right): © Dallas Events Inc. | Shutterstock

151 (left): © Maxfx | Dreamstime.com

152 (right): © Noam Armonn | Shutterstock

153 (left): © Marilyn Zelinsky-Syarto

154 (right): Courtesy of Obrien & Schridde

155 (left): Courtesy of Brookstone

156 (left): Courtesy of The Container Store

156 (right): © Grahamtomlin | Dreamstime.com

157 (left): © Ncn18 | Dreamstime.com

Chapter 14: Halls & Stairs

159 (left): © Manoj Valappil | Shutterstock

160 (left): © Brad Calkins | Dreamstime.com

Dreamstime.com
206 (left): © Anna Adesanya
207 (left): © Raymond Kasprzak | Dreamstime.com
208 (left): © Joanne Zh | Dreamstime.com
208 (right): Courtesy of ADT Security
209 (left): © Joe Mamer | Dreamstime.com
210 (left): © Anna Adesanya
210 (right): © Barbara Krueger
211 (left): © Barbara Krueger
212 (left): Courtesy of Stacks and Stacks
212 (right): Courtesy of Stacks and Stacks
213 (left): Courtesy of Stacks and Stacks
214 (left): © Barbara Krueger
214 (right): Courtesy of Clarity

215 (left): Courtesy of Wikipedia Commons

Chapter 19: Landscaping & Gardening
216 (left): © Anna Adesanya
216 (right): © Anna Adesanya
217 (left): © Beisea | Dreamstime.com
218 (left): © Nancy Kennedy | Dreamstime.com
218 (right): © Mark Payne | Dreamstime.com
219 (left): © Elena Elisseeva | Dreamstime.com
219 (right): © Claudiodivizia | Dreamstime.com
220 (left): © Ken Cole | Dreamstime.com
220 (right): © Ryan Kelm | Shutterstock.com

221 (left): Courtesy of Advantage Trim & Lumber Co.
222 (left): Courtesy of Oxo
222 (right): © Marilyn Zelinsky-Syarto
223 (left): © Marilyn Zelinsky-Syarto
223 (right): Courtesy of Bosch
224 (left): © Eli Mordechai | Dreamstime.com
224 (right): © Barbara Krueger
225 (left): © Claus Mikosch | Dreamstime.com
226 (left): © Caroline Hedges | Dreamstime.com
226 (right): © Blueenayim | Dreamstime.com
227 (right): © Lisa F. Young | Dreamstime.com

INDEX

A

agility, 6–7
aging, xii–1
Alzheimers, 58–59, 89, 142, 169, 178
appliances, kitchen
    built-in cooktops, 64–65
    microwaves, 66–67
    placement, 70–71
    refrigerators, 68–69
    stoves, 60–61
    wall ovens, 62–63
    washers and dryers, 68–69
area rugs, 30–31
arthritis helpers
    door handles, 72–73
    gardening, 222–23
    innovative solutions, 80–81
    kitchen tools, 78–79
    levered faucets, 74–75
    soap and water, 76–77
    vacuums and brooms, 82–83
automobile access, 16, 17

B

banisters, 160–61
bathroom
    fixtures, 84–95
    tubs and showers, 96–107
bathtubs
    fixtures, 98–99
    transfer seats, 100–101
    types of, 96–97
bedrooms
    bed height, 134–35
    bed transfer slings, 140–41
    big beds *vs.* twins, 136–37
    emergency pull cords, 142–43
    light controls, 144–45
    mattresses, 138–39
    remote controls, 144–45, 190–91
brooms, 82–83

C

canes, 8
carpet, 26–27
cataracts, 171
chair rails, 160–61
chairs
    dining room, 118–19
    easy, 112–13
closets, 146–47
color
    combining patterns, 176–77
    contrasting walls and floor, 172–73
    distinct edges, 174–75
    flooring patterns, 34–35
    linear elements, 178–79
    poor vision and, 168–69
    yellowing and, 170–71
computers, 128–29
cooktops, built-in, 64–65

D

dementia safety, 58–59, 89
dens
    bookcases, 122–23
    televisions, 124–25
desks, 126–27
dimmer switches, 116, 144–45, 162–63, 203
dining room
    chairs, 118–19
    tables, 120–21
door handles, 72–73
doorknobs, 3, 12, 18–19, 20–21
doorways
    exterior hardware, 18–19

counters, kitchen
    edge treatments, 38–39
    location, 42–43
    work surfaces, 36–37

interior modifications, 20–21
  patio, 180–81
  pocket doors, 22
  remodeling interior, 22–23
  thresholds, 14–15
dryers, 68–69

E

elevators, 164–65
emergency
  call buttons, 94–95
  pull cords, 142–43
entries
  doors, 12–13
  vehicle, 16–17
entry doors, 12–13

F

fine motor skills, 2–3
fixtures, bathroom
  emergency call buttons, 94–95
  faucets, 86–87
  grab bars, 92–93
  medicine cabinets, 88–89
  sink adaptation, 84–85
  toilets, 90–91
flooring
  area rugs, 30–31
  carpet, 26–27
  edge treatments, 28–29
  hard surface, 24–25
  patterns, 34–35
  throw rugs, 32–33
flower beds, raised, 224–25

G

garages
  door openers, 210–11
  extra space in, 16–17
gardening
  alternatives, 226–27
  arthritis, 222–23
  lighting, 216–17
  limited mobility, 224–25
gas detectors, 206–7
grab bars, 92–93

H

hallways, 158–59, 162–63
hand strength, 2–3
hardware, door, 18–19
home offices
  bookcases, 122–23
  computers, 128–29
  desks, 126–27
  laptop tables, 130–31
  organizing paperwork, 132–33

K

kitchen
  appliances, 60–71
  counters and sinks, 36–47
  storage, 48–59

L

landscaping
  garden lighting, 216–17
  levels and topography, 220–21
  surfaces, 218–19

lifts (chair lifts), 164–65
lighting
  ambient, 194–95
  bedroom, 144–45
  canisters, 117
  garden, 216–17
  hallway, 158–59
  illuminated switches, 162–63
  living room, 110–11, 116–17
  medicine cabinet, 88
  recessed, 196–97
  sensors, 200–201
  skylights, 192–93
  switches and switch plates, 202–3
  task, 198–99
linoleum floors, 24–25
living room
  easy chairs, 112–13
  lighting and layout, 110–11
  lighting fixtures, 116–17
  sofas, 108–9
  tables and storage furniture, 114–15

INDEX

locks
    cabinets, 88–89
    doors, 3, 18, 21, 73
    windows, 182–83, 184–85

M
macular degeneration, 168–69
mattresses, 138–39
medicine cabinets, 88–89
memory loss, 10–11
microwaves, 66–67
mobility, 8–9
motor skills, 2–3

O
organization
    closet, 146
    collectibles, 152–53
    drawers and shelves, 148–49
    linens, 150–51
    memorabilia, 156–57
    photographs, 154–55
    travel, 212–13
ovens, 62–63

P
patio doors, 180–81
pill organizers, 11, 89
pocket doors, 22

R
ramps, 9, 166–67, 175
refrigerators, 68–69
rug tape, 31, 32–33

S
screen locks, 13, 180
security, 208–9
shower
    enclosures, 106–7
    fixtures, 104–5
    stalls, 102–3

sinks, kitchen
    considerations, 40–41
    faucets and helpers, 46–47
Solatubes, 193
skylights, 192–93
smoke detectors, 206–7
sofas, 108–9
stairs
    chair rails and banisters, 160–61
    elevators, 164–65
    helpers for, 166–67
    lighting, 162–63
stone floors, 24–25
storage
    closets, 146–47
    collectibles, 152–53
    drawers and shelves, 148–49
    home office, 122–23, 126–27, 132–33
    kitchen, 48–59
    linen, 150–51
    living room, 114–15
    memorabilia, 156–57
    photographs, 154–55
storage, kitchen
    dementia safety, 58–59
    drawers, 54–55
    interior cabinet modifications, 52–53
    pantry shelves, 50–51
    pull-out shelves, 48–49
    wheelchair accessible, 56–57
stoves, 60–61

T
tables
    coffee, 114–15
    dining room, 120–21
    laptop, 130–31
telephones, 214–15
televisions, 124–25
thermostats, 204–5
thresholds, 14–15
    ramps, 9, 166–67

throw rugs, 32–33
tile floors, 24–25
toilets, 90–91
transfer
    seats, 100–101
    slings, 140–41
travel organization, 212–13
TTY, 215

V
vacuums, 82–83
vehicle entries, 16–17
vinyl floors, 24–25
vision
    aging process, 4–5
    color choice and, 168–69
    combining patterns, 176–77
    contrasting walls and floor, 172–73
    distinct edges, 174–75
    linear elements, 178–79
    yellowing, 170–71

W
walkers, 8
washers and dryers, 68–69
wearable emergency buttons, 94–95, 142–43, 209
wheelchair access
    elevators, 164–65
    kitchen modifications, 44–45
    kitchen storage, 56–57
    stair helpers, 166–67
windows
    coverings, 186–87
    custom, 182–83
    light and glare, 188–89
    patio doors, 180–81
    remote controls, 190–91
    sliding, 184–85
wood floors, 24–25